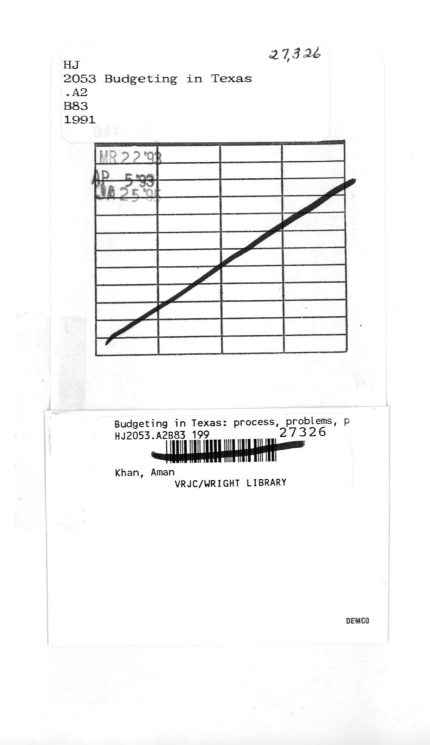

BUDGETING IN TEXAS
Process · Problems · Prospects

Edited By
AMAN KHAN

UNIVERSITY
PRESS OF
AMERICA

Lanham • New York • London

Copyright © 1991 by
University Press of America®, Inc.
4720 Boston Way
Lanham, Maryland 20706

3 Henrietta Street
London WC2E 8LU England

Library of Congress Cataloging-in-Publication Data

Budgeting in Texas : process, problems, prospects
/ edited by Aman Khan.
p.   cm.
Includes bibliographical references.
1. Budget—Texas.   I. Khan, Aman.
HJ2053.A2B83   1991
353.97640072'22—dc20   91-3790 CIP

ISBN 0–8191–8305–9 (cloth : alk. paper)

The paper used in this publication meets the minimum requirements of
American National Standard for Information Sciences—Permanence
of Paper for Printed Library Materials, ANSI Z39.48–1984.

Contents

IV. BUDGET RELATED TOPICS

V. LOCAL BUDGETING

Preface

Although the recent debates over budget deficit in the Congress have made it all too familiar, the word "budget" still conjures up images in the public's mind of alien terms and concepts, and of thousands of numbers crammed in large documents. While these are manifestations of budget, they are not what budgeting is all about. Budgeting is about people and politics, their goals and ideas. It is about competing needs, relative strengths of alternative views, and compromises. It is also about resource scarcity, about managing and delivering services, and about accounting for the resources used for those services and results accomplished.

Budgeting is at the heart of all government activities. Without it, most governments will come to a standstill. Much of the discussion on budgeting in the literature in recent years has focused on federal and, to a large extent, on local governments with very little attention given to state budgeting. Yet, budgeting is just as important to state governments as it is to federal and its local counterparts. Recent budget cuts in the federal government coupled with declining federal assistance, have forged a "new partnership" in which the state governments are called upon to bear an increasingly greater burden of public service provision. If current economic and political trends in the country are any indication of the future, then this partnership is here to stay for a long time. This obviously means that more attention must be given to state governments, their problems, and their ability to deal with the new challenges.

This book presents a glimpse of budgeting in Texas as seen through the eyes of some of its leading practitioners and academicians in the state. It does not attempt to offer a rigorous assessment or prescription for "best practices." Rather, it attempts to describe, as clearly and simply as possible, the nature of Texas budget, its background, and related perspectives that confront the state. It is hoped that the broad, non-technical manner in which the various elements of Texas budgeting are presented in this text will be of interest to an average reader.

As the table of contents shows, this book is the result of a concerted effort; it would not have been completed without the direct support of many individuals, including those whose names do not appear on the table. I am grateful to all of the authors involved in this project, individuals who clearly have supported the idea of a textbook on Texas budgeting. Clarke E. Cochran, Jerry Perkins, and Chuck Fox of the Department of Political Science at Texas Tech University offered the initial support for this project. Sheila Beckett, Director, Governor's Office of Budget and Planning; Larry Copp, LBB Assistant Director of Budget; and Dale Craymer, acting Staff Director for the Select Committee on Capital Construction provided valuable assistance during different stages of this project.

Lee Deviney of LBO, Carl Prestfeldt of Financial Reporting Section in the Comptroller's Office, and Anita Zinnecker of Health and Human Services Department merit special mention for their help with data and other information. Sylvia Silvers provided valuable editorial suggestions, while Iftekhar Hussain prepared the book in its final form for publication. These people were true assets.

Finally, a special thanks to my wife, Teresita Khan, for her patience, persistence, and love that kept me going through it all.

Aman Khan
Lubbock, Texas

1

BUDGETING IN TEXAS: AN OVERVIEW

Aman Khan

Budgeting in Texas, like the national budget, is the state's single-most important decision making function. It sets the state's goals, objectives, and priorities as well as determines the means for achieving them. Since the economic crunch of the mid-eighties, budgeting has become even more important as an instrument for raising revenue, allocating funds, and coordinating various state activities. Like the national budget, the process is complex and time consuming.

This chapter presents a broad, general overview of the principal elements of the Texas state budget system. It begins with a brief description of the budget environment, followed by a simple discussion of the budget cycle, its key characteristics, and the current state of the capital budget. The chapter ends with a brief narrative of the major constraints within which budget decisions are made and their implications for budget outcome.

Budget Environment

A budget is a collective undertaking. A successful budget is the result of successful interaction among many individuals, their ideas and efforts. In Texas, five groups of individuals are most responsible for designing the state budget and its contents. They are: (1) the Governor and his Office of Budget and Planning (GOBP); (2) the Director of Legislative Budget Board (LBB) and the analysts in the Legislative Budget Office (LBO); (3) the Comptroller and the analysts in the Economic Analysis Center; (4) the finance and appropriations committees in the Legislature; and (5) the various agencies and their managers. There are also others, outside the government, who play a critical role in this process. They are the media, the interest groups, the lobbyists and, of course, the individual taxpayers.

These individuals, or actors, as they are frequently referred to, do not play the same role, or exercise the same amount of influence in budget decision making. The constitution, hard economic realities, and political considerations often dictate the terms and set the boundaries within which the individual actors exercise their

1

roles and responsibilities. Historically, the Legislative Budget Board – an arm of the Legislature, has exercised the greatest weight in the state budget process. This is an exception, rather than the rule, since there are not too many states in the country where the legislature still enjoys a greater say in the budget process. In most states, the budget making activities are centralized in the executive branch. LBB's success has been primarily due to its experience with the budget process that goes back to its inception in 1949.

The Budget Cycle

Budgeting is a cyclical process, consisting of a number of distinct phases. Each phase involves a sequence of activities and each activity, in turn, takes place in a specific time period. These phases of the process from one fiscal year (FY) often overlap phases from other fiscal years.

Most fiscal years are twelve months long, which is a reasonable length of time to execute a budget. Texas is one of the handful of states that deviates from this procedure. It operates on a biennial, or two-year long fiscal year, divided into twelve-month periods. The fiscal year begins in September 1, following a legislative session that lasts for one hundred and forty days. The state Constitution permits the Legislature to meet once every two years, on the second Tuesday in January of every odd-numbered year. Considering the size of the budget, and the fact that the Legislature meets only once every other year, the length of the session seems rather short for a lengthy discussion on a wide range of issues and problems facing the state.

The Preparation Phase

The cycle begins when the various operating agencies receive detailed instructions for putting together budget requests. The instructions are jointly prepared by the staff of the Legislative Budget Board and the governor's Office of Budget and Planning. Unlike most states, Texas has a dual budget system in which both these agencies play a vital role. After the budget requests are prepared and submitted, joint hearings with the LBB and GOBP begin and the two agencies start to independently prepare a proposed budget. The two budgets do not always coincide; in fact, they frequently differ inasmuch as the two branches of government – the executive and the legislative – differ in their perspective of the future needs of the state. The proposed budgets are then submitted to the Legislature for appropriation and the second phase of the cycle begins.

The Appropriation Phase

The budgets of the LBB and GOBP are essentially proposals; they do not automatically guarantee the money needed for state expenditures. Appropriations must be made. Appropriation is a legislative function, and it is where the greatest political battle for the "purse" takes place. Legislative consideration of the budget

2

begins immediately after the proposed budgets are submitted to the House Appropriations and the Senate Finance committees, and from there to various subcommittees. Subcommittees conduct hearings with each state agency and after the hearings are completed, the committees begin to prepare their respective version of the General Appropriations Bill for passage by the two houses. A Conference Committee, consisting of ten members – five from finance committee and five from appropriations committee – is appointed to iron out the differences and to prepare a report (which must be approved by both houses) for submission to the governor.[1]

The governor has the power to accept or veto any item of expenditure without vetoing the entire bill. However, the Legislature retains the ultimate authority in the sense that it can override the governor's *item-vetoes* with a two-thirds majority, but, in practice, these vetoes are final. Once signed by the governor, the bill becomes law, and the budget becomes effective immediately.

The Implementation Phase

The passage of the bill and its signing by the governor does not quite end the budget cycle; it merely sets the stage for the next set of activities. The approved budget needs to be implemented. Implementation allows the funds to be used by various agencies to carry out the approved programs and policies of the state. The LBB, GOBP and all affected agencies are involved in this process. Also involved during this phase is the Office of the Comptroller for maintaining controls at the fund, appropriation, and cost center levels to ensure that expenditures are not made in access of budgetary authority.

Appropriations are legal authorization to expend funds; they do not provide an ironclad guarantee that the agencies will receive these funds appropriated for them. The administration has the authority to hold back, supplement, or transfer funds when confronted with serious economic or natural problems. Thus, there is often a difference in the budget that is being implemented from the one originally proposed by the two agencies and subsequently approved by the Legislature and the chief executive. The final budget is usually the one at the end of the fiscal year when the process of implementation is complete.[2]

The Audit and Evaluation Phase

The cycle ends with an audit of state finances and an evaluation of various programs undertaken during a fiscal year. The objectives of these activities are to ascertain the extent to which the state has (1) complied with the spending requirements, (2) presented the results of its operations and the changes in financial positions in accordance with the generally accepted accounting procedures (GAAP), and (3) the extent to which the completed programs have achieved their stated goals and objectives. The state auditor and the program evaluation section of the Legislative Budget Board are the principal actors during this final phase of the cycle.[3] Although it can be conducted any time during the year, the process generally begins after the end of the fiscal year covered by the current budget.

Budget Components and Characteristics

All budgets have certain elements in common; they provide an exhaustive array of information on revenue and expenditures. These sources of information are the centerpiece of a government's policies and serve as reference points for future public and legislative debate. Yet, it is not quite as simple as going through a government budget document and digesting its contents which are often classified as sources of revenue, fund groups, organizational units, and objects of expense. This creates a problem for an occasional reader, or one who is not familiar with the mechanics of budgetmaking. This section presents a brief description of some of these elements.

Sources of Revenue

The state collects revenue from a variety of sources. These sources are essentially the same for all fifty states, although the states differ markedly in their reliance on them. By far, the largest source from which the state derives its revenue is taxes, federal income accounts for the second major source, and the remainder come from interest on investment, licenses and fees, revenue from public land, and miscellaneous other sources. Table 1 presents these sources and the magnitude of their revenue for most recent years.

TABLE 1
State Revenue By Source (in $millions)
FY 1985 - FY 1990

Source	1985	1986	1987	1988	1989	1990*
Tax Collections	10,721	10,232	10,266	12,365	12,906	13,161
Federal Investment	3,470	4,106	4,078	4,515	5,043	5,307
Interest on Investment	1,001	1,105	1,084	1,169	1,222	1,112
Licences, Fees, etc.	848	1,136	1,233	1,456	1,483	1,530
Land Income	556	855	281	268	266	286
Other Revenues	400	961	898	585	558	482
TOTAL	16,996	18,395	17,840	20,358	21,478	21,878

Source: Legislative Budget Board, *Fiscal Size Up*. Austin, TX: LBO, 1986-90.
* Estimated Figures.

As the table shows, tax revenue is the principal source of state income, averaging about 60 percent of total revenue. *Sales tax* continues to provide the lion share of all tax revenues. Three types of sales taxes are presently used by the state: (1) *general sales taxes*, which are broad-based and collected from the sale of most items; (2) *excise taxes*, which are levied on the sale, manufacture, and use of particular items, such as liquors, gasoline, and cigarettes; and (3) *franchise taxes*, which are collected on the gross revenue of certain types of business activity, such as utility companies. Of these three categories, general sales tax is the most important, accounting for the bulk of state tax revenue. It has increased significantly in recent years, from about 39 percent in 1980 to 53.6 percent in 1989, and is expected to increase even further.[4]

Another important category of tax revenue is the *severance taxes*, which are collected on the production of oil and natural gas. There are seventeen states in the country that currently levy some type of severance taxes, but only Texas, Alaska, Oklahoma, Montana, Wyoming, and some other energy producing states depend heavily on it for their income.[5] Revenue from this source has declined considerably in recent years, following a sharp decline in oil prices after it had reached its peak in 1980 when it accounted for 38.2 percent of all tax revenue in the state.[6] In FY 1989, it yielded a meager 9.1 percent and is expected to decline even further as the federal government continues to rely on foreign imports.[7] The recent events in the Persian Gulf have reversed this trend somewhat, but it is unlikely that it will actually reach the stage of early 1980's again.

Despite the increases in general sales tax and problems in the oil market, Texas still has one of the lowest per capita tax burden in the nation. In 1988, for instance, an average Texan paid only $57.6 for every thousand dollars in personal income, ranking it 46th among the 50 states.[8] The state does not levy a property tax, which is collected by cities, counties, and special districts. The state Constitution prohibits the imposition of such a tax. The state also does not have a personal or corporate income tax, although the pressure for both has been increasing for some time. Only three other states – Nevada, Wyoming, and Washington – do not presently have an income tax.

The Fund Structure

Government revenues are organized by funds. Unlike the private sector, government revenue comes from a number of different sources, some of which have terms and conditions that restrict their use for certain activities. A fund structure helps control as well as increase accountability by ensuring that resources segregated by funds are used for their intended purposes. There are eight different categories of funds currently maintained by the state, with over 200 different accounts.[9] Theoretically, there are no limits as to the number of funds or accounts a government can maintain at any one time, but it is generally accepted that the number should be minimum to be consistent with operating and legal requirements, and to maintain sound financial administration.[10] The following presents a brief description of these funds:

The General Revenue Fund is the largest and accounts for all revenues collected by the state except for those required by law to be deposited in another fund. Included in this category are taxes, charges and fees, and income from federal government. Currently, about 63 percent of all revenues are accounted for by this fund.

Special Revenue Funds consist of over 150 different accounts and are collected from restricted or earmarked sources. These funds have grown in recent years as the government interest has shifted more toward finding new ways to finance programs without raising taxes. By restricting charges and fees, the

5

government can easily generate the needed revenue for these programs. The State Highway Fund, the Available School Fund, and the Water Development Fund are among the best examples of this type of fund.

Debt Services Funds, the third category of funds, have 20 different accounts. They are maintained by the state to pay for principal and interest on long-term debts. Many of the activities in this category include the servicing of bonds issued by Water Development Board, and the General Land Office/Veterans Land Board.

Capital Projects Funds consist of 14 different accounts and are maintained by the state to accumulate funds from the proceeds of bond issues, federal grants, or transfer of revenue from other funds. These funds are mostly used to acquire, repair, or construct major capital facilities. Among the beneficiaries of these funds is the Public Finance Authority, which has been responsible for majority of developmental activities in recent years.

Enterprise Funds, the fifth category of funds, are similar to private sector operations. They are self-supportive in the sense that costs of providing goods and services to the public are recovered through user fees and charges. There are nine such enterprise operations in the state. They are: (1) the state Highway Agency, (2) the Guaranteed Student Loan Corporations, (3) the Hospital Equipment Financing Council, (4) the Surplus Property Agency, (5) the State Bar, (6) the Department of Commerce, (7) the Turnpike Authority, (8) the Department of Correction, and (9) the Water Development Board. Together, these operations constitute the second largest depository of state revenue, next to the general fund.

Administered by the state, the *Pension and Retirement Funds* are used to provide for retirement benefits to state employees. The contributions from employees and the employer as well as earnings from investment of these contributions are used to finance these funds. Included in this category are (1) the Teacher Retirement Fund, (2) the Employees Retirement Fund, (3) the Judicial Retirement Fund, (4) the Law Enforcement Fund, and (5) the Fire Fighter's Pension Fund.

Trust and Agency Funds comprise the seventh category of funds. There are 15 different accounts in this group for which the state acts as a trustee on behalf of individuals, private organizations, or government agencies. These funds are used largely as a clearing device for assets held by the state and cannot be used for any other operations except to cover administrative costs.

Finally, there is the *Internal Service Fund*, which is used to account for the financing of services, rendered by a designated agency for other agencies in the government. The Purchasing and General Services Commission presently serves as the internal service fund for the state.

In addition, the government also maintains two separate account groups, one for general fixed assets, and the other for general long-term debt. The purpose of these account groups is two-fold: (1) to account for all property, plant, and equipment of the general, special revenue, capital projects, and debt services funds, known collectively as *governmental fund;* and (2) to account for bonds, notes,

6

capital leases, and other long-term debt, which are financed through governmental and expendable trust funds. General fixed assets and long-term debt for colleges and universities are accounted for separately in their respective funds.

The financial position and operations of each of these funds and account groups are presented separately in the Annual Financial Report as a system of self-balancing statements consisting largely of each agency's assets, liabilities, equity, revenues, expenditures, and transfers. As noted previously, revenues organized by and accounted for in these funds are based on the purposes for which they are to be used and the means by which the activities are to be monitored and controlled.

Expenditure Categories

Texas is one of the fastest growing states in the nation. In the past two decades, its population has grown more rapidly than any other state with the exception of California and Florida. To keep pace with this trend, the state expenditure has also grown at a fairly rapid rate. Each new budget presented to the Legislature marked an increase over the previous ones. Between 1980 and 1990, for instance, expenditures grew by more than $13 billion, from over $10 billion to over $23 billion respectively. In real terms, after adjusting for inflation and population growth, this represents about a sixteen percent increase, or 1.5 percent per year.

Table 2 presents a breakdown of these expenditures for most recent years. According to the table, education is the largest component of state expenditure, accounting for 42.2 percent of the 1990-91 biennium budget. Compared with the 1988-89 level, this represents about 10 percent increase and the trend has been fairly consistent. On a per capita basis, however, Texas ranks 29th in the country – way below California, Michigan, New York, and other populous states.[11] Rising enrollment in public schools and institutions of higher education, along with a general salary increase accounted for much of this growth.

TABLE 2
State Expenditure By Category (in $millions)
Biennium Levels 1982-1991

Category	1982-83	1984-85	1986-87	1988-89	1990-91
Education	12,469	14,430	16,827	18,105	20,092
Health and Human Services	6,118	6,784	7,752	8,962	11,838
Transportation	3,194	3,818	5,386	5,155	5,216
Employee Benefits	2,226	2,501	2,958	3,036	3,860
Public Safety & Corrections	976	1,362	1,580	1,963	2,536
General Government	860	1,237	1,477	1,460	2,569
Natural Resources	656	661	737	492	727
Regulatory Agencies	123	199	237	299	387
General Provisions	0.0	0.0	289	77	333
TOTAL	26,622	30,992	37,243	39,549	47,558

Source: Legislative Budget Board, *Fiscal Size Up*. Austin, TX: LBO, 1982-91.

The next important category is the Health and Human Services, which comprises almost 25 percent of the state budget. In the last few years, it has been increasing at a much faster rate than any other category in the state, reaching an all time high of $11.8 billion during 1990-91 biennium. Of this, human services alone consume 70 percent of the combined expenditure. Federal funds received either on a grant basis, or as matching funds for specific expenditures, such as medicare catastrophic coverage, nursing home reform, welfare reform, and hunger prevention provide the majority of the funding.

Another notable category of expenditure where substantial growth has taken place in recent years is employee benefits. The 1990-91 biennium budget records a 21 percent increase in employee benefits over the previous biennium level. Several factors have contributed to this growth. Important among them are rising contribution to social security, employee group insurance premium, and a general increase in payroll.

Although it constitutes a small portion of the total budget, the expnditure for general government has increased steadily over the years. Since 1989, however, it has been increasing at a relatively faster rate due in part to a number of major restoration programs undertaken by the state. Among the beneficiaries of this growth are the Public Finance Authority for debt services of general obligation bonds, the state Preservation Board for the restoration of state capitol and other buildings, the Purchasing and General Services Commission, and the Office of the Attorney General.

Transportation and public safety are two other minor, but important, categories; together, they account for almost 17 percent of the total state budget. Growth in the transportation sector has been modest due in part to a decline in federal support since the early eighties. Other minor categories, such as natural resources, and regulatory agencies account for less than 3 percent of the budget.

The Capital Budget

All budgets belong to one of two categories: operating or capital. An operating budget deals with recurring expenses, such as wages and salaries, contractuals, materials and supplies, travel and utility, etc. A capital budget, on the other hand, deals with non-recurring long-term expenditure plans, programs, and projects. Unlike most operating activities, capital projects and programs are costly, and once in place, they cannot be moved easily without serious irretrievable costs. With few exceptions, most governments have a separate capital budget that brings together in one place a diverse array of capital projects, classifies them by programs, costs, sources of funds, and time of completion. The process is complex and difficult, since there are no hard and fast rules as to what constitutes a capital expenditure, or what criteria should be used to select a capital project, and how it should be financed.

The Magnitude of Capital Expenditure

Capital expenditures are the foundations of future economic growth and development. Without the infrastructure of roads, bridges, buildings, equipment, and vehicles, most governments will find it difficult to survive. Yet, investment in this vital area of government has been declining in recent years.

In Texas, capital outlays account for about 11 percent of total government expenditures. The trend is consistent with a majority of the states, and the federal government in particular, which spends roughly the same amount on capital outlays each year.[12] Table 3 presents the share of state expenditure on capital outlays for most recent years. However, in contrast to the federal government, which allocates most of its capital outlays on military equipment, approximately 70 percent of this expenditure in the state goes to highway constructions and educational facilities, and the rest into buildings, utilities, vehicles, and equipment.

TABLE 3
Capital Outlay Expenditure (in $millions)
FY 1981 - FY 1989

Fiscal Year	Capital Expenditure	Total Expenditure	% of Total
1981	1,483	11,368	13.0
1982	1,222	12,074	10.1
1983	1,336	13,539	9.9
1984	1,293	14,349	9.9
1985	1,244	16,527	7.5
1986	2,026	18,710	10.8
1987	2,044	17,872	11.4
1988	2,447	19,440	12.6
1989	2,374	21,237	11.2

Source: Comptroller of Public Accounts, *State of Texas Annual Cash Reports.*
Austin TX: Office of the Comptroller, 1985-1989.

State of the Capital Budget

Texas is one of the few states that currently does not have a separate capital budget. Being an oil-rich pay-as-you-go state, Texas has always paid cash for its capital expenditures. This system worked well until the mid-eighties when the state's oil-depleted finances were not enough to pay for court-mandated improvements for its prisons and health programs. In 1987, for the first time ever, the state issued general obligation bonds to pay for capital improvements. The same year, the regular session of the 70th Legislature established the Select Interim Committee on Capital Construction to review the development of a capital budget process. The Committee report focused on four principal areas of capital budget development, namely planning, budgeting, financing, and monitoring.[13]

In order to maintain quality, efficiency, and growth need of public services, a government needs to periodically acquire, replace, or upgrade its capital facilities. *Planning* helps provide for systematic and orderly acquisition, maintenance, and replacement of these facilities. The Committee recommended the development of a long-term consolidated plan, prepared for every two years, before the beginning of each regular session of the Legislature. The plan would include, among other things, an inventory of existing capital facilities and equipment, an assessment of future capital needs, and an estimate of the cost of capital improvements. As of 1987, thirty six states have consolidated long-term plans, 24 of which do so by statutes, and 23 publish "needs assessment" as a part of this process.[14] Only a few of the Texas state agencies, such as the Department of Highway and Public Transportation prepare any type of long-range budget plans.

The Committee also recommended the adoption of a separate capital budget. Among the many advantages, a separate capital *budget* would allow each agency's capital requests to be prioritized relative to the needs of other agencies and would provide a better means for identifying the exact capital needs and sources from which the selected projects and programs will be financed. Historically, capital appropriations in the state were made as a separate line-item within each agency's section of the over-all budget bill and were difficult to compile. The 71st Legislature restructured the appropriations bill so that budget authority for capital outlay could be itemized (in the first rider for each agency) and presented in a summary fashion at the end of the budget.[15] The bill also made some additional changes in the capital budget preparation process. For instance, it required that instead of submitting capital requests as separate line-items, each agency justify individual projects, identify their purpose, describe the costs and benefits associated with each project, and finally, prioritize them so that it would be consistent with the zero-base budgeting (ZBB) format currently used by the state.

One of the major issues in capital budgeting is to determine what sources of *financing* to be used in funding individual capital requests, and how seriously a government should rely on each alternative funding source for the entire budget. The current realization in the state is that long-term financing should be emphasized as a method of payment for non-recurring capital facilities, such as prisons, hospitals, office buildings, etc. These items are used over a long period of time, and it makes sense to pay for them as they are used. Moreover, in light of today's slow-growth economy, very few states in the country can afford to pay cash for all its capital requirements. The state, however, does have a good credit rating, which should work to its advantage in financing the current and future capital needs.

Finally, a capital budget development process would not be complete without some form of *monitoring* activities. It has been a common practice with most state and local governments to use funds appropriated for capital improvements for various other activities, when necessary. Since most capital facilities extend over a number of years and the fact that many governments lack proper oversight, safeguarding against this practice is not always possible. With adequate review and monitoring, the governments can, however, keep track of the progress in capital improvement activities and ensure that funds raised or appropriated for this purpose are utilized accordingly. The state Bond Review Board, which was established during the legislative session prior to the work of the

Select Interim Committee on Capital Construction, fills an important gap in this regard. The Board, consisting of the Governor, Lt. Governor, House Speaker, Treasurer, and the Comptroller oversees the issuance of bonds by the agencies and lease purchasing of equipment.

Budget Constraints

Budgeting does not take place in a vacuum. Budgets, as instruments of economic and political decision making, are very much affected by economic and political constraints. The nature of these constraints determines whether a government should increase spendings, cut down programs, or continue to provide services at the current level of consumption. This final section briefly looks at three such constraints and discusses their impact on budget decisions.

The Balanced Budget Requirement

Unlike the federal government, state and local governments are required, by law, to maintain a balanced budget.[16] A balanced budget simply means the revenues will either exceed or be equal to expenditures. Most governments, however, find it difficult to balance their budgets. Besides economic and political uncertainties, the need to borrow funds for capital outlays frequently leads to budgets that are difficult to balance. Since capital expenditure constitutes a part of the overall budget, it can easily add to this problem.

Since 1980, state governments have been accumulating deficit at the rate of about $10 billion a year. The combined debt for all fifty states currently stands at about 9 percent of the total national debt.[17] In Texas alone, the long-term debt jumped from $2.4 billion in 1980 to almost $7 billion in 1989, and is expected to reach almost $12 billion by the end of the decade.[18]

Political and Economic Uncertainties

Budgets are about estimates of future revenue and expenditures. Estimates are not actual values, and even the best econometricians may not always produce the best estimates. Time lag, lack of proper understanding of the complexities of the real world and, more importantly, political and economic uncertainties can greatly affect the budget estimates. The oil-embargo that hit the nation in the mid-seventies is a case in point. It took the economists and politicians by surprise. Inflation and unemployment both began to climb at the same time, putting the economy on a spin in defiance of all accepted laws of economics, and forcing the government to drastically reduce services and resort to various austerity measures.

In FY 1986-87, the Texas state budget suffered a major setback, resulting again from an oil crisis, but of a somewhat different nature. Earlier, in 1985, the Legislature had passed a $37.3 billion budget for the 1986-87 biennium based on a revenue projection of $37.2 billion, which left little margin of error.[19] The assumption on which the projection was based was that the economy would grow at a modest rate and the oil prices would decline from about $32 a barrel to $25 in 1986, and to $24.15 in 1987. Unfortunately, increased production by OPEC and other non-OPEC members created a glut in the market and the price dropped to $15 a barrel in February 1986, leading to a budget deficit of $1.3 billion for the remainder of the biennium.

Exacerbating this crisis was the fact that the state's tax structure was not able to capture economic diversification which had been initiated in the early eighties. Tax revenue was still depending heavily on those segments of the economy that are most vulnerable to economic contraction.

Constitutional and Legal Restrictions

Interestingly, all three levels of government in the country operate under an added constraint that some funds be set aside for specific purposes, or programs. Constitution and legal requirements prohibit the use of these funds for any other purpose, which substantially reduce the budgetary discretion of these governments. Over 75 percent of the federal budget, for instance, is regarded as *uncontrollable* in the sense that these could not be touched because of prior commitments.[20] The government has very little discretion over these expenditures, which mostly include fixed costs, such as interest on national debt, long-term contracts, and payments to state and local governments.

For Texas, the Permanent University Fund is a good example, which, according to the state Constitution, can only be spent by the University of Texas, and the Texas A&M system. Similarly, revenue generated from motor fuel tax and automobile license fees are earmarked for education and public roads. There are literally dozens of other activities for which funds have been committed and cannot be transferred for other uses. Only the general fund, which is largely supported by sales taxes, is unrestricted and can be used for any program or activity.

Beyond constitutional limits, there are also legal ones. For instance, the state must pay interest on debt as well as social security, and retirement contributions for its employees. Recently the state was under a court order to improve its school finances. In July 1990, the state raised the sales tax from 6 percent to 6.25 percent to partially offset this problem, and to address other human services needs.[21]

The state also operates programs that are partly funded through federal matching grants; the federal government pays between 50 and 90 percent of a program's cost with the state paying the remainder. The states have very little option in this regard, but to fulfill the matching requirements; failure to do so may mean losing the program altogether.

These and other constraints facing the state are not typical of Texas; nearly every state and local government in the country has to deal with them. Budgeting would definitely be much more simple without them, but there is no guarantee that the states would do a better job if no such constraints existed. On the positive side, however, some constraints, especially those which are legal and constitutional in nature, can bring about a sense of discipline in the budget process. Whether they are successful or not, theoretically at least, they can control government spendings, maintain a balance between revenue and expenditures, and limit the size of budget deficits.

Conclusion

In conclusion, budgeting is about allocation and management of scarce resources, based on ideas, logic, and analysis. The development, appropriation, and implementation of government budgets take place in an environment of tight schedules, conflicting goals, unanticipated problems, legal obstacles, and tense negotiations within a political milieu. Recent innovations in budget practices are an attempt to moderate these pressures, while maintaining the goals of rational allocation among competing needs and priorities.

Obviously, there is a diverse range of environments and issues that shape the budget policies and determine their outcomes. Similarly, there is a diverse range of tools and approaches that influence budget decisions and affect budget practices. As these practices evolve, reinforcing the evolutionary nature of budgeting, there is a need to constantly remind the practitioners as well as those interested in the subject of the timeless requirements that make budgeting such a challenging exercise: efficiency, accountability, and comprehensiveness.

Notes

1. State of Texas, *Text of Conference Committee Report.* Senate Bill No. 222, Governor's Veto Proclamation. Austin, TX, 1989.
2. F.A. Piduch, "Adapting the Budget During the Execution Phase to Changed Conditions," in D. Axelrod, *Budgeting for Modern Government.* New York, NY: St. Martin's Press, 1988: 169.
3. See, for example, the 1989 *Texas Annual Financial Report* prepared by the Office of the Comptroller of Public Accounts, the Legislative Budget Board's *Performance Report* submitted to the 71st Legislature for further discussion on it.
4. Legislative Budget Board, *Fiscal Size Up: 1990-91.* Austin, TX: LBO, 1990: 2-8.
5. S.B. Hansen, "Extraction: The Politics of State Taxation," in V. Gray and others (eds.), *Politics in the American States.* Boston, MA: Little-Brown and Company, 1983.
6. Legislative Budget Board, *Fiscal Size Up: 1982-83.* Austin, TX: LBO, 1982: 2-5.
7. Legislative Budget Board, *Fiscal Size Up: 1990-91.* Austin, TX: LBO, 1990: 2-8.

8. Legislative Budget Board, *Fiscal Size Up: 1990-91*. Austin, TX: LBO, 1990: 3-3.

9. Office of the Comptroller, *Annual Financial Report*. Austin, TX: Office of the Comptroller, 1989.

10. Municipal Finance Officers Association, *Government Accounting, Auditing, and Financial Reporting, 1988*. Chicago, IL. MFOA, 1988: 11.

11. Legislative Budget Board, *Fiscal Size Up: 1990-91*. Austin, TX: LBO, 1990: 3-9.

12. U.S. Department of Currency, *Governmental Finances*, GF 85, No. 5. Washington, DC: Bureau of Census, 1987: 5.

13. B. Sims and R. Williamson, *Report on Capital Construction*. Austin, TX: Interim Committee Report, 1989.

14. National Conference of State Legislatures, *Capital Budgeting and Finance: The Legislative Role*. Denver, CO: 1987.

15. Legislative Budget Office, "Implementing the Capital Budget: Background Information." Austin, TX: LBO, 1990.

16. The state of Vermont is the only exception, which does not have a balanced requirement.

17. Advisory Government on Intergovernmental Relations, *Significant Features of Fiscal Federalism*. Washington, DC, 1987: 8-9.

18. Interim Committee Report, op. cit., 3-7.

19. Legislative Budget Board, *Fiscal Size Up: 1988-89*. Austin, TX: LBO, 1988.

20. L. LeLoup, *Budgetary Politics*. Brunswick, OH: King's Court Communications, Inc., 1986: 51-61.

21. Legislative Budget Board, *Fiscal Notes*. Austin, TX: LBO, November 1990: 5.

2

THE TEXAS MACROECONOMY

Kay Hofer

The Lone Star state, long a citadel of the banking, oil, cattle, farming and insurance industries has an economic base that is unmatched by that of any of the remaining forty nine states in terms of natural resources, potential for diversity and scale. The state's unique economic picture began with the discovery of oil at Spindletop in 1901. This discovery, set against the history of political and individual independence from the days of the Republic, was instrumental in the development of a state economy that has been closely tied to energy-related industries and that many have called a "boom or bust" economy. The "boom or bust" cycles of the Texas economy are reflected in business attitudes and ventures as well as state policy and politics affecting the macroeconomy. Being Texan was associated by individuals in other states with oil, bold economic ventures, and plenty of money. Folklores of national cartoons, movies, and television shows projected Texans as individuals who think big, talk big and exude success. Texas was "oil" and cattle. Texas was able to maintain a status of one of the lowest tax states while revenue surpluses directly related to the severance tax often flowed into the state coffers. The position of energy and energy-related industries such as mining and petrochemicals in development of the state's economy resulted in a heavy dependence on such interests for revenues to finance business ventures as well as activities of state and local government. Oil, gas and energy-related production along with agriculture dominated the state's economy for almost the entire century. Until the late 1980s, the energy industry has also played a vital role in insulating Texas from economic downturns occurring nationally.

Between 1901 and 1983, the Texas economy developed in such a manner that as much as twenty-five percent of the state's economy was directly related to energy and energy development. Economic diversification for the state was not a formal macroeconomic policy advocated by public officials. In more recent years, however, the state has moved from a narrow track of primary dependence of the economy on the energy industry with few policies of state or local government directed to economic development to one in which economic diversification is reflected in activities of the Governor's office as well as through direct and indirect financial assistance from the state. Before turning our attention to the current status of the Texas economy, some attention should be separately devoted to the role of industries that currently dominate or dominated the economy throughout most of the century – energy (oil and gas), agriculture, and banking. As energy and energy-related industries still rank first with regard to economic effect and unemployment in the Texas economy, we begin with an examination of that impact.

Energy-Related Industries In The Texas Macroeconomy

Texas has been a major supplier of petroleum needs of the United States since the discovery of Spindletop on January 10, 1901. Although other fields preceded the discovery near Beaumont, Texas, Spindletop was the first salt dome oil discovery. Texas oil production skyrocketed after Spindletop, increasing 426 percent by the end of 1901. In 1902, Spindletop alone accounted for ninety four percent of total state oil production. Today, one third of the nation's oil reserves lie in Texas. Additionally, the state ranks first among the fifty in refining capacity, accounting for over twenty seven percent (27.39%) of the total for the United States. Thirty three refineries have a crude oil capacity of 4,145,900 barrels per calendar day. Refineries in California and Louisiana, ranking second and third respectively, have a refinery capacity only half that of Texas. Although dependence on foreign oil is increasing, Texas remains a major source of crude, providing close to thirty percent of the nation's total oil. In 1983, prior to the collapse of oil prices, the petroleum industry in Texas provided an average of 350,533 jobs with a payroll of $10,487,481,180. Estimates of the direct and indirect impact of oil and gas extraction (refining, petrochemicals, and gasoline marketing) and related industries on the Texas macroeconomy run as high as fifty percent. Heavy machinery enterprises and petrochemical factories are also closely tied to the oil and gas industry with such factories producing roughly forty-one percent of all United States' petrochemicals. Few, if any, sectors of the economy in Texas are spared from the effects of a change in oil prices.[1] The effect of the collapse of oil prices in the early 1980s on the Port of Houston serves as an example of the ripple effect that occurred throughout the Texas economy. Houston port volume dropped about fifteen percent as shipping of steel pipe and machinery exports related to the petroleum industry decreased. The impact on the Texas economy would have been even more severe if Houston did not serve as the number one port for Mexico. The economic stimulation associated with service for Mexico acted as a buffer against the downturn in the Houston economy directly associated with the falling oil prices. In 1987, the Port of Houston handled 112.5 million tons and was ranked third overall in the United States; only New York and New Orleans were ranked ahead of Texas, in first and second place respectively. The largest import commodities in 1987 were petroleum and petroleum products at 31.4 million tons. In the late 1980s, imports of petroleum and petroleum products coupled with increased agriculture exports have offset the decrease in value of tonnage occurring in the first part of the decade.[2]

As long as the oil "boom" lasted, Texas had little to concern itself about with regard to the economy or management of state finances. The petroleum industry remained the largest taxpayer to both state and local government throughout the twentieth century. A severe decline of the oil industry, however, began in 1981. The impact of the decline ("oil bust") on the Texas economy was dramatic. "Each time the price of a barrel of oil fell one dollar, state government lost approximately $100 million in revenues. ... Oil which once sold for $39 a barrel, fell below $10 in early 1986. ... 25,000 Texans lost their jobs for each dollar drop in oil prices."[3] By 1986, the world price of oil had declined to a new low, and the State Comptroller projected revenue shortfalls of $3.5 billion for the biennium of FY 1986-1987. The impact of this decline in oil prices was immediate and direct in the mining industry of the state. Almost all mining activities in Texas are related to oil and gas extraction (over 95%), and this sector of the economy was the most hard hit of any during the early 1980s. Although employment in mining began to grow in 1987, the mining sector has yet to recover completely from the oil "bust."[4] The oil "bust" (sharp decline in world oil prices) resulted in state revenue shortfalls due to heavy dependence on the oil and gas severance taxes. Surplus revenues were no longer generated without added or increased taxes. Increasing taxes dramatically was not a comfortable political option for most Texas lawmakers during the peak of an economic downturn with rising unemployment levels. Table 1 shows the change in the proportion of state revenues from severance taxes between 1955-1989.

TABLE 1
Proportion of State Revenues from Oil and Gas Severance Taxes
1955 to 1989

Year	Percent	Amount
1955	31.0%	$125 mil.
1965	17.0%	$207 mil.
1970	14.0%	$307 mil.
1975	18.0%	$518 mil.
1982	27.0%	$2.2 bil.
1984	24.0%	$2.4 bil.
1985	20.2%	$2.2 bil.
1986	15.5%	$1.5 bil.
1987	11.5%	$1.2 bil.
1988	8.5%	$1.0 bil.
1989	9.1%	$1.2 bil.

Source: Comptroller of Public Accounts, Texas Annual Cash Report, 1982, 1984, 1986, 1989.

Texas is also a major supplier of natural gas within the United States, particularly to California and the New England states. Natural gas is also supplied in large quantities to the Central and Southeastern states. Texas is first in proven reserves of natural gas with 24.99% of United States' total, and natural gas production in Texas constitutes 47.3% of the United States' total production.[5] Texas gas reserves are projected to carry the state well into the next century. With the state's large reserves of natural gas, the Texas economy can be accelerated beyond projected growth levels if demand for gas as a clean burning fuel associated with fewer pollutants increases during the 1990s.[6]

Current national clear-air legislation passed in June of 1989 should give the natural gas industry a boost. Vehicles can be converted to gas; gas burned in conjunction with coal at power plants reduces pollutant emissions; and gas is economical and clean burning. The natural gas industry may hold the key to the performance of the Texas macroeconomy in the 1990s providing both a boost to the economy as well as a cushion for any downturn in the petroleum industry. In 1987, the Fuel Use Act of 1978 was rescinded. This act had prohibited the use of natural gas for new industrial power plant boilers. By 1989, federal price controls on natural gas had also been lifted. These recent legislative changes at the national level signal what may be a very bright future for the natural gas industry. In Texas, more than fifty percent of current drilling activity is for gas exploration.[7] Such exploratory activity coupled with the presence of known gas reserves places Texas in the forefront as a major supplier of energy during the 1990s. In addition to the apparently bright future for the gas industry in the state, West Texas has been identified as a prime target for the development of solar power in the 1990s. Solar power can be produced at significantly lower costs than nuclear power without the accompanying risk to the environment. A California based firm has opened numerous successful plants there and is looking to Texas as a natural location for production of this clean, economical energy source.[8]

Crude oil and gas are, however, minerals that are not renewable and the risk of depletion increases each year. The risk of depletion must be set against the prospect of a future decline in oil prices when considering the potential for impact in the Texas economy. A severe decline of oil prices to $12 a barrel or less for a sustained period could slow the state's economic recovery in the foreseeable future by as much as fifteen percent of projected growth rates.[9] Oil prices began to rise in 1987 and have fluctuated between $15 and $18 a barrel in the late 1980s. Recovery of the oil industry has begun to occur. Only if oil prices remain below $12 a barrel for an extended period of time would the rate of growth of the Texas economy be effectively slowed. Such a sustained period of decreased oil prices remains unlikely in light of bringing Iraq under the quota system during the OPEC meeting in Vienna in November of 1988. Since the decline in oil prices, Texas petroleum production has turned from exploration to production in fields that are rapidly becoming depleted. Though the Texas economy remains closely related to the petroleum industry, the impact of such decrease in oil prices in the future would have less of an impact on the macroeconomy than that of the early 1980s. While oil demand is projected to increase annually (1 to 1.5%), the state's dependence on oil severance tax revenues had declined from a high of 27 percent in 1982 to only 8.5 percent of total state revenues in 1989. This change in revenue dependence provides some insulation from the impact of a change in world oil prices. The future of the petroleum industry in the area of exploration, however, remains closely related to world oil prices as current prices will not support exploration for new fields and sources.[10]

In short, the energy business has been big business in Texas for close to one hundred years. The Texas economy floated on the revenues from oil, gas and related industrial development. The revenue from the severance taxes that rolled into the state Treasury constituted an average of almost one-fifth of all state revenues even as late as 1983 and generated almost as much revenue annually as all payments received from the federal government. While the impact in 1990 of a change in the oil industry remains significant, that impact has been considerably

1 8

lessened, the change in oil prices upward or downward no longer automatically signals a return of a "boom" or "bust" period for the state.

The Role Of Agriculture In The Texas Macroeconomy

The significant place of Texas in agriculture enhanced the state's macroeconomy outlook during the "boom" period of the late 1970s and early 1980s. Texas leads the nation in the number of farms and ranches and farm/ranch acreage. As measured by cash receipts for agriculture, Texas ranks third following California and Iowa. Texas normally leads the nation in the livestock industry as well as in wool and mohair production. The state also continues to rank first in number of cattle feedlots. Additionally, Texas either leads or is among the nation's most significant producers of rice, grain, sorghum, spinach, watermelons, and cotton. Cotton and wheat remain the state's most important crops and together account for a combined total of 37 percent of total crop production.[11] Prior to the downturn of agriculture in the 1980s, it was estimated that "... over 17,000 businesses in Texas (including farms, gins, commodity brokers, warehouses, oil mills, and textile mills) [were] affected by the production of cotton alone, contributing to 58,000 jobs and $3 billion in revenue in 1982."[12] The state has 657 active gins in operation, but during the recession, the number of running bales ginned decreased from 5,508,519 in 1981 to 2,240,874 in 1983. The agriculture slump of the early 1980s hit Texas agriculture workers and family farmers hard. The average number of farm workers hired decreased from 223,000 in 1980 to 205,000 in 1983. Even after the downturn, the impact of the agribusiness on the Texas macroeconomy remains significant. If all aspects of the agribusiness are combined (provisions of supplies, credit, service and marketing), the impact of agriculture on the state's economy exceeds $33 billion each year.[13]

During the past ninety years, the macroeconomy of Texas developed on this fairly narrow track dependent upon either expendable natural resources or agriculture production that was closely tied to profitable energy prices. Agriculture income in Texas, however, mirrored the national picture. High energy costs coupled with poor weather conditions, depressed crop prices and high real interest rates of the early 1980s led to a serious decline in the agribusiness across the entire United States. With such a high level of agricultural production in the state, Texas was hard hit by the decline of agriculture by 1983. Farmland values in Texas decreased 32 percent between 1985 and 1989 compared to 12 percent for the United States. Between 1981 and 1988, 34,300 farmers left the business in Texas; almost 23 percent of those were under thirty five years of age. The loss of younger farmers indicate fewer farmers in the future to replace those who retire. Cash receipts for agriculture production fell from $9.6 billion in 1982 to $9.0 billion in 1983. With farm prices decreasing, participation in government programs increased dramatically between 1982 and 1988. Even the King Ranch signed up for the first time for the government programs. Table 2 shows change in the percentage of farmers participating in government programs in 1982 and 1988.

19

TABLE 2
Participation of Texas Farmers in U.S. Government Programs 1982 and 1987 by
Commodity

Commodity	1982 Percent Participation	1988 Percent Participation	Percent Change
Wheat	48%	85%	77%
Corn	29%	87%	200%
Sorghum	47%	81%	72%
Rice	78%	92%	58%
Barley	46%	78%	70%
Oats	14%	30%	114%

Source: Farm Facts, Office of Farmer Assistance Programs at the Texas
Department of Agriculture, September 9, 1988.

Participation in government farm programs provides price support for agricultural commodities. During periods of declining commodity pricing, participation in the programs may make the difference between a farmer going out of, or remaining in the agribusiness. Participation in federal government programs, however, generally carries the requirement of planting a reduced level of the crop for which the price support is received. High participation generally indicates a gap between parity (the cost of raising the crop) and market price. While record numbers of farmers were signing up for government farm programs in the late 1980s, the federal government was projecting a scheduled phase out of such programs. President Bush's FY 91 budget proposal calls for continued phase out of such government programs. By August of 1988, the number of farms and ranches had dipped to the lowest level since 1910 when the trend away from small family farms first started. The number of Texas farms and ranches declined fifteen percent between 1985 and 1988 with the state losing an average of 168 farmers and ranchers a week in 1988.[14] Added to these problems, adverse weather conditions dealt Texas farmers yet another blow. The drought occurring in 1988 was determined to be the worst since that of the 1930s with crop and livestock damage estimated at $1.36 billion. After the downturn of agriculture in 1983, a slow improvement in farm conditions had been projected throughout the remainder of the 1980s if adverse weather conditions did not increase crop losses. These fairly optimistic projections were effectively changed when the drought of 1988 was followed by a more serious drought in 1989 and a devastating freeze in December of 1989. In the Rio Grande Valley, the freeze, unprecedented as measured by severity and duration further devastated the agribusiness. The near zero temperatures destroyed all crops including nursery stock necessary for replanting of the citrus orchards. President Bush declared nine counties of the Valley disaster areas. The harvest of 1989 had been projected as the first full harvest following the freeze of 1983 which had come to devastating the citrus industry. Recovery that began to occur in 1987 has been further slowed by these recent events.

While the farmers and ranchers of Texas suffered economically from the 1988 drought, a four-state survey of retail food prices indicated that major beef packers and food processors profited. Retail prices of beef jumped an average of

20

10.4 percent in Texas a cattle producers were forced to sell off their base herds. High feed costs coupled with drought-killed grasslands resulted in price decreases of up to 15 percent to producers. A 1988 survey conducted by the Texas Department of Agriculture attributed the variance in pricing to the control of about seventy percent of feedlot cattle slaughter nationally by ConAgra Inc., IBP Inc., and Cargill Inc., a subsidiary of Excel Corporation. The American Meat Institute, a national grade association representing the meat packing and processing industry denied the survey results. According to the Texas Agriculture Commissioner, the results in Texas remained out of line with those of previous surveys that had been conducted over many years. Jim Hightower (Texas Agriculture Commissioner), Jim Nichols (Minnesota Agriculture Commissioner), and Steve Mauere (Ohio Agriculture Director) held a joint press conference on June 30, 1988 in front of the Chicago Board of Trade to focus national attention on the growing gap between rising consumer prices and falling farm prices that they felt could not be attributed to drought-related economics. In light of the impact of the drought of 1988 on the state, South Texans turned to the federal government for emergency relief, and the state removed the sales tax on hay, corn, oats, and other feeds consumed by farm and ranch animals as well as wildlife. The sales tax relief was designed to improve the economics of the agriculture situation as well as promote progressive wildlife and conservation practices.[15]

Responding to current trends and projections for a slowing in agribusiness development, Governor Clements had signed an executive order in 1988 establishing the Governor's Task Force On Agricultural Development in Texas. The Task Force is composed of twenty six members who represent farm and ranch production as well as commodity groups and agricultural organizations and leaders in private agribusiness and education. The primary purpose of the Task Force is to assist with keeping Texas competitive in farming. The Task Force found that the state is losing cast sums of money by sending its agricultural product out of state for processing rather than retaining the value added to commodities through in-state processing. The difference between the raw commodity price and the processed price constitutes what is called "value-added" loss to the Texas economy. The Texas Department of Agriculture as well as the Texas A&M University system have long pushed for increased agricultural processing in the state.[16] The impact of the "value-added" loss is illuminated in the following example:

> Texas onions net growers in South Texas 12 cents a pound, but they are returned to state supermarkets and restaurants after processing in Philadelphia as onion rings costing more than $2 a pound. Farmers sell cotton for $450 a bale to mills in Georgia, North Carolina or Tennessee, but once that cotton is processed into threads it costs Texas clothing manufacturers $24,000 to buy it back and use it to make shirt and jeans.[17]

Texas produces one-third of the United States' cotton crop and 97 percent of the domestic-produced mohair. These agricultural commodities have successfully made the transition into current markets. The real profits are, however, currently exported out of state as part of the price spreads between raw wool and retail products is estimated to be $1.50 per pound (raw wool) and $50.00 per pound (finished wool product).[18] Research at Texas A&M indicated that the value-added by in state processing could increase the state's economy by $10 billion annually. Over 133.2 million acres in the state are devoted to agriculture

21

use, and the industry is second only to oil and gas production. The potential for impact in the Texas macroeconomy is significant.[19]

As part of the approach to diversification of agriculture, Texans have turned once again in recent years to an old industry. Prior to Prohibition, there were more than twenty-five wineries in the state. By the time that Prohibition was repealed, only one winery remained. In recent years, rejuvenation of the wine industry that began in the 1970s has accelerated with impetus from the University of Texas experimental research programs. The University of Texas began to experiment with growing vines on its arid West Texas lands. Vines that produced excellent grapes for wine were identified, and eventually, the University of Texas lands were commercialized in a joint venture through leasing the lands to a French and Texas consortium of investors. Wines from this project are bottled under the label of Ste. Genevieve, and this area that began as a University of Texas experimental station may one day be one of the largest wineries in the country. Over 30,000 acres in the Bakersfield winery area have been identified a potential vineyards. To retain a Texas bond, a winery must remain at least fifty one percent Texas owned, and, by 1985, there were sixteen such wineries in Texas. The wine industry in the state continues to grow both in size and in excellence. In 1987 and 1988, the Llano Estacado winery near Lubbock won gold, silver, and bronze awards for wines submitted in international competition.[20] Such diversification of the agribusiness is one key to keeping Texas agriculture competitive in future years.

While the economic impact of agriculture in the state has increased in recent years, the face of agriculture has changed over time to that of a less labor-intensive industry. Between 1940 and 1984, the number of producers was reduced from 23 percent to 2 percent of the Texas population. Agribusiness suppliers had increased, however, from 17 percent to 25 percent during the same time period.[21] Since 1981, 18,000 cattle operations in the state have been discontinued. Beef production and feedlot operations have shifted heavily to larger operations. Between August of 1981 and March of 1987, the number of farm equipment dealers decreased in the state from 9,651 to 7,290.[22] Agriculture and agriculture-related employment is not projected to grow as rapidly in the future as other sectors of the Texas macroeconomy. The agribusiness will become progressively less labor intensive over the remainder of the decade. The long-range trend in agriculture is for continued and increased mechanization coupled with a change in farm sizes to fewer, but larger tracts. These trends are expected to accelerate and continue throughout the remainder of the 1990s.

Banking And The Texas Economy

The rather narrow base of the Texas economy in the late 1970s and early 1980s closely tied the banking industry to agribusiness, petroleum industries and related economic developments. Financial transactions in the state occur through banks, saving and loan firms, and many of the more than two thousand insurance companies licensed to sell insurance to the state. The Texas banking industry had developed in a somewhat unique manner. Regulation of banks and other financial institutions in Texas is lodged, for the most part, in the Finance Commission consisting of nine individuals appointed by the Governor and confirmed by the Senate for six-year overlapping terms of office. Until 1987, the Texas Constitution prohibited branch banking, i.e., banks doing business in more than one physical location. The prohibition against branch banking was circumvented in the 1970s through "bank holding corporations." These corporation purchased subsidiary banks outright or obtained a controlling interest in other banks while maintaining their separate corporate identities.[23] The responsibility for chartering state banks is vested in the State Banking Board which is composed ex officio of the State Treasurer, the Banking Commissioner and a gubernatorial appointee. These political connections allowed the banking industry in the state to bypass the Constitutional requirements against branch banking and thus contributed to the failure of large numbers of savings and loans during the 1980s as many that failed were part of large holding corporations. Today, the banking industry in Texas is consolidating. Interstate banking and branch banking are also increasing. "Four of the five largest Texas banks are owned by banking companies based out of state."[24]

Banks in Texas were caught up in the real estate "boom" of the late 1970s and early 1980s. The construction industry is also closely tied to performance of the macroeconomy, and the status of lending institutions has a direct impact on this industry. The "boom" in the construction business of the 1970s began a sharp decline in late 1983. The "boom" had been tied to the rapidly increasing immigration rates and oil prices.[25] When oil prices dropped, unemployment increased, foreclosures and bankruptcies rapidly followed, and the value of real estate took a sharp plunge. A substantial number of bank failures have been attributed to real estate and real estate development loans. For example, Texas Commerce Bankshares is the state's second largest banking organization. Almost thirty percent (29.7%) of its 1989 losses were attributable to its Austin branch, a heavy real estate lender.[26] The sharp decline in real estate even led to the bankruptcy of former governor John Connaly who had invested heavily in real estate development. Even as late as January of 1990, it was estimated that in Austin "... 65 percent of apartments, at least half of downtown office buildings and most of the major hotels now belong either to the federal government or to the financial institutions that lent developers billions of dollars during the '80s real estate boom."[27] The situation in Austin was not dissimilar from that of Houston, Dallas and other cities hard hit by the downturn in the Texas economy.

Texas and Oklahoma led the nation in the number of banks that failed in 1986. By September 22, 1989, one hundred thirteen banks in Texas had failed with the year not yet over. Of these 1989 failed banks, more than forty four were part of two large bank-holding companies. Forty of the failed banks were from First Republic Bank Corporation which became NCNB Texas National Bank, the state's largest bank. As of the third week in September, 1989, Texas bank failures constituted 70.6 percent of all bank failures in the nation. Even more independently chartered banks are predicted to fail in Texas during 1990; projections are that about eighty will fail in 1990. Yet, according to an analyst for Paine Webber Inc., the worst is behind the state. Although the failures are projected to continue, the absolute numbers should be fewer in the future.[28] The numbers of banks that have failed in Texas since the recession of 1981 are shown in Table 3.

23

TABLE 3
Bank Failures in Texas – 1982 through 1990

Year	Bank Failures	
1982	42	
1983	48	
1984	80	
1985	120	
1986	138	
1987	184	
1988	200	
1989	200	(projected)
1990	80	(projected)

Source: Compiled data from Farm Facts, Texas Department of Agriculture, September, 1988, and July, 1989, and San Marcos Daily Record, September 22, 1989.

The economy in Texas has begun to stabilize, but the banking industry lags from eighteen to twenty four months behind changes in the macroeconomy. Bank failures in Texas are predicted to continue for at least two more years as the result of previous decisions even if the economy of the state continues to grow. The combination of the decrease in oil prices and the decline in agriculture and related industries coupled with high unemployment and record bank failures resulted in a downturn of the Texas macroeconomy unprecedented since the 1930s. The state has yet to fully recover. The economic "bust" of the early to mid 1980s, however, had a positive impact in that the recession prompted the development of innovative strategies to bolster state revenues and diversify the Texas economy.

The Years Of Economic Downturns And Revenue Shortfalls

The years from 1970 through 1982, the "boom" years for Texas, ended as quickly as they had begun. Until 1983, the state had revenue surpluses in the range of a billion dollars annually from the rapid growth of severance taxes associated with high world prices. Accompanying the rapid decline in oil prices that began in 1981 were other changes in the national economy that had a direct effect on the state. Revenue sharing funds also began to steadily decline after 1981. General revenue sharing had increased the state's dependence on federal dollars over the seven-year life of the program. Additionally the program was slated for phase out and expiration in September of 1986. Compounding these revenue shortfall problems were additional decreases in federal grant dollars. The consolidation of numerous categorical grants into block grants at the federal level as part of the Omnibus Appropriations Bill of 1981 had reduced federal dollars coming into the state for entitlement and infrastructure, putting yet another drain on decreasing revenues. The economy spiraled from a period of "boom" to one of "bust" with record numbers of foreclosures, farm failures, bankruptcies, record slumps in the mining and real estate sectors, and a virtual halting of the construction business.

By 1983, the world price of oil had declined to a new low, and the State Comptroller projected revenue shortfalls of up to $3.5 billion for the biennium of FY 1986-1987. The shortfall was tied primarily to the sharp decrease in revenues from the severance tax coupled with the added burden of economic slump and decreased federal dollars coming into the state. A special session of the legislature was called in 1984 to deal with the revenue shortfall; taxes were increased to fund education and highways. The tax increases of 1984 were insufficient to resolve the problems associated with declining revenues set against rising costs and demands for government service. In 1986, Governor Mark White called two special sessions of the legislature to deal with the state's continuing revenue-shortfall problems.[29]

In 1987, the National Governors' Association and the National Conference of State Legislatures reported that poor economic performance coupled with reduced federal funding had forced almost one half of the states to reduce current fiscal year budgets. Budgets in seven states were cut by nineteen percent or more and in four states by five percent or more. Federal grants for capital development in the areas of highways, urban development, transportation, and environmental protection had been substantially reduced between 1980 and 1986, placing greater demands on state coffers simply to maintain current program levels. State and local expenditures for capital development increased dramatically in 1986 to offset federal cuts.[30] The Community Development Block Grant declined by 16 percent between 1982 and 1987, and the Reagan administration proposed termination or phase out of all other community and economic development grants in the FY 1988 budget. Federal grants to state and local governments (excluding income support programs) were reduced thirty-seven percent between 1980 and 1987. The overall reduction in federal aid amounted to five percent of total state budgets by the end of 1986. By the end of 1987, most states ran a deficit of about one percent of total outlays.[31] Federal Revenue in Texas declined from $4,109,472,582 in 1986 to $4,078,102,385 in 1987. Net revenues dropped from $17,951,954,127 in 1986 to $$17,524,097,514 in 1987, a decrease of 2.4 percent. State expenditures in 1987 were decreased by 4.5 percent from those of 1986.[32] Texas was faced with absorbing the brunt of the decrease in federal funds from budget cuts to offset the growing national deficit in an economy already beleaguered by the impact of the decline in the state's two most significant industries – petroleum and agriculture.

In a search for additional revenues, the Texas legislature turned in 1986 to increases in the sales tax, the gasoline tax, cigarette tax, alcohol tax, the corporate franchise tax and proposals to legalize pari-mutuel wagering. User fees such as college tuition, driver's licenses, entrance fees for recreational facilities, circuit court filings and auto safety inspections were increased. Pari-mutuel wagering was projected to compensate for a large portion of the state's revenue shortfall. Proposals were also introduced for the addition of a state lottery. Evidence suggests, however, that pari-mutuel wagering is not the panacea of new revenue that proponents often claim. Twenty-five of the twenty seven states which have pari-mutuel wagering have had to change or adjust the percentage of the state's share of revenues in order to attract the industry. The Legislative Budget Board estimates that the revenue from pari-mutuel wagering will generate $101 million in revenues for the state by 1992; however, that revenue would represent less than one half of one percent of total state revenue needs. Pari-mutuel wagering on horse and dog racing in Texas was legalized in a November, 1987, referendum. Initial revenues to the state were projected to be $3.59 million in the 1988 budget year and $22 million in 1989 and $20.3 million in 1990. Additional evidence suggests that state lotteries do not make a significant contribution to state revenues with the average percent of state own source general revenue falling below 2.0 percent. Administration costs are high relative to the returns generated by such lotteries and, in some cases, may run as high as 22 percent of lottery sales. Often the net revenue receipts are less than one percent of total state revenues.[33]

In his FY 89 Budget Message, President Reagan had specified the problems that he considered to be significant and recommended changes to increase management of the national budget. As he took office in January of 1989, President Bush promised a continuation of the "no new taxes" policy and emphasized a focus on improved government efficiency and integrity. His view of national fiscal affairs, however, did not signal a major departure from that of the Reagan administration. For FY 90, the U.S. budget cut federal grants to state and local governments once more. The cuts amounted to almost half as a share of GNP between 1980 and 1988 (2.2% of GNP in 1980 compared to 1.3% of GNP in 1988). In terms of real dollars, grants to state and local government were cut by more than one third, especially in the area of local government benefits such as economic development, transportation systems, state and local judicial grants. Remaining domestic discretionary programs had also been cut substantially during the 1980s. Real outlays were cut by more than 25%.[34]

The intergovernmental transfer of funds from the federal government to state and local government can, therefore, be expected to continue at relatively the same or reduced levels throughout the 1990s. States will have to accept an increasing financial burden and compensate for any required changes through state policies and development of new revenue sources. Decreases in intergovernmental transfers in federal funds will continue to have a major impact on the macroeconomy of state and local government due to the size of the public sector.[35] At the turn of the century, the public sector was only 5% of the national GNP. At the current time, government remains ranked as the third largest employer of Texas. As the majority of state expenditures are constitutionally required or the result of federal programs and mandates, the changing role of the national government and reallocation of expenditures will take an ever increasing share of the state budget and require adequate financing and tax base for generation of the appropriate revenue levels. During February of 1990, the Texas legislature has once again been called into special session to find a solution to financing primary and secondary education. Local government tax bases in many areas are insufficient to provide the necessary funding levels. Because of the decline in property values, many local school districts have already increased taxes to such a point that local taxpayers are eligible to call for, and are calling for, tax rollback elections. Bond elections are going down to defeat in other local areas. The shrinking local tax base will mean that efforts to improve funding for education will most likely fall to the state legislature.

It is estimated by the University of Texas Bureau of Business Research that "... every dollar spent in education will save about six dollars in future prison and welfare costs."[36] To compete effectively for the kind of economic development that Texas needs and move into the skilled labor market, education will have to be improved. Governor Mark White stated that, "Education is the oil and gas of the future."[37] If Texas is to be competitive in the current "boom" of high tech industry, the state will have to supply a skilled labor force. Future economic development of the state hinges on the type of labor force that is developed along with the accompanying business development. Low skill, low wage industries may only succeed in placing additional financial burdens on the state, and the absence of skilled labor primarily attracts this type of industry and business.

Texas has a constitutional limit on the level of allowable state debt which results in a "pay-as-you-go" approach to government finance. State debt levels cannot simply be increased each fiscal year to the total amount of a projected deficit as is the case with the federal government. As the state continues to experience tight budgets during the early 1990s, demands for state expenditures appear to be on the increase. Agencies in the state that account for sixty percent of the state budget are either under federal court orders to improve services or constitutional provisions requiring increased expenditures related to growing client numbers.[38] The state will need a stable, growing economy as well as increased revenues simply to meet the demands for services and programs placed on state and local governments.

Economic Transition

In 1984, the per capita average tax burden in Texas was $615, and the state ranked last in the ratio of taxes to personal income, first in reliance on severance taxes, and the fourth in sales tax reliance. In 1986, Texas state government ranked forty-seventh in per capita state government spending and forty-sixth in taxation. In 1986, 61.3 percent of state revenue came from taxes; 22.1 percent from federal grants and 16.6 percent from miscellaneous sources. The state had been able to maintain low taxes primarily because of the revenue from oil and gas severance taxes.[39] For the year ended August 31, 1989, 60.1 percent of state revenues came from taxes. Oil and gas production taxes were 5.4% of total revenue, and federal grant income was 23.5% of all revenues. In 1987, Texas ranked forty-eighth in general expenditures of state government per $1,000 of personal income ($86/$1,000 of personal income compared to $251 for Wyoming and average of $115/$1,000 for the U.S.). State expenditures were reflective of the level of taxes. In that same year, Texas ranked forty-ninth in revenue/$1,000 of personal income ($106.89/$1,000 of personal income). When measured in dollars per capita or percentage of personal income, taxes remain lighter in Texas than in most states. However, if taxes are measured in terms of effective tax rates, Texas taxpayers now pay a higher effective federal tax rate than individuals in states with an income tax. The federal 1986 tax reform eliminated the sales tax deduction but retained the deduction for state income tax. This change of the national tax structure contributed to the regressivity of the Texas tax system. Individuals at the lower end of the income spectrum will pay a higher proportion of their income in state taxes than will their counterparts in other states.[40] The 1970 census had ranked Texas thirty-fourth in median family income and in 1973, the state ranked thirty-third in per capita income. In 1985, Texas ranked forty-third in per capita income ($12,572) and forty-seventh in state expenditures ($165.21 per person). Projections for per capita income for the year 2000 in 1982 constant dollars are $15,153 with the state moving to twenty-first place among fifty. However, the projections are for the state to move into fifth place with regard to tax liability per person. In 1987, Texas had a median income of $13,819. The level of income in the state does not appear to be related to level of government expenditures in the state.

Texas has always expressed a preference for low taxation which made the state's revenue levels dependent on urbanization, industrial growth, natural resources, and the world market. Between 1980 and 1986, the state's population increased 17.3 percent with a net migration increase of 9.3 percent; Texas ranked fifth in the nation in population increase. In terms of largest numerical increase, Texas ranked second in the nation for the period from 1980 to 1986 in spite of inmigration decreases that began in 1983. The state's rapid population growth of 1980 through 1982, occurred on the heels of a net migration and population growth increase of 13.2 percent between 1970 and 1980. The most significant increase in net population for the state occurred in 1982. With net inmigration nearly doubling between 1981 and 1982, Texas looked for a continued population "boom." Property values rapidly increased, and real estate developers began large scale projects in record numbers anticipating a continuation of the pattern. The long period of sustained and rapidly increasing population growth of the 1970s through 1982, made the bitter pill of the severe economic downturn even more difficult to swallow. While the population of Texas continued to grow, the decline in population growth mirrored the decline in the energy industry. Population growth rates in Texas began to fall off sharply after 1983. Between 1986 and 1989, as measured by net migration, more individuals moved out of the state than into the state. The growth in population that helped to offset further decreases in revenues related to energy and natural resources during the mid-1980s will slow for the remainder of the decade. The net gain in population is expected to be in the range of an average increase of 0.92 percent for the decade of the 1980s compared to 1.96 percent average increase for the decade of the 1970s. The bulk of the population growth will be in the major metropolitan areas of Texas. Such patterns of urban population growth are like a two-edged sword. When a downturn in the economy occurs, the effect is most evident in the changes in unemployment rates for these same major metropolitan areas with heavy concentrations of business and industry. During the downturn of the mid-1980s, unemployment rates increased dramatically in the major metropolitan areas and were highest of all in Houston which was more closely tied to the energy industry than were other major metropolitan areas of the state.[41]

During the 1960s and 1970s, unemployment in Texas had seldom exceeded 3.5% to 4.0%, about half that of the national average. By June of 1986, the unemployment rate for nonfarm occupations had reached 10.0 percent, the highest level since the 1930s.[42] The bulk of unemployment occurred in the petroleum, mining, agriculture, and construction industries. The pattern of unemployment in the state has changed significantly since the move toward economic diversification

2 8

was started in 1986. While increases in employment in the manufacturing and services sectors occurred in the late 1980s, employment in mining and construction have decreased substantially. The face of agriculture employment has also changed dramatically. In 1940, 30 percent of the state's work force was employed in agriculture. By 1970, only 6 percent were employed in agriculture. In 1988, most of the gains in employment were in business, health and other services. Employment also increased in state and local government due to upgraded in state's education, corrections, and mental health/mental retardation systems. Services accounted for over half of the new jobs in fiscal 1989. Employment in retail sales and trade are also increasing.[43] Table 4 shows Texas' agricultural employment by sector of the economy for 1985 to 1992.

TABLE 4
Texas Nonagricultural Employment Annual Growth Rates 1985 to 1992

Occupation	1985-87	1987-92	1985-92*
Mining	-16.3	0.0	-4.9
Manufacturing	-3.6	1.6	0.1
Construction	-11.7	0.3	-3.3
Transportation Communication Public Utilities	0.4	2.2	1.7
Finance, Insurance Real Estate	-0.4	1.7	1.1
Wholesale, Retail Trade	-1.7	2.0	0.9
Services	3.0	1.9	2.2
Government	2.5	1.4	1.7

Source: Comptroller of Public Accounts.

Houston is leading the state's expansion with almost a third of all new Texas jobs over the past two and a half years. By the summer of 1989, unemployment in Houston fell to its lowest level since 1982, the peak of the "boom." Dallas has also begun to recover. Employment rose slightly in 1989. The San Antonio area tourism industry helped the city to ride out the recession with no significant decreases in unemployment. Employment in the Fort Worth area increased by more than 2.0 percent between 1988 and 1989. Fort Worth, like San Antonio, escaped job losses during the 1986-1987 recession; however, employment growth came to a halt. As the Fort Worth, Austin, and San Antonio areas are heavily dependent upon the aerospace and defence industries, employment growth may be adversely affected by the proposed cuts in the national defense budget for FY 1991. Austin was Texas' fastest growing city but has been the slowest of the metropolitan areas to experience economic recovery. With the slump in the high-tech industry, real estate, construction, and finance, Austin experienced a severe and prolonged economic downturn during the state's recession. Between August of 1988 and August, 1989, Austin began to once again record an increase in employment.[44]

Economic Diversification

Areas of Texas heavily dependent upon the petroleum or agriculture industry were hardest hit by the economic downturn that began in 1983. The efforts on the part of political and business leaders to assure that the state's macroeconomy no longer ran on such a narrow track resulted in the economic diversification of the late 1980s. While this diversification has been instrumental in the state's economic recovery, the potential for insulation of the Texas economy from national economic downturns has also changed. "... compared to ten years ago, nonagricultural employment in Texas today is 62% less sensitive to unexpected changes in real oil prices and 338% more sensitive to unexpected changes in national employment."[45] Projections are for the Texas' economy to be much more vulnerable to national business cycles during the 1990s.[46]

> ... the state's economic diversification efforts has a dark side that changes Texas' historical relationship with the U.S. economy. "We used to say,'What's good for the country is bad for Texas,' or 'When the nation gets pneumonia, Texas sneezes.'" Now it's different. ... Now as the nation goes, so goes Texas.[47]

With the United States economy experiencing the longest sustained periods of economic expansion, the immediate future of the Texas economy would appear to fairly stable. The rate of growth in the national economy was projected to be moderate during 1989, averaging 2.5 percent when final figures are computed. This same growth rate in the economy is projected for 1991. While the sustained growth has occurred in the macroeconomy, the pace of growth has varied widely across sectors of the economy with minicycles occurring in energy, farming, and manufacturing. The national economic stability has been enhanced by a move to a service economy which is more stable than manufacturing. The sustained period of growth in the national economy is projected to continue in 1990 if inflation is kept under control. With the closer ties to the national economy, performance of the state's macroeconomy will depend more heavily in future years on political decision makers.[48] Downturns in the macroeconomy will signal revenue shortfalls and economic adjustments for all levels of government.

The intergovernmental fiscal system changed dramatically during the 1980s. The federal government shifted an increasing responsibility to state and local government at the same time that federal support for long-standing programs was reduced. In 1987, nearly one-half of the states reduced expenditures from budgeted levels and thirty-three adopted new taxes; Texas was one of these.[49] In 1987, Texas increased its sales tax from 5.25% to 6.0% and extended the base of the tax to include a variety of services. As the financial burdens of the mid-1980s increased, Texas turned increasingly to non-guaranteed debt (revenue bonds) to finance development of the infrastructure. In 1987, total state debt was $5,328,886,000. Of this $2,080,588,000 was full faith and credit; the remainder was non-guaranteed. Of the net long-term debt remaining, the proportion that is non-guaranteed debt is even larger; $2,091,407,000 of net long-term was non-guaranteed in 1987 compared to $643,703,000 of full faith and credit net long-term debt.[50] The pattern has continued with revenue bonds increasing as a portion of state debt from 25 percent in 1988 to 28.7 percent in 1989.[51]

The low point in Texas economy was during 1986-87 as measured by the real gross state product (GSP). Not all sectors of the state economy experienced the downturn from 1985-1987. Services, government, transportation, communication, and public utilities experienced positive growth compared to a real GSP annual rate of -2.5 percent in 1986 and -1.9 in 1987. The manufacturing sector of the economy ranked second (trade is first) in contributing to the gross state product. The service sector, particularly medicine, health and business experienced the highest growth rate between 1985-1987. The mining sector (oil and gas industries) extraction was the hardest hit during the economic downturn; also hard hit were construction, finance, and real estate.[52] The non-farm employment rate is projected to experience positive growth during 1990-1992. A recovery of the mineral sector is not projected unless world oil prices increase. Most of the growth in the manufacturing sector during this period was generated by six industries: nonelectrical machinery, electronics and electronic equipment, chemical and allied products, petroleum and coal products, food and kindred products, and transportation-equipment. Electronics and electronic equipment or high-tech manufacturing is one key to future economic expansion in the state.[53] In order to be competitive in these industries, however, local business will have to expand into overseas markets. At the current time, estimates are that fewer than twenty-five percent of Texas' high-tech industries are engaged in overseas market. With the expanding markets in Europe and Japan and the changes occurring in the Soviet Bloc, the scope of overseas markets will be closely related to the expansion and success of high-tech industries.[54]

In order to begin a period of economic recovery, Texas has been faced with the need to diversify the economy and develop a macroeconomy that was not primarily dependent upon the energy industry. Certain states such as Missouri and Arkansas had linked economic development to education. Skilled labor is vital to attracting industries that will increase economic development. "Skilled labor doesn't simply happen on its own – it is the product of an efficiently run, adequately funded system of public education."[55] In 1984, educational reforms had moved Texas from thirty-eighth of the fifty states to a median position in educational support. In 1986, however, Texas was the only state to cut its general appropriations to higher education; higher education budgets were the source of 38 percent of funding cuts made for that year. The funds for higher education were cut even more deeply in 1987. By 1989, funding for higher education had not returned to 1985 funding levels. The Foundation School Budget which provides the bulk of state funding for Texas public schools was also significantly decreased in 1986. Such cuts send a message to business and industry that the state has decreased its focus on creating a supply of "skilled" labor which is essential for the development of high-tech industry.[56] With forty-nine community colleges and thirty-five universities, the state has the resources to provide a steady supply of "skilled" labor if the funding is aligned with policies and educational structures.[57] Such industries as MCC, Sematech, Superconducting Supercollider require skilled labor. Without such skilled labor, capability and productivity of the work force declines. Educational funding is a critical state issue. Nationally,

... more than half of the workers entering the labor force lack the ability to perform even moderately complex tasks such as reading blueprints or understanding equipment operating instructions. While the capability of our work force is declining, Japan's economic success can be attributed at least in part to their investment in education. Japan's literacy rates is 95 percent, whereas ours has slipped to about 80 percent.[58]

Even though Texas is in a median position, the state ranks far below other states against which we compete for economic development in the area of educational financing. "New York, ranked second among the states in educational funding, spent two-thirds more per student than Texas."[59] New York also ranks far ahead of Texas in the area of economic development.[60]

Economic performance in future years will be more closely related to structuring of a macroeconomy that has fully developed manufacturing and service industries coupled with availability of a skilled labor force. The challenge for the future will be to continue to develop a diversified and stable state economy. By 1986, Texas had at least twenty-one different programs, funds, offices, and commissions dedicated to economic development in order to try to improve the state economic prospects.[61] Since the mid-1980s, the emphasis in the state has been on the importance of building indigenous or "home-grown" companies. The building of "home-grown" companies is known as "incubator development." Although the state lags behind New York and Pennsylvania, Texas is among the ten leading states in business incubator development. The growth of such programs across the United States has increased from slightly above fifty in 1984 to more than three hundred and fifty in 1989. Varieties of names are used to describe incubator development – enterprise or business and technology center, innovator center. In essence, the incubator provides a protected growth environment including economic conditions to support development of a new business.[62]

The incubator seeks to link effectively talent, ideas, capital and know-how to leverage, entrepreneurial talent, accelerate the development of new companies, and thus spread the commercialization of technology. ... The newest of the Texas incubators, the Austin Technology Incubator, is unique in that it is a joint venture sponsored by UT-Austin, the City of Austin, the Austin Chamber of Commerce, and private donors with a focus on developing new technology-based businesses.[63]

The incubator strategy is innovative and encourages diversification as well as providing jobs and a boost to local economies. As of August, 1989, one hundred thirty three companies operated in the Texas incubators. Each such contribution to economic development provides an opportunity for insulation against a downturn in the macroeconomy.

Economic growth between 1983 and 1989 has averaged 2.5-3.5 percent in the United States, setting all peacetime records. The pace of this economic growth has varied dependent upon the sector of the economy. Greater diversification of a state's economy provides an increased opportunity for variance in the effects of an economic downturn. Growth of the Texas economy is projected to be 3.0% in 1990 increasing to 4.1% in 1991. The latest figures for 1989 showed an increase in the Texas GSP of 2.7% for the year.[64] The national recessionary trend of 1981

32

through 1983 was magnified in Texas as energy and agribusiness constituted the narrow tracks on which the economy of the state ran. Because of the close relationships of these industries to the price of petroleum, economic recovery in Texas was projected to lag behind that of the nation. The economic downturns and problems occurring in other states were simply magnified in Texas. Indeed, while the latest, 1989, economic indicators show that the state's economy is growing and experiencing recovery, Texas continues to lag behind economic recovery occurring in much of the rest of the nation. Texas has historically depended on its natural resources for the value of the state's economic climate, but the world economy is shifting from one based on natural resources to an economy based on high technology, information and services. The state's economy can no longer afford to run on the narrow tracks of the pre-1986 years. Table 5 shows the percentage increase in total income for sectors of the economy for Texas, the United States and selected regions of the country.

TABLE 5
Percent Change in Income Shares for Texas, Geographic Regions, and the United States, 1987 – 1988.

Geographic Unit	Total % Change	Min- ing	Const- ruction	Manu- factur- ing	Whole sale/ Retail	Finance Insurance Real Estate	Ser- vices	Gov.
Florida	9.0	7.5	7.5	7.3	10.7	8.6	9.7	8.5
NewYork	7.7	7.6	6.9	4.6	7.3	9.8	9.5	7.7
California	7.4	8.7	8.2	5.5	10.8	6.9	8.5	6.5
Texas	4.8	2.8	-2.1	7.1	5.5	4.0	7.5	4.3
U.S.	7.3	4.0	6.9	6.2	8.9	8.5	9.5	6.2
New England	9.5	7.8	9.3	4.2	10.6	10.1	12.9	9.3
Mideast	8.1	2.4	9.1	4.9	8.9	10.1	10.2	7.3
Southeast	7.7	2.8	6.8	5.8	9.4	7.7	10.1	6.1
Far West	7.7	12.6	9.5	6.3	10.6	6.8	8.6	6.4
Great Lakes	7.2	-1.0	9.4	7.3	8.2	9.9	8.7	6.5
Plains	5.4	4.0	4.1	6.9	8.4	6.6	8.8	5.4
Southwest	4.9	3.8	-0.9	6.8	5.8	3.3	7.5	3.6

Source: U.S. Department of Commerce Survey of Current Business, April, 1989 (latest figures available)

Indeed, Texas continues to rank behind other states of similar size and diversity such as California and Florida as well as behind the United States and all eight regions included in the Department of Commerce Survey of Current Business. In general, Texas ranks above the South Eastern states but below the other regions in growth in personal income. Texas ranked above all census regional averages for growth in manufacturing for the period 1987-1988 except the East North Central and below all regions for growth in wholesale/retail trade. The U.S. Department of Commerce Bureau of Economic Analysis showed the growth in Texas personal income to be 2.7% for the third and fourth quarter of 1988 compared to 6.2% for the same period during 1987. Projections are for per capita income to grow from $15,337 in 1989 to $16,188 in 1989. The data revealed increases in mining with a

33

slight reordering of contribution to the state's economic growth. Manufacturing was first, services second, transportation and public utilities third and wholesale/retail trade fourth.[65]

The 1988 GAAP report of the Texas Comptroller of Public Accounts, Economic Analysis Center shows the state's net worth has risen to $48.8 billion or an increase of 11.2% over 1987. The state's liability also increased, jumping 10.3% over 1987 with a total of 11.8 billion in 1988. State revenues did, however, grew faster than expenditures in 1988. Total state revenues rose 13.2% in 1988. Revenue from the sales tax increased 11.2% between September of 1988 and July of 1989. Other areas of sizeable increase included revenues from motor fuels, hotel and motel tax and taxes such as cement, sulphur and miscellaneous gross receipts not identified separately. The areas of most significant decrease included, in order of significance, telephone tax, franchise tax, insurance companies tax and oil production tax.[66] The Texas Comptroller's 1989 Cash Report showed continued improvement and diversification in the Texas economy. Revenues increased 5.5% between 1987 and 1988. Population growth was increasing, and Texas is projected to have the second largest state population by the mid-1990s if current trend continues. Temporary taxes such as the franchise taxes that were increased as the result of the economic downturn in 1986 were allowed to expire at the end of 1989. The oil production tax which had experienced a reduction of 30.7% between 1986 and 1987 showed positive growth. Revenues from the natural gas production tax which had decreased 17.2% between 1986 and 1987, increased 19.9% above the 1988 revenues and accounted for 5.2% of total tax collections. The projected cuts in federal funding proposed in the FY1989 national budget did not occur, and, in 1989, Texas received an increase of 11.7% over fiscal year 1988 in federal funding.[67]

In 1987, the Texas Bond Review Board was created by the 70th Session of the Legislature. The first annual report of the Bond Board was issued in November of 1988. The report showed that improvement in the Texas economy and state finances during the FY 1987 fiscal year had resulted in increased confidence in Texas general obligation bonds. The yield rates on Texas bonds had risen steadily after the state's financial strength was weakened by the oil "bust." Texas bond ratings were decreased by Standard and Poor's and by Moody's in March of 1987. By 1988, investors demanded less of a premium for Texas' bonds due to the state's improved economy.[68] Louisiana as well as Texas was hard hit by the decline in world oil prices. The report compares the current economic conditions of the two states, and notes that:

> Louisiana's general obligation debt is currently trading at yields higher than any other state in the U.S. The state's poor position is attributed to lack of diversification in the state's economy and the state's failure to put its finances in order as oil prices declines cut into state revenues. Texas' relative trading strength is testimony to the underlying strength of the state's non-oil economy and the resolve of the state's leadership to keep state finances on an even keel, despite oil-related state revenues.[69]

Conclusion

Had Texas not moved to diversify the macroeconomy, the economic situation might mirror that of Louisiana. However, the future looks bright for continued recovery and sustained growth in Texas. Diversification of the state's macroeconomy, coupled with the development of indigenous enterprises, diversification of agribusiness, and strengthening of the financial network has resulted in a macroeconomy that should be able to sustain positive growth even in the wake of a national recession. Should a severe recession occur nationally, the diversification of the Texas economy will, at a minimum, insulate a certain sectors of the economy against the type of economic downturn experienced by the entire economy of the state during 1986 and 1987. The nature of the macroeconomy will more closely resemble the national economy which experiences variable cycles of contraction and expansion or "minicycles" that vary by sector of the macroeconomy. Unemployment rates are projected to remain stable for the state through the year 2000, varying between 6.5% and 5.3%. The Texas gross state product is projected to increase between 3.7% and 22.4% through the year 2000. The state should continue to gain population at more stable rates of increase and experience a continued and sustained increase in personal income levels. Most of the growth in employment is projected in manufacturing and high technology. If the national economy does not experience a major downturn, Texas should not experience a repeat of the major recession of the 1980s. That's good news for all state budgetmakers!

Notes

1. P.L. Adkisson, "Big Cash Drop is Waiting Out on Texas' Farms," *Houston Chronicle*. June 26, 1988.
2. *An Analysis of the President's Budgetary Proposal for Fiscal Year 1988.* Washington, D.C.: Congressional Budget Office, 1987.
3. "Analysis: Bank Profits Big, Protection Thin," *San Marcos Daily Record.* October 10, 1989.
4. Jane Baird, "Houston Area Banks Found Insolvent as Failures for Year in Texas Climb to 29," *Houston Post.* May 27, 1988.
5. *Bonded Debt of the State of Texas.* Austin, Texas: Office of the State Auditor. November, 1988.
6. *Budget of the United States Government Fiscal Year 1988.* Washington, D.C.: Government Printing Office 1988.
7. *Budget of the United States Government Fiscal Year 1988.* Washington, D.C.: Government Printing Office 1989.
8. *Budget of the United States Government Fiscal Year 1988.* Washington, D.C.: Government Printing Office 1990.
9. "Clements Plans Ag Task Force," *Dallas Morning News.* May 3, 1988.

10. "Even in Tough Times Houston Port Delivers," *San Marcos Daily Record*. December 22, 1988.

11. *Farm Facts*. Austin Texas: Office of Farmer Assistance Programs at the Texas Department of Agriculture, July 1989.

12. *Farm Facts*. Austin Texas: Office of Farmer Assistance Programs at the Texas Department of Agriculture, September 1988.

13. *Fiscal Notes*. Austin, Texas: Economic Analysis Center of the Texas Comptroller of Public Accounts, September 1989.

14. *Fiscal Size Up Seventieth Texas Legislature 1988-1989*. Austin, Texas: Legislative Budget Board, 1988.

15. Joe Fohn, "Hightower: Middlemen Using Drought to Hike Beef Prices," *Express*. July 16, 1988.

16. R.H. Kramer and Charldean Newell, *Texas Politics*. New York: West Publishing Company, 1987.

17. Kirk Lalendorf, "More Failures, Slow Recovery Expected," *Austin American Statesman*. January 1, 1990.

18. S.H. Lee, Hightower Alleges Profiteering on Drought," *Dallas Morning News*. August 2, 1988.

19. S.H. Lee, "An Arid Outlook for Family Farms," *Dallas Morning News*. August 16, 1988.

20. W.E. Maxwell and Ernest Crain, *Texas Politics Today*. New York: West Publishing Co., 1978.

21. Stuart McCorkle, Dick Smith, and J.C. May, *Texas Government*. New York: McGraw-Hill, 1974.

22. Bill McCann, "Natural Gas Ready to Take the Spotlight," *Austin American Statesman*. January 1, 1990.

23. Bill McCann, "Solar Power Comes Out of the Shadows," *Austin American Statesman*. October 8, 1989.

24. Clifton McCleskey, et al., *The Government and Politics of Texas*. Boston: Little, Brown and Company, 1978.

25. "NCNB Profits Jump 77 Percent in 1989; Chemical Suffers Loss," *Austin American Statesman*. January 19, 1990.

26. Kyle Pope, "Austin Firms in Global Marketplace," *Austin American Statesman*. January 1, 1990.

27. Raul Reyes, "Pari-Mutuel Delay May Not Hurt Budget," *Dallas Times Herald*. August 2, 1988.

28. *Rethinking Texas Taxes. Final Report of the Select Committee on Tax Equity, Volume 1*. Austin, Texas: Reproduction Division of the Texas House of Representatives, 1989.

29. *Summary of Texas Annual Financial Report: Cash Basis--For the Year Ended August 31, 1988*. Austin, Texas: Comptroller of Public Accounts, 1989.

30. *Summary of Texas Annual Financial Report: Cash Basis--For the Year Ended August 31, 1989*. Austin, Texas: Comptroller of Public Accounts, 1989.

31. *Survey of Current Business*. "Regional Perspectives," Washington, D.C.: U.S. Department of Commerce, Bureau of Economic Analysis, April 1989.

32. Gary Taylor, "Texas Has More Ties to U.S. Economy," *Austin American Statesman*. January 1, 1990.

33. *Tax and Data Book and Staff Draft Tax Policy Options*. Select Committee on Tax Equity, Austin, Texas: March 1988.

34. *Texas Agricultural Facts*. Austin, Texas: Texas Department of Agriculture and the United States of Agriculture, October 6, 1989.

35. *Texas Almanac 1986-1987 Sesquicentennial Edition.* Dallas: A.H. Belo Corp., 1985.

36. *Texas Annual Financial Report Cash Basis--For the Year Ended August 31, 1988.* Austin, Texas: Comptroller of Public Accounts, 1988.

37. *Texas Annual Financial Report Cash Basis--For the Year Ended August 31, 1989.* Austin, Texas: Comptroller of Public Accounts, 1989.

38. *Texas Annual Financial Report. Audited GAAP Edition for the Year Ended August 31, 1987.* Austin, Texas: Comptroller of Public Accounts, 1987.

39. *Texas Annual Financial Report. Audited GAAP Edition for the Year Ended August 31, 1988.* Austin, Texas: Comptroller of Public Accounts, 1988.

40. *Texas Bond Review Annual Report.* November 1988.

41. *Texas Business Review.* Austin, Texas: Bureau of Business Research, June 1989.

42. *Texas Business Review.* Austin, Texas: Bureau of Business Research, February 1989.

43. *Texas Business Review.* Austin, Texas: Bureau of Business Research, April 1989.

44. *Texas Business Review.* Austin, Texas: Bureau of Business Research, August 1989.

45. *Texas Economic Outlook.* Austin, Texas: Comptroller of Public Accounts, October 12, 1989.

46. *The Book of the States 1986-1987 Edition.* Lexington, Kentucky: The Council of State Governments, 1986.

47. *The Book of the States 1988-1989 Edition.* Lexington, Kentucky: The Council of State Governments, 1987.

48. Kim Tyson, "Real Estate Opportunities Entice International Investors," *Austin American Statesman.* January 1, 1990.

49. "1990 Semiconductor Industry Forecast Anything But Rosy," *Austin American Statesman.* January 1, 1990.

50. *Texas Annual Cash Report 1988* and *Texas Annual Cash Report 1989.*

51. *Texas Annual Cash Report 1989.*

52. *Texas Business Review.* June 1989.

53. Ibid.

54. Kyle Pope, "Austin Firm Lags in Global Marketplace," *Austin American Statesman.* January 1, 1990; and "1990 Semiconductor Industry Forecast Anything But Rosy," *Austin American Statesman.* January 1, 1990.

55. *Texas Business Review.* February 1989.

56. Kramer and Newell, 1987; *Texas Annual Cash Report 1989*; and *Texas Business Review.* February 1989.

57. *Texas Business Review.* February 1989.

58. Ibid.

59. U.S. Department of Commerce, Bureau of Economic Analysis, *Survey of Current Business.* April 1989.

60. Ibid.

61. Kramer and Newell, 1987.

62. *Texas Business Review.* August 1989.

63. Ibid.

64. *Economic Outlook.* October 12, 1989.

65. United States Department of Commerce, Bureau of Economic Analysis, *Survey of Current Business.* April 1989.

66. *1988 Texas Annual Financial Report.*

67. Ibid.
68. *Texas Bond Review Board Annual Report, 1989.*
69. Ibid.

3

NEW DIMENSIONS IN INTERGOVERNMENTAL RELATIONS

James B. Reed

The challenge of budgeting at the state and local level has become increasingly complex as the roles and relationships of different levels of government have changed over the last ten to fifteen years. Nationally, a complex mix of circumstances and events has contributed to the changing intergovernmental landscape. These events and trends include: the state and local tax revolts of the late 1970's and their aftermath; the "new" federalism of the Reagan years with its decreased funding to state and local governments yet decreased responsibilities; the balooning of the federal budget deficit to immense proportions; the increasing internationalization of the U.S. economy; federal tax reforms in 1986; and boomeranging energy prices. The upshot of these events and trends is that state and local governments have had to shoulder an increasingly greater fiscal burden or responsibilities transferred from the federal government. More service delivery and greater regulation of the private sector has required increased revenues to fund the new responsibilities. States have also regulated new policies in areas where the federal government is perceived to be inactive or ineffective. Budgeting under these conditions has become a complex endeavor, requiring a search for new resources, the increased use of performance-based evaluations of government programs, and the innovative application and re-deployment of limited financial resources.

Analysis of revenue trends shows the relative growth of subnational governments. State and local governments in 1986 collected 44.1 percent of all government revenue compared to 38.4 percent in 1970, while the federal share declined from 61.6 percent to 55.9 percent over the same period. On a per capita basis, state and local government revenue rose from 42 percent of all revenue collected in 1970 to 48 percent in 1986.[1] This growth of state and local revenue has occurred to accommodate new spending needs prompted by shifting federal programs and by new state initiatives, and to keep pace with inflation and rising costs of providing government services. The expansion has also occurred under the constraints of balanced budget requirements. Forty-nine states (Vermont being the exception) have some form of balanced budget requirement and most impose restrictions to local government spending.[2] Yet, while new duties were given, often the tools to carry out the new duties were not available. State taxing and regulatory authority has been subject to preemption by the federal government, and likewise, local revenue producing ability has been constrained by state legislation. Intense intergovernmental competition for financial resources has been the result.

In Texas, these intergovernmental events have brought changes relative to both governance and the way government is financed. Other chapters of this book discuss these changes from different points of view, focusing, for instance, on adapting budgeting processes to fit new circumstances. This chapter will highlight one particular change in governance--the proliferation of special purpose government or special districts, and profile the evolution of the use of bonds in Texas state government financing. To put these case studies in a broad perspective, the first section of this chapter will characterize the evolving relationship between the federal government and state and local entities and briefly describe the policies and circumstances that have brought change. This discussion of federalism highlights the implications for budgeting where appropriate.

Federalism In The 1980's

The concept of federalism, as embraced by the framers of the U.S. constitution, was to provide for self-governance by Americans through a division of political power between the national government and the states. The Constitution defines certain powers delegated to the federal government and other powers, not delineated, are reserved to the states. However, events of the past decade have brought about a pronounced erosion of state authority in the federal system, though its roots were in the explosion of federal programs in the 1970's.

Some scholars of federalism have argued that the actual practice of Constitutional federalism is a contradictory exercise because no affirmative limit is placed on Congress' power with respect to the states. The Tenth Amendment to the Constitution, which reserves to the states powers not delegated exclusively to the national government nor explicitly denied to the states is in essence, the empty set, unless Congress restrains its exercise of restrained powers.[3] Thus, the constantly expanding power of the federal government with an accompanying reduction in state independence should come to be expected. Various cures for this federalism contradiction have been proposed, including constitutional amendments.

Episodes of the past decade that have reconfigured intergovernmental relationships include the continued growth of unfunded mandates to state and local government, declining federal funding for shared programs and grant activities, the growth of the debt and the annual budget deficit to immense proportions, and Supreme Court decisions such as *Garcia* and *South Carolina*.[4]

Unfunded Mandates

The unrestrained growth of partly or wholly unfunded federal mandates to state and local government is a continuing source of frustration for subnational governments. State and local officials in recent years have been charged with enforcing federal standards, implementing federal policies, and contributing fiscal resources in areas such as clean air, highway traffic speeds, bilingual education, water quality, prison improvements, and billboard removal. States often must fund new programs, or at minimum, match a federal dollar amount with state dollars. Federal judicial decisions in Texas have mandated policy changes in the areas of prisons, and mental health and mental retardation. The need to fund a mandated program increases competition among other budget areas for available funds. States, through national lobby organizations, have unsuccessfully pushed for full federal reimbursement of additional costs incurred in implementing new federal statutory mandates.[5]

Another common approach involves withholding funding in an area (federal highway funds) to accomplish another federal goal (uniform minimum drinking age). This "crossover sanction" has created resentment on the part of state officials who watched another state-regulated area give way to federal intrusion.[6] As it stands now, a state choosing to defy federal mandates with crossover highway aid sanctions could possibly lose 110 percent of its highway funding.[7] (A more recent example is the threat of cutting off education funds to the states unless the federal drug program is implemented.) Crossover sanctions inject much uncertainty into state budget processes since it is often difficult to predict whether the state will enact the mandated policy in time to prevent a loss of funds.

Preemption of state laws by the three branches of the federal government is another way state power is undermined. State policies in the areas of product liability, cable TV, taxation, telephone access, coastal zone management, licensure of certain professions, and motor vehicle safety regulations have been superseded in recent years.[8] The 101st Congress is considering legislation of hazardous materials transportation that would preempt traditional state authority in registration, permitting, and assessing fees on hazardous materials transportation.[9]

Preemption is triggered by many factors including the desire for uniform national regulations, federal perceptions that state programs are ineffective, and poor communication between federal and state officials. Unjustified federal preemption has been called the "sleeper issue of the 1980's."[10] When the numerous preemptive actions of the past are viewed as an overall policy thrust, some believe that states are becoming less viable partners in the federal system. Clearly, federal actions are needed in areas where states fail to act or where intestate cooperation is lacking. But in policy fields traditionally and adequately governed in the states, federal intrusion has been unwelcome. A recent victory for states in the fight against preemption occurred in the first session of the 101st Congress. States were heartened by passage of a House of Representatives amendment to HR 1465 to protect state oil spill liability and compensation fund statutes by a 279-143 margin.[11]

Declining Aid

The amount of aid available to states in federally funded programs has declined as well. The Reagan Administration, under the philosophy of returning power to the states, restructured numerous categorical grant programs and created "block grants" with fewer strings attached. However, the end result of grant consolidation was usually a reduction in overall funding, requiring states and local

41

governments to fund the difference. In 1981, President Reagan successfully persuaded Congress to consolidate 77 categorical programs into seven new and two revised block grants at funding levels approximately 25 percent less than the previous year's funding for the categoricals.[12]

Federal aid to states and local government peaked in 1978 at 26.5 percent of state and local funding and had fallen to an estimated 17.1 percent in 1989. As a percentage of federal outlays, state-local aid has fallen from 17 percent in 1978 to 10.9 percent in 1989.[13]

Texas has fared better than the average state. Federal aid to the state in 1978 amounted to $3.3 billion in 1987.[14] After adjusting for inflation this amounts to an increase of 3.7 percent, compared to a drop of 14.8 percent after inflation for all states. Aid to Texas as a percentage of all federal aid was 4.2 percent in 1978 and 4.5 percent in 1987. However, this masks the nature of the tax dollar flow between Texas and the federal government. In 1978, Texas sent $1.35 to the federal government for every dollar it received. In 1986, the amount had risen to $1.46 to rank Texas last among the states in return on the federal dollar.[15] In 1987, Texas ranked second to last in per capita federal aid, at $289 per person, compared to a US average of $437.[16] This figure will likely increase since Texas has been more aggressive in its pursuit of federal dollars in the post-oil boom years.

A perennial problem with federal funds is instability. The "vagaries of federal budget policy" and the rate at which the state applies for reimbursement under various grant programs contributes to year-to-year instability.[17] Thus, state and local budget officials must make a variety of assumptions and rely on past experience to factor federal aid into budget formulation. Volatility of federal aid is exacerbated during times of economic stress as seen when "sequestration" under the Gramm-Rudman-Hollings Act is threatened, causing across-the-board budget cuts.

Federal Deficit Spending

The immense federal budget deficit and geometrically expanding national debt have also changed the face of intergovernmental relations. Since 1980, the national debt has grown from $914 billion to $2.58 trillion in 1988. Interest on the debt is now the fastest growing part of the federal budget. According to John Shannon, former Director of the Advisory Commission on Intergovernmental Relations (ACIR), "The changing fiscal fortunes of the national government now stands out as the single most important factor reshaping relations between Washington and the fifty state-local systems. It has transformed the expansive 'Great Society' federalism of the 1980's."[18] This budget-driven federalism takes many forms including restrictions on state and local authority, unfunded mandates, preemption, and invasions of state and local revenue sources. A recent strategy of federal officials is to restrict use of trust funds for highway and airport projects to make the deficit appear smaller.

If costs continue to be shifted to state and local government, the so-called "leaf-blower fiscal strategy,"[19] these entities need sufficient authority to accommodate fiscal pressure within the limits of their own choosing, according to Robert B. Hawkins, Jr., Chairman of ACIR. He has stated, "The federal government cannot expect states and localities to pick up costs while hampering or invading their revenue-raising abilities and policy making authority."[20] In the absence of a major new revenue source for the federal government, states and localities can expect to keep tapping their own resources to increase revenues for new initiatives and to keep pace with inflation and population growth. In addition, states will need to protect their revenue sources from federal intrusion, particularly in the traditional state domain of consumption taxes.

Supreme Court Decisions

Two recent U.S. Supreme Court decisions, that further tilted federalism to the national government side, have alarmed state and local governments. In February 1985, the court ruled that Congress had authority under the Constitution to regulate the wages and hours of state and local government employees. The ruling in *Garcia v. San Antonio Transit Authority* reversed an earlier court decision (*National League of Cities v. Usery*) which held that Congress did not have the power to force states to comply with the minimum wage and overtime provisions of the *Fair Labor Standards Act* in areas of traditional governmental functions. The Tenth Amendment, it turns out, would not shield states from federal regulations as they had hoped. The court majority in the 1985 decision concluded that states should seek redress for unduly burdensome laws and protect their sovereign interests through the political process rather than through judicial review.[21]

Critics of the decision worry that the concept of federalism embraced by the *Garcia* court gives the national legislature sole discretion in determining the relationships between the national government and the states. Others contend the decision correctly interpreted the constitutional intent behind federalism. The various arguments reveal the "federalism" contradiction as stated in the Advisory Commission on Intergovernmental Relations report *Reflections on Garcia and the Implications for Federalism*:

> The American system of government is a federal system comprised of a limited national government and sovereign states in which the national government may do anything Congress deems it should, unless the Constitution expressly forbids it from doing so; and there exists no express Constitutional prohibitions on Congress' ability to regulate the actions of the states.[22]

The report expresses the opinion that: "Constitutional crisis produced by this contradiction must also come to a head in the near future, because techniques used to cope with it have about run their course."[23]

The 1988 Supreme Court decision in *South Carolina v. Baker* overturned its 1895 ruling in *Pollack v. Farmers Loan and Trust Company* which held that municipal bond interest is immune from federal taxation. Congress has given municipal bonds tax exempt status through legislation, but that could change as Congress seeks additional ways to battle the federal deficit.

In its *South Carolina* discussion, the court wrote:

> The Tenth Amendment limits on Congress' authority to regulate state activities are set out in *Garcia v. San Antonio...Garcia* holds that the limits

are structural, not substantive -- i.e., that States must find their protection from congressional regulation through the national regulation process, not through judicially defined spheres of unregulable state activity.[24]

Through the tax-exempt status of bonds may not change soon, further regulation of the bond market by the federal government is a virtual certainty. The implications for state and local budgeting of the *South Carolina* decision and other federal policies are discussed further in the case study on financing through bonds.

The intrusion of the federal government into state and local policy arenas has been recognized and partially mitigated, at least in the executive branch, by Executive Order 12612 "Federalism" issued by President Reagan in October 26, 1987. The order calls for federal agencies to: allow for maximum discretion on the part of state officials in administering federal programs; refrain from establishing national standards for programs; preempt state laws only when provided for by statute; and refrain from submitting legislation that would interfere with the independence of states.[25] Congress, though, has not seriously debated any proposals that would help ensure that the federalism implication of legislation are considered. Among the proposals being advanced are the following: establishing federalism subcommittees; requiring federalism assessment similar to environmental impact statements; requiring reimbursement of costs incurred by states and localities to implement federal mandates; and a federalism convocation to periodically assess the status of federalism and propose changes for Congress and state legislatures to consider.[26]

The changing face of intergovernmental relations is complex and only some of the multiple causes and effects have been described. An excellent analysis of such trends has been compiled in *Readings in Federalism: Perspective on a Decade of Change* by the Advisory Committee on Intergovernmental Relations.[27]

Intergovernmental Case Studies

These new intergovernmental relationships are brought into perspective in Texas in the case studies below. The first relates to governance. In the early to mid-1980's many rapidly growing Texas cities faced cutbacks in federal aid. Just as the federal government used its "leaf-blower" to transfer its fiscal problems to states, cities have, to some extent, done the same to special districts. Marked growth in the number and financial size of special districts has been the result.

Second, the present and future use of bonds to finance Texas state government needs is analyzed. From 1970 to 1987, the growth of bond issuance by state government was dramatic, particularly revenue bonds. In the wake of the bond restrictions contained in the Tax Reform Act of 1986, bond issuance has declined. The financing whiplash effect of federal tax reform and its implications for state finances is examined.

Special Districts

Federal intergovernmental aid to Texas has declined as a percentage of state and local government revenue. In 1978-79, federal aid totaled 17.0 percent of state and local revenue, falling to 11.6 percent in 1986-87. Municipal government has suffered an even more precipitous decline in federal aid, from 13.7 percent to 5.1 percent of total revenue over the 1978-79 to 1986-87 time period.[28] The complete elimination of federal revenue sharing to cities in 1986 was a major contributing factor. The percentage decline in federal aid combined with rapid growth in many Texas cities during the same time strained the ability of local officials to provide services. As a result many urban areas, particularly Austin and Houston, experienced growth of special districts, especially municipal utility districts. These special districts enabled subdivision development to continue in areas when the center city was unable or unwilling to incur the infrastructure expense associated with new development.

A special district is a unit of government created to serve a defined geographical area for the purpose of carrying out one or more specific function(s). In Texas, certain kinds of districts are authorized by the Texas constitution, others can be created under general law procedures, and the legislature may also provide for the creation of districts. The preponderance of special districts in Texas have a water-related function such as water supply, sewage treatment, flood control, irrigation, and/or navigation. Water districts are subject to continuing supervision by the Texas Water Commission, though they have control over their own revenues with the ability to assess and levy taxes and issue bonds.

Statewide the number of special districts grew from 1,425 in 1977 to 1,892 in 1987, an increase of 33 percent.[29] This outpaces the 26 percent population growth of the same period. Moreover, the growth in special district revenue, expenditures and bonded indebtedness grew at a pace that far surpassed population growth (see Table 1). On a per capita basis, special district debt grew from $287 to $895 from 1977-78 to 1986-87.

TABLE 1
Special District Finances ($1,000's)

Year	Revenue	Expenditures	Bonded Indebtedness
1977-78	$ 752,100	$ 959,400	$ 3,826,000
1986-87	3,785,865	4,090,166	15,034,000
Percent Increase	403%	326%	293%
Inflation Adjusted	215%	174%	157%

Source: U.S. Department of Commerce, Bureau of Census, *Governmental Finances* 1977-78 and 1986-87.

As a percentage of all local government revenue the proportion attributable to special districts increased from 7.2 percent in 1977-78 to 12.4 percent in 1986-87. If school districts are excluded (since special districts do not provide any educational services), the percentage special districts account for rises even more from 13.3 percent in 1977-78 to 20.6 percent in 1986-87.[30]

Implications of Special District Growth

The growth in number and financial resources of special districts raises several important questions related to efficiency, equity, responsiveness, accountability, and self-governance. Defenders of American populism claim that the most democratic governments are those closest to the people. Power must be dispersed among small, limited, and multiple governments if the democratic goal of individual freedom is to be attained. A recent ACIR study on the organization of local political economy examined, among other issues, why citizens historically prefer metropolitan reform efforts that involve substantial consolidation of jurisdictions.[31] The study shows that the minimum size unit for providing a public good or services can often be small, the size of a typical neighborhood, for instance. The smaller the unit, the greater the homogeneity of the community and, hence, the more similar the preferences of the residents. Thus, services can be more easily and efficiently provided when preferences are similar. (The study makes a distinction between "provision" and "production" of public goods and services in a local public economy.) "Basically, provisions refer to decisions that determine what public goods and services will be made available to the community. Production refers to how these goods and services will be made available."[32]

The study also argues that a multiplicity of local jurisdictions serves several useful purposes, including increasing the sensitivity of local government officials to diverse citizen preferences, increasing efficiency by more closely matching the distribution of benefits to the economic demand of communities, and enabling citizens and tax payers to hold public officials accountable to a small identifiable community interest. In examining the issue of whether proliferation of local governments is undesirable, one must balance the values associated with increased responsiveness of service provision with the costs of organizing and operating each additional unit. Citizens must be empowered to create "optimal patterns of order" for themselves, the ACIR argues. Governance, or the rules by which citizens choose to be governed should be viewed community-wide, dependent not on a metropolitan government, but on multiple local governments within a framework of rules.[33] Public works construction initiated by special districts, in particular, benefits from the more responsive, less cumbersome regulations that results from smaller, more efficient units of provision.

Based on its actions over the years, it appears that the Texas legislature has largely adopted the view that responsive local governance depends on opportunities for citizen choice that can allow a more creative and efficient local public economy to emerge. Nearly 30 types of special districts can be created under Texas law. Furthermore, the 71st Legislature authorized the creation of another type of special district -- the municipal management district. This type of district would be empowered to provide funding within cities to preserve, maintain and enhance the economic health of the area, to promote public transportation and to enhance aesthetic beauty.[34] Texas is ranked third in number of special district governments in the U.S. at 1892, after Illinois with 2,783 and California with 2,734. In comparing the number of special districts to state population figures, Illinois has one district for every 4,162 residents, Texas has one for every 8,874 residents, and California has one for every 10,118 residents.[35]

Critics of special district growth, particularly municipal utility districts, have concerns that affected homeowners are often unaware of the existence of such districts, and as such the districts are not democratic and not accountable bodies, and that overlapping jurisdictions increase competition for tax dollars. Concerns about the inability of numerous special districts to address regional problems also exists.

The first concern is critical. Despite disclosure requirements, many homeowners are unaware that they have purchased property in a special district. This can contribute to minimal participation by district residents, thus diminishing accountability. Voter participation in elections for utility board members rarely exceeds 5 percent in the typical case.[36] Over time homeowners do seek and acquire positions as directors of utility district boards, but often the most critical decisions concerning the future of the district have been made by the original developer-appointed board. These decisions include determining the initial scope of the capital expenditures, the hiring of district consultants (general manager, attorneys, engineers, financial advisors), and the structuring and sale of bonds to pay for district improvements. Holders of district bonds often exercise unseen but significant control over district decisions because they have financed the developer's project and the developer's board members work to protect those investments.[37]

Overlapping jurisdiction assessing ad valorem taxes on properties within their boundaries is another issue. A single property in the South Austin Growth Corridor MUD #1 in Austin, Texas, for example, pays taxes to five different taxing entities. No one assesses the impact of such overlapping taxes, except for the bond rating agencies when a district prepares to sell bonds. The rating agencies are concerned about a district's ability to repay a debt with property taxes if other jurisdictions also assess ad valorem taxes for their debt retirement and operations. The impact on the individual homeowner can prove burdensome.

Due in part to previous excesses, municipal utility districts operate in a fairly restrictive environment. As is the case with other units of local government, effective tax rates are subject to rollback if the year-to-year increase exceeds 8 percent. A public hearing is required if the increase is projected to exceed 3 percent. The Texas Water Commission must review and approve a variety of activities that MUDs undertake. To address the issue of disclosure, the 71st Legislature passed a bill which requires sellers of real property to notify interested buyers of certain tax rate and district bond debt information before entering into a binding contract.[38]

The broader issue of addressing regional problems such as air pollution, natural resources degradation, transportation gridlock, land use patterns, and landfill construction in a setting of multiple local governments is a vexing dilemma. Self-interested local governments cooperate if they anticipate benefits, but become uncooperative if adverse consequences are perceived. Thus, regional agencies are often needed to address cross-jurisdictional issues. Given sufficient authority, regional agencies, particularly in the environmental area, are a necessary mechanism for addressing regional problems.

Special districts fill intergovernmental gaps created by the inability or failure of general purpose government to meet citizens needs. A resultant trend has been growth in the number and financial influence of special districts as cities strain to cope with declining federal aid and the need for infrastructure improvements to accommodate growth. When properly governed, special districts allow communities with particular preferences that may not coincide with existing local government boundaries, to organize to provide a limited set of goods and services in an efficient manner.[39] As abuses are uncovered in such arrangements, the legislature and other oversight bodies take steps to control the abuse. Legislative action to address a variety of problem areas was undertaken in the recent session relative to river authorities, hospital districts, MUDs and county-wide districts with bond issuing authority.

State Government Financing Through Bonds

One of the more significant areas affected by the intergovernmental dynamics described in this paper is bond finance. Actions taken at the local level, such as the Tax Reform Act of 1986 and the *South Carolina* decision, have critical implications for public finance decisions involving bonds at the state and local level. This is because bond financing has become an increasingly important method of paying for needed capital improvements, particularly for state government in Texas. Bond issuance by state and local government increased dramatically in the ten years prior to 1987. In 1987 debt issued by state and local government nationally amounted to $46.2 billion, and rose to $204 billion in 1985 in anticipation of restrictions to be imposed by the Tax Reform Act of 1986.[40] Nationally, debt issued in 1986 amounted to $142.5 billion, falling to $94 billion in 1987. Further, the overall size of bonds outstanding has expanded 250 percent since 1978 to $720 billion.[41] In Texas, outstanding bonded indebtedness for all governments has grown from $19.6 billion in 1980 to $40.9 billion in 1986, generally mirroring the growth at the national level.[42]

The growth in bonded indebtedness prior to 1987 has many causes, including: tight budgets brought on by economic hard times; the drop in federal aid and state and local governments in financing areas such as prisons, housing, and water supply; increased state and local concern for long-range capital planning; the enhanced value of the tax-exempt status of bonds in times of high interest rates; the increased use of revenue bonds and new instruments of debt to avoid constitutional debt limits and bond elections; and the public demand for infrastructure improvements.[43] However, the need for increased oversight and disclosure brought on by events such as the defaults of bonds issued by the Washington Public Power Supply System (WPPSS) produced new restrictions on the bond market in the form of the Tax Reform Act of 1986. (Previous laws passed by Congress, the Tax Equity and Fiscal Responsibility Act of 1982, and the Deficit Reduction Act of 1984 also placed restrictions on the use of Tax-exempt financing.)

The Tax Reform Act of 1986 affected Texas in at least two ways. First, the deductibility of the sales tax, Texas' primary source of revenue, was repealed thereby increasing taxes for individuals. Second, the use of tax exempt bonds for

4 8

certain private activities was severely curtailed, particularly for sports and convention facilities, air and water pollution control facilities, industrial parks, and privately owned airports, docks and wharves. As noted above, bonding has become an increasingly popular method of funding state government capital improvements over the years and as such, curtailment of bonding ability reduces flexibility in budgeting options. The Act specifies criteria as to the amount if private activity that is allowed in order to retain tax-exempt status. If the bonds are characterized as tax-exempt private activity bonds, they would fall under the volume cap established by the Tax Reform Act for each state. Activities subject to the volume cap include mortgage revenue bonds, student loan bonds, hazardous waste disposal facilities, private solid waste facilities, sewage treatment facilities, among others.[44] The Act also imposes provisions restricting arbitrage and advance funding and includes other provisions that generally reduce the attractiveness of tax-exempt bonds.

Revenue Bonds

Prior to 1986, bond issuance, particularly revenue bonds issuance by Texas state agencies grew significantly. (Revenue bonds are different from general obligation (GO) bonds or tax bonds in that GO bonds are backed by general tax revenues and the "full faith and credit" of the issuer. Revenue bonds are repaid with monies generated by the operations of the bonded facility.)

Revenue bonds have become increasingly popular in the last several years as a way to finance public works and capital improvements reflecting, in part, the struggle of state and local governments to make ends meet. Much of the growth in outstanding public debt both nationally and in Texas since 1970 is due to the increased use of revenue bonds to fund traditional capital projects. Of the $6.98 billion outstanding bonded indebtedness of Texas state agencies as of March 31, 1988, 64 percent was due to revenue bond issuance.[45] Revenue bonds are typically issued to fund construction of long-term capital projects such as power plants, water systems, sewage treatment facilities, housing, hospitals, pollution control, nonprofit hospitals, electrical facilities, and industrial development.

A key concern of bond buyers in recent years is the financial strength of the state of Texas. In March 1987, Moody's downgraded the bond rating for the state from Aaa to Aa due to concerns about the state's economic base and revenue structure. (Standard and Poor's also downgraded Texas' rating.) Several actions have been taken by the state specifically to reassure potential investors in Texas bonds. One is the publication for the first time of general purpose financial statement for the state as a whole using generally accepted accounting procedures (GAAP).[46] Uniform accounts for all state agencies will assist the bond rating agencies in determining the relative risk associated with a particular bond issue.

Implications of Bond Market Restrictions

Restrictions embodied in the Tax Reform Act of 1986 relative to the issuance of tax-exempt debt have had the following results:

• Fewer non-governmental projects can be financed on a tax-exempt basis.

- Fewer opportunities arise to earn arbitrage income by investing bond proceeds.
- Greater volatility and limitations on refinancings mean timing is more important.
- More burdensome procedures surround the issuance process.
- Lower underwriting spreads, fewer deals, and constraints on flotation costs mean intense competition and fewer firms.
- Institutional investor demand is at low ebb and demand of the individual investor, directly or indirectly, reigns supreme.[47]

For state and local governments, the timing of the bond finance restrictions could not have been worse. Strapped by tight budgets in the early 1980's many entities delayed investment in infrastructure. A report by the National Council on Public Works in 1988 recommended increasing annual spending on infrastructure from $45 billion to $90 billion.[48] The combination of TRA and the *South Carolina* decision inhibit the financial planning of state and local government by reducing their fiscal capacity and limiting their ability to finance necessary improvements. The net result could be a decline in national economic competitiveness and greater long-term costs. Efforts have been underway to ease some restrictions imposed by the TRA. The budget reconciliation bill for FY 1990 included provisions to ease arbitrage regulations for tax-exempt bonds and softened accounting rules to help the investor using the alternative minimum tax calculation.[49]

Conclusion

In intergovernmental relations over the last decade, the playing field has shifted and the rules of the game have changed. Subnational levels of government have struggled with the federal government over the growth of unfunded mandates, the decline in federal aid, the massive increase in the federal budget deficit and national debt, and judicial decisions like *Garcia* and *South Carolina*. Two resulting developments have been described here: the growth of special districts in Texas and the reduced ability of state and local officials to obtain long-term debt financing for infrastructure and other capital needs.

Despite the shifting tide of the intergovernmental ocean, the state and local governments have proven resilient and innovative in their response to the trends and events identified in this chapter. In areas such as education, economic development, and environmental protection, governors and state legislators have turned to their own resources and come up with innovative and workable approaches. Education reform efforts have been underway for many years in the states as state leaders have taken the lead in advancing excellence in education through increasing teacher compensation and training, establishing centers of excellence, and equalizing state aid to school districts. In economic development, which has become closely linked to education, states have moved to nurture entrepreneurs, stimulate technological innovation, and help business adapt to the changing economy. Environmental protection has been on state agenda as well in the area of ground water protection, forcing hazardous and radioactive waste cleanup at federal sites, and taking concrete steps to address global climate change. These actions taken as a whole can be viewed as the emerging antidote to the imbalanced state of federalism currently tilted toward national predominance.

Texas has actively taken part in the state-based policy renaissance. Though the current program for state aid to school districts must be significantly revamped after the *Edgewood v. Kirby* decision, House Bill 71 in 1984 made substantial strides in education reform, with an accompanying tax bill to pay for it. Despite economic hard times, the state has won nationwide competitions to host high-technology firms like MCC (The Microelectronics and Computer Technology Corporation) and Semetech in Austin and the Department of Energy's superconducting supercollider in Ellis County. Economic development has been further enhanced by establishing a state department of commerce in 1987. In environmental protection, Texas has, among other programs, established a state hazardous waste cleanup effort, promoted the use of alternative motor fuels, moved to encourage the recycling and reuse of scrap tires and instituted a groundwater protection and cleanup program.

With emerging state prominence in these fields, the state-local relationship will need to be enhanced as the direct federal-local relationship declines. Unnecessary state regulation, unfunded mandates and bureaucratic procedures burden locals in a manner similar to federal policies that shackle local officials. The state-local relationship in Texas in dollar terms is overwhelmingly related to education; 95 percent of state aid to local governments in 1986 went to education.[50] The U.S. average is 63 percent.

The biggest concern of local government is state imposed limitations on taxing authority. The property tax power of a county is limited to a cap of 80 cents per $100 of assessed valuation, of which no more than half can be for debt service programs. Also, county voters have the right to approve up to a 15 cent tax for road and bridge operations and 30 cents for farm-to-market road operations and debt. General-law cities can levy up to $1.50 per $100 of assessed value, with a 50 cents maximum for debt service. Home-rule cities are limited to $2.50 per $100 valuation overall, with a ceiling of one dollar for payment on debt. Particularly for cities and counties, response to changing revenue situations is impaired by the inability to act quickly and with flexibility. Texas cities are using all available taxing options, while counties are struggling to implement state imposed mandates relative to emergency response planning and jail standards.[51] The options for relief include legislative action increasing local revenue flexibility, and sufficient state aid to accompany mandatory programs. Otherwise local governments face the unhappy options of service cuts or continuing the pattern of deferred spending and investment. Restrictions on cities and counties in taxing ability has been a contributing factor to the growth of special districts, which have fewer restrictions of their taxing authority.

The *Garcia* decision in a sense "deregulated" the federal government, allowing it to exercise policy leadership in virtually any domestic policy area.[52] Yet, despite fiscal situations of the national government has given the states and units of local government the opportunity to seize the initiative in many policy areas. This situation has been characterized as competitive federalism, where "federal, state and local governments must now compete head on for the political and fiscal support of federalism's ultimate arbitrators -- the voters/taxpayers."[53] Perhaps this competition will help restore the plenary powers of the states as intended by constitutional authors and regulate the federal government to more of a special district role with specific and limited assigned functions in areas such as foreign affairs, defense, and interstate commerce.

Among the challenges to be faced in the emerging era of competitive federalism are the following:

- A decline in national prosperity brought on by recession, the trade deficit and federal budget actions to reduce the deficit.
- Continued pressure for state and local tax increase as the federal government continues to mandate programs, preempt revenue sources, and impinge on tax immunity.
- The possibility of more federal preemption of state and local economic authority to create a more uniform national marketplace to compete with the unified European Economic Community in 1992.

For Texas, in particular, many challenges loom:

- Reassessing policies towards local governments to increase local flexibility to respond to changing economic conditions.
- Adjusting to a down-sized federal defence budget and absorbing cuts at military installations and reduced work for military contractors.
- Revamping the state revenue system to ensure balance, stability, efficiency, and equity.
- Legislating a new finance system for education in the wake of the *Edgewood* decision to equalize educational funding of all local school districts despite the local tax base.
- Effectively dealing with escalating health care costs brought on by obligatory medicaid payments, an aging population, and more expensive medical technology.

These challenges and others will continue to test the American federal system and strain the budgets of all levels of government.

Notes

1. U.S. Department of Commerce, Bureau of Census, *Statistical Abstract of the United States*. Washington, D.C.: U.S. Government Printing Office, 1989: 267.
2. Texas Legislature, Select Committee on Tax Equity, *Rethinking Texas Taxes*. Vol. 2. Austin, Texas: Texas House of Representatives, Jan. 1989: 534, 545.

3. Advisory Commission on Intergovernmental Relations, *Reflections on Garcia and its Implications for Federalism.* Washington, D.C.: ACIR, Feb. 1986: 12 - 14.

4. Ibid., 34, 39.

5. See for example National Conference of State Legislatures, *Goals for State-Federal Action 1989-90.* Denver, Colorado: NCSL, 1989: 80.

6. Norman Beckman, "Developments in Federal-State Relations: 1984-85," in Council of State Governments, *Book of the States 1984-85.* Lexington, Kentucky: CSG, 1984: 427.

7. National Conference of State Legislatures, *Federal Update* 3, no. 13, December 1, 1989: 3.

8. ACIR, *Readings in Federalism: Perspectives on a Decade of Change.* Washington, D.C.: ACIR, May 1989: .116 and K.L. Schmitt, "Licensing and Regulation: States v. the Federal Government," *Intergovernmental Perspective.* Vol. 15, no. 3, Summer 1989: 33.

9. See HR 3229 introduced by Rep. Glenn Anderson of California.

10. ACIR, "Readings in Federalism," op. cit., 116.

11. National Conference of State Legislatures, *Federal Update* 3, no. 13, December 1, 1989: 4.

12. ACIR, "Readings in Federalism," pp. 79-81.

13. R. B. Hawkins, Jr., "Rebalancing the Federal Budget and the Federal System," *Intergovernmental Perspective.* Vol. 14, no. 4, Fall 1988: 13.

14. U.S. Department of Commerce, *Statistical Abstract 1989.* p. 271, and CSG, *Book of the States: 1980-81*: 608.

15. Tax Foundation, *Facts and Figures on Government Finance.* Baltimore, Maryland: The John Hopkins University Press, 1988: 151.

16. U.S. Department of Commerce, *Statistical Abstract 1989*: 271.

17. Select Committee on Tax Equity, *Rethinking Texas Taxes.* Volume 2: 78.

18. Quoted in Norman Beckman, "Developments in Federal-State Relations," CSG, *Book of the States, 1988-89*: 438.

19. Fred Brown, "The Leaf-Blower Strategy for Managing Governmental Fiscal Policy," *Denver Post.* September 27, 1989: 7B.

20. Hawkins, "Rebalancing the Federal Budget," p. 14.

21. ACIR, "Reflections on Garcia," p. 2.

22. Ibid., 14.

23. Ibid.

24. 108 S.C. 1355 (1988).

25. ACIR, "Readings in Federalism," p. 127.

26. Beckman, "Developments in Federal-State Relations, 1988-89," op. cit., 442.

27. ACIR, "Readings in Federalism," 1989.

28. U.S. Department of Commerce, Bureau of Census, *Governmental Finances,* for the years 1978-79 and 1986-87.

29. U.S. Department of Commerce, Bureau of Census, *Census of Governments,* for the years 1977 and 1987.

30. U.S. Department of Commerce, *Governmental Finances* 1978-79 and 1986-87, and James B. Reed, *Trends in Texas State and Local Government Finance.* Austin, Texas: Texas Advisory Commission on Intergovernmental Relations, December 1983: 40-41.

31. This point of view is argued in ACIR, *The Organization of Local Public Economies*. Washington, D.C.: ACIR, December 1987: 49-50.

32. Ibid., 1.

33. Ibid., 50.

34. 10 Tex. Sess. Laws '89, Ch. 1056, Sec. 4.

35. U.S. Department of Commerce, *Census of Governments 1987*.

36. Institute of Public Administration, *Special Districts and Public Authorities in Public Works Provision: Report to the National Council on Public Works Improvement*. New York, New York: IPA, August 1987: 164.

37. V.M. Perrenod, *Special Districts, Special Purposes: Fringe Governments and Urban Problems in the Houston Area*. College Station, Texas: Texas A&M University Press, 1984: 117.

38. 9 Tex. Sess. Laws '89, Ch. 935.

39. ACIR, "Local Public Economies," op. cit., 25.

40. Select Committee on Tax Equity, "Rethinking Texas Taxes," op. cit., 559.

41. Ronald Snell and Tony Hutchinson, eds., *States and the Bond Markets*. Denver, Colorado: National Conference of State Legislatures, December 1988: 49.

42. Texas Legislative Budget Office, *Perspectives on the Bonded Indebtedness of State Government in Texas*. Austin, Texas: LBO, March 1987: 3.

43. Snell and Hutchinson, "States and the Bond Markets," op. cit., 4-6.

44. Texas Legislative Budget Office, "Perspectives on the Bonded Indebtedness," p. 24.

45. Texas Bond Review Board, *Analyzing and Reporting Texas State Debt*. Austin, Texas: TBRB, July 1, 1988: 1.

46. Texas Comptroller of Public Accounts, *Texas: GAAP Edition, Annual Financial Report*. Austin, Texas: Office of the Comptroller, 1988.

47. Snell and Hutchinson, "States and the Bond Markets," op. cit., 46-47.

48. Beckman, "Developments in Federal-State Relations, 1988-89," op. cit., 440.

49. National Conference of State Legislatures, *Federal Update* 3, no. 13, December 1, 1989: 1.

50. S.D. Gold and Brenda M. Erickson, "State Aid to Local Governments in the 1980's, *State and Local Government Review*. Vol. 21, no. 1, Winter, 1989: 13.

51. Select Committee on Tax Equity, "Rethinking Texas Taxes," op. cit., 122, 129.

52. John Shannon, "Competitive Federalism - Three Driving Forces," *Intergovernmental Perspective*. Vol. 15, no. 4, Fall 1989: 18.

53. Ibid.

4

THE LEGISLATIVE BUDGET BOARD IN THE STATE BUDGET SYSTEM

Jim Oliver

When the Texas Legislature created the Legislative Budget Board in 1949, Texas became one of the first states to establish a budget system where the Legislative branch of government was given a significant role in the initial process of formulating budget recommendations. Other states have more recently established within the Legislative branch the organization and staff resources dedicated to a budget system which, like Texas, results in a partnership with the executive branch in the budget process. However, the Texas budget system involves the Legislature in the state budget process as much, or more, than in any other state. The following sections describe the various constitutional and statutory responsibilities of the Texas Legislative Budget Board and the Governor in the process.

Prior to the creation of the Legislative Budget Board in 1949, the State Board of Control, an operating agency that can best be described as the state's purchasing and property services agency, had the statutory responsibility of collecting and compiling state agency budget requests. The Governor had been designated the "Chief Budget Officer of the State" by a state statute in 1931, but served as little more than a conduit in the transfer of information compiled by the Board of Control to the Legislature. In the absence of a more comprehensive budget system, the primary effort at developing a state budget was conducted by the committees of part-time Legislature, with little or no support staff, which met in regular sessions for 140 days every two years. The inadequacy of this system, combined with a growing state and an ever-increasing demand for state services provided the impetus for strengthening the budget process for state government in Texas.

The Creation Of A Dual Budget System

The primary responsibilities given to the Legislative Budget Board when it was created in 1949 included the development of budget recommendations; the inspection of property, equipment and facilities of state agencies; the conduct of

55

hearings related to agency budget requests; and the preparation of a budget and a general appropriations bill for introducing at each regular session of the Legislature.

Composition of the ten-member Board, as provided by the statute, consists of the Lieutenant Governor as Chair; the Speaker of the House of Representative as Vice Chair; the Chairs of the House committees on Appropriations and Ways and Means; the Chairs of the Senate committees on Finance and State Affairs; and two members each from the House of Representative and Senate, appointed by the Speaker and Lieutenant Governor, respectively.

The statute which created the Board authorized the Board to appoint a Director and necessary staff. The organization of the staff -- commonly referred to as the Legislative Budget Office -- reflects the original responsibilities of the Board as well as responsibilities that have been added over the years. Each of the three organizational sections -- the Budget Section, the Program Evaluation Section, and the Estimates and Operations Sections -- is headed by an Assistant Director.

In 1951, the Legislature established, in the Governor's Office, budgetary responsibility and authority similar to that which had previously been placed in the Legislative Budget Board.

Since 1951, Texas has had a dual budget system that serves the Executive and Legislative branches of government in a manner which recognizes the unique constitutional and statutory responsibilities of each branch and which provides separate organizational support dedicated to their unique requirements.

A Description Of The Budget Process

The primary responsibilities of the budget system are to provide for the analysis of budget proposals and the formulation of budget recommendations for legislative considerations, and to facilitate the legislative appropriation process by providing timely and accurate information on budget issues. The primary goal of the system is the final enactment of a general appropriations bill which accurately reflects legislative priorities in the allocation of limited resources to unlimited needs. A description of the process follows.

In Texas, the Legislature meets in regular session for 140 days every two years, convening the second Tuesday in January of odd-numbered years. Generally, appropriations are made for a two-year period which begins September 1 following a regular session and are limited by the Texas Constitution to the amount of revenue estimated by the Comptroller of Public Accounts to be available during that period. Strict application of the "pay-as-you-go" provision is an important constraint on the budget process.

The budget process begins with the drafting of budget instructions for use by agencies in preparing request proposals (Figure 1). The drafting of these

Texas Biennial Budget Cycle

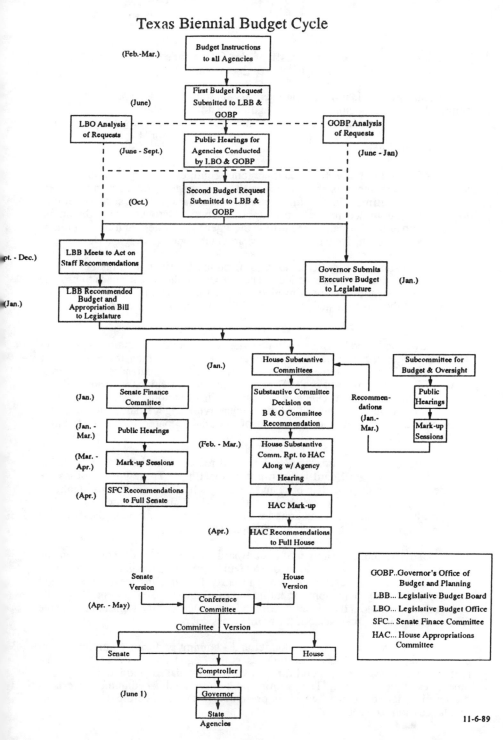

(Feb.-Mar.) **Budget Instructions to all Agencies**

(June) **First Budget Request Submitted to LBB & GOBP**

LBO Analysis of Requests

GOBP Analysis of Requests

(June - Sept.) **Public Hearings for Agencies Conducted by LBO & GOBP** (June - Jan)

(Oct.) **Second Budget Request Submitted to LBB & GOBP**

pt. - Dec.) **LBB Meets to Act on Staff Recommendations**

(Jan.) **LBB Recommended Budget and Appropriation Bill to Legislature**

Governor Submits Executive Budget to Legislature (Jan.)

(Jan.) **House Substantive Committees**

Subcommittee for Budget & Oversight

(Jan.) **Senate Finance Committee**

Substantive Committee Decision on B & O Committee Recommendation

Recommen- dations (Jan.- Mar.)

Public Hearings

(Jan. - Mar.) **Public Hearings**

(Feb. - Mar.) **House Substantive Comm. Rpt. to HAC Along w/ Agency Hearing**

Mark-up Sessions

(Mar. - Apr.) **Mark-up Sessions**

(Apr.) **SFC Recommendations to Full Senate**

HAC Mark-up

(Apr.) **HAC Recommendations to Full House**

Senate Version

House Version

(Apr. - May) **Conference Committee**

Committee | Version

Senate **House**

Comptroller

(June 1) **Governor**

State Agencies

GOBP..Governor's Office of Budget and Planning

LBB... Legislative Budget Board

LBO... Legislative Budget Office

SFC... Senate Finace Committee

HAC... House Appropriations Committee

11-6-89

57

instructions is a joint effort of staff of the Governor's Office of Budget and Planning and the staff of the Legislative Budget Board.

Joint budget instructions are sent to all state agencies approximately 10 months before the beginning of the regular biennial legislative session. These instructions establish the format and informational content of budget requests to be developed and submitted by the agencies to the Governor, Legislative Budget Board, and the Legislature.

After a three- or four-month agency budget preparation period, the completed budget requests are returned to the two budget offices for independent analysis and, ultimately, for funding recommendations. A second request document is submitted to the two budget offices in October. This document contains updated information regarding the agency's request and also contains actual expenditure data for the state fiscal year which ended on August 31.

From June through September, joint public hearings are conducted with each agency by the two budget offices. The purpose of these hearings is to provide the budget staff and agency administrators with an opportunity for in-depth discussion of the program, activities, and funding levels which are requested by the agency.

After the public hearings, each Legislative Budget Board examiner develops detailed budget recommendations for every agency for which the examiner is responsible. These recommendations are reviewed and finalized by an internal Board of Review composed of the Directors, and other Legislative Budget Board staff. The purpose of the review is to examine justifications, ensure consistency with overall guidelines provided by the Legislative Budget Board, and check for uniformity in the pattern and the format of material prepared for the Legislative Budget Board's review.

After cleaning the Board of Review, staff recommendations are presented to the Legislative Budget Board in open public meetings. These presentations are intended to inform the Board, in brief and concise terms, of the programs highlights of the budget requests and recommendations. Staff members are prepared to propose alternative recommendations for the board's consideration in the event the staff's recommendations are not totally acceptable.

Usually, the Legislative Budget Board makes its final decision on the recommended budget by the middle of December prior to a regular session. From then until the regular session convenes in early January, the legislative budget document and the general appropriations bill draft are prepared and printed. The budget document and bill draft are distributed to members of the Legislature and the Governor during the first week of the regular session.

The Governor's Office of Budget and Planning performs a similar budget examination and recommendation process as the Legislative Budget Office. The recommended levels of expenditure, however, are based upon the goals and objectives of the Governor. The recommendations are published in the Governor's proposed budget document, which is presented to the Legislature soon after the regular session convenes.

With the convening of the regular session, the Legislative Budget Board staff becomes actively involved in the legislative process by providing staff services to the House Appropriations Committee, House substantive committees on appropriative matters, and the Senate Finance Committee. With the approval of the respective committee Chairs, The Legislative Budget Board Director assigns Assistant Directors to supervise and coordinate staff services to the committees and subcommittees.

Immediately following the introduction of the recommended general appropriations bill in the House and Senate and their referral to committee, the Senate and House committees and subcommittees schedule hearings with each state agency. Usually, the committees begin rewriting the referred bills after agency hearings are completed. During these "mark-up" sessions, the Legislative Budget Board staff participates as requested by providing information and by assisting the committees in translating into bill draft from the decisions regarding committee adjustments to the recommended appropriations.

After the House and Senate have passed their respective versions of the general appropriations bill, a Conference Committee is appointed to resolve the differences, and the Legislative Budget Board staff provides support to the Conference Committee. The staff identifies issues and provides analysis, information, and recommendations as requested by the committee. The staff is also responsible for recording the committee's decision in its mark-up sessions and for translating those decisions into the dollar detail of a general appropriations bill.

The Conference Committee report on the General Appropriations Bill must be approved by both houses of the Legislature. Under the "pay-as-you-go" provision of the Texas Constitution, the bill is sent to the Comptroller of Public Accounts for certification that the total appropriations will be within the limits of the Comptroller's estimate of anticipated revenues. Finally, the appropriations bill is sent to the Governor for his consideration of item vetoes and for final approval. The bill then becomes effective on the first of September, the beginning of the state fiscal year.

The Texas Approach To Budget Analysis

The budgetary approach used in Texas is a composite of budget techniques that evolved from the zero-based budgeting system and includes those elements of that system which have proven most useful and are most applicable to the information needs and analysis required by the Governor and the Legislature.

The Texas budget system identifies all substantive aspects of agency operations in terms of programs and activities, establishes alternative levels of financing for each program and activity within an agency, projects the expected accomplishments of each alternative funding level using workload and performance indicators, and depicts the agency's priorities for funding the alternative levels. The system provides the Legislature, Governor, and each budget staff with comprehensive information concerning funding requirements needed to accomplish desired results.

The Evaluation of State Programs

In 1973, the Legislature directed the Legislative Budget Board to establish a system of performance audits and program evaluations, resulting in the creation of the Program Evaluation Section. Analysis of agency operations and evaluation of programs are an integral part of the Texas budget system. The implementation of the legislative directive resulted in highly formalized and specialized system for the evaluation of state government programs.

The Program Evaluation Section consists of a separate staff of program analysts with specific assignments. The staff provides a comprehensive and continuing review of the programs and operations of each state agency, and prepares for each regular session of the Legislature a performance report which evaluates a particular aspect of each state agency for program effectiveness and operating efficiency in terms of legal responsibilities as measured by costs, workload efficiency, and data and program output standards.

The findings and recommendations of the program evaluation staff are reviewed and adopted by the Legislative Budget Board and are presented to the Legislature in a formal report designed to provide the appropriation process with more complete information on which to base budgetary decisions. Program analysts, along with the budget examiners, assist legislative committees during the the process of developing and enacting a final appropriations bill.

Fiscal Notes on Pending Legislation

In 1973, the Legislature also directed the Legislative Budget Board to establish a system of expenditure or diversion of state funds. The fiscal note must contain a projection of cost estimates for each of the first five years following the effective date of the proposed legislation, and the note must state whether or not costs will be involved after that period. The statute requires that the fiscal note be attached to the legislation throughout the legislative process, including submission to the Governor.

Beginning in 1977, the rules of the House and Senate extended the fiscal note system to bills that would have statewide impact on units of local government. This action was taken in response to the concern of local government officials, particularly of cities, about legislation that would require or cause increases in local government costs without related funding from the state.

Since its inception, the fiscal note system has provided timely information on proposed commitments. The system encourages communication between agencies and legislators regarding legislative intent of proposed legislation, thereby improving understanding between the Legislative and Executive branches of state government. In 1989 regular session, Budget Board staff prepared and delivered over 7,000 fiscal notes to committees.

Constitutional Limitation on Growth in Appropriations

In 1978, Texas voters approved a constitutional amendment to limit the rate of growth of appropriations from state tax revenues not dedicated by the constitution to the estimated rate of growth of the state's economy. As a result, Texas now has two constitutional limits on appropriations: (1) the limit which is linked to the growth of the state's economy, and (2) the long-standing "pay-as-you-go" limit.

In 1979, the Legislature, by statute, placed with the Legislative Budget Board the responsibility for determining the constitutional limitation on appropriations adopted by the voters in 1978. The statute requires publication of the items of information along with the procedure used in computing the limit. The Legislative Budget Board is required by statute to hold public hearing on the limit and the methodology used in the calculations. Once approved, the Board is required to submit the information and the limit that it has approved to a committee consisting of the Governor, Lieutenant Governor, Speaker of the House, and the State Comptroller. The committee has 10 days in which to change the items or approve them; the committee can permit them to become legally binding by not meeting.

The budget recommendations of the Legislative Budget Board may not exceed the limit adopted by the committee unless authorized by majority vote of the members of the Board from each House. The Board is directed by statute to include the limit in transmitting its budget recommendations to the Governor and each member of the Legislature.

The constitution provides that the Legislature may provide appropriations in excess of the limit only by adopting a resolution, by record vote of a majority of the members of each House, finding that an emergency exists.

Budget Execution Authority

Prior to 1985, little authority existed between legislative session for the Governor or the Legislature to change the amounts or the purposes of appropriated funds. In November 1985, the voters adopted a constitutional amendment authorizing the Legislature to require prior approval of the expenditure of appropriated funds or to authorize the emergency transfer of appropriated funds. The Legislature, in 1987, enacted legislation to implement that constitutional authority. The legislation authorized the Governor, between legislative sessions, to propose that a state agency be prohibited from spending all or part of an appropriation, or that an appropriation made to a state agency be transferred to another agency, or that it be retained by the agency and used for a purpose different from or additional to the purpose for which the appropriation was originally made. The Governor may propose a change in the time that an appropriation is distributed or otherwise made available to a state agency. However, there are some constraints to these actions as they apply to federal funds, constitutionally dedicated funds, and state aid to school districts.

In order for the Governor's proposal to become effective, it must be approved by the Legislative Budget Board. If the Budget Board modifies the Governor's proposal, the Governor must approve the modification.

There are a number of procedural requirements and restrictions throughout the process, and the Legislature may also exercise the constitutional authority by use of riders, or special provisions, in the General Appropriations Act.

Automation in the Legislative Budget Office

The Texas Legislative Budget Office is supported by a mainframe-based legislative data processing system under the operation of the Texas Legislative Council. The Legislative Budget Office and the Legislative Council provide programmer support and system design for all integrated mainframe applications relating to the Legislative Budget Office.

Budgeting and Appropriations

The Texas Legislative Budget Office has developed two computer applications to assist with the general appropriation process. These applications are the Automated Budget and Evaluation System of Texas (ABEST) and the General Appropriation Processing System (GAPS).

The ABEST system provides the budget system information base and application technique for approximately 280 state agencies. Budget data are stored for each stage of the budget process. The initial stage begins with the budget request information submitted by the state agencies. Subsequent stages include the Legislative Budget Board recommendations, Governor's recommendations, House appropriation stages, Senate appropriation stages, and the finally enacted version of the General Appropriations Act. Budget information is stored for the various programs and activities of each state agency, including detail by object of expense and funding source. The budget information for each stage may be translated into appropriations bill line items.

Additional information contained within ABEST includes: workload performance measures associated with expenditure and funding levels; capital outlay budgets; and personnel budget data. A large number of standard reports are available from the system that may be used to analyze and compare the information between the various stages of the appropriations process.

The GAPS system is the automated system used to produce the general appropriations bill. The system can produce a document for one state agency, a group of agencies, or an entire appropriations bill. Input into the GAPS system comes from two sources. The quantitative information for the appropriations bill is transferred from the ABEST system, while the text portion of the appropriations is maintained by a separate software system. The text portion of the appropriations bill is merged with the quantitative information from ABEST to produce a complete general appropriations bill.

Fiscal Notes

The Fiscal Note Procedure System is an application that allows the Legislative Budget Office to track "on-line" the fiscal note processing from the moment a request for a fiscal note is received by the office to its completion and return to a legislative committee. The system tracks the staff assigned responsibility for writing the fiscal note, the status of the request for information from agencies affected by the bill, and the date the bill will be heard in the committee.

School Finance Modeling

The Legislative Budget Office has developed a computer application to provide budget estimates and related information concerning the funding of primary and secondary public education. The application is also a research tool used to evaluate the impact of proposed statutory changes on both statewide costs and on district-level allocations. The estimates provide assistance to members of the Legislature in analyzing proposals for restructuring finance law.

The public education computer model contains data relevant to the calculation of state aid for over 1,000 Texas school districts. These include, for example, student attendance counts, tax rates, property values, district size, and numerous other variables, both current and projected. The model provides estimates for the current biennium and four years into the future. A large number of analytical and statistical reports can be produced by the system and these are used to demonstrate the impact of proposals on state costs, equity, educational programs, individual districts, and other criteria, and to compare funding proposals to each other or to current law.

Criminal Justice Modeling

The Legislative Budget Office has designed and programmed a computer model which simulates selected dynamics of the adult corrections system in Texas. The model provides an important tool for analysis of policy alternatives, as well as for producing forecasts of demand for prison capacity. The model groups convicted felons into 32 offense categories corresponding to the provisions of the Texas Penal Code. An analyst may model the impact of one or more policy changes related to any or all offense categories, as well as changes in number of persons sentenced under each category. Policy alternatives related to sentences, release mechanisms, and renovations may be modeled. The model is being expanded to address adult probation policy and related correctional programs.

The model also produces estimates for a future period of five years at quarterly intervals. Forecasts and analyses, assisted by the model, support various Legislative Budget Office responsibilities, including production of fiscal notes and policy impact statements for legislation and development of budget recommendations.

Conclusion

In conclusion, in the late 1940's the Texas Legislature determined that it would play a strong role in the state budget process. As a significant step toward accomplishing that objective, the Legislative Budget Board was created in 1949. In the years that followed, the legislature continued to regard its role in the budget process as one of the most, if not the most, important of its constitutional responsibilities. Consequently, it frequently turned to the Legislative Budget Board when it wanted to increase available information, strengthen analytical capability, or expand its budget oversight authority. The development of the zero-based budgeting system, fiscal note system, the program evaluation system, budget execution authority, and computer modelling capabilities are all examples of efforts to improve the legislature's capability to make the right choice when presented with many competing alternatives.

There is no basis for assuming that the legislature's demand for timely, reliable budgetary information will diminish in the foreseeable future. Whether that need continues to be served by a central fiscal staff such as the Legislative Budget Office or by decentralized staff attached to substantive committees, leadership offices, or partisan organizations, only the future will tell.

5

THE BIENNIAL BUDGETING CYCLE

Charles W. Wiggins and Keith E. Hamm

Today, a majority of American state governments operate on pure annual session and budget cycles, whereby a one-year budget plan for the next fiscal year as proposed by the governor and, usually after some modifications, enacted by the legislative branch. A notable minority, or around fourteen, employ a budget cycle which can be characterized as a "mixed," or hybrid, form, and involves practices whereby either (1) the governor prepares a two-year budget but the legislature appropriates on an annual basis or (2) the governor proposes and the legislature approves a biennial budget, but this measure is subjected to legislative review and modification prior to the commencing of its second fiscal year. Finally, only eight states, including Texas, relay upon a pure biennial budget cycle, with appropriation decisions being made simultaneously for each fiscal year of the next two-year budget period.

Why does Texas use a pure biennial budget cycle? Why, as observers have queried, is Texas the only large, industrial state in the U.S which continues to utilize biennial budgeting? What are the prospects for Texas changing to a one-year budget cycle as have the bulk of other states since the 1940s? In this chapter, we will attempt to address these questions, drawing to a major extent upon key events in the political history of the state, several factors surrounding recent unsuccessful efforts to alter the budget cycle, as well as the attitudes of two key elite groups toward such change.

Historical Background/Constitutional Framework

In many ways, the origins of the biennial budgeting system go back to the general atmosphere, or circumstances, surrounding the post-Civil war period.[1] For a brief period following the Civil War, Texas operated under a constitution placed only a limited number of restrictions on the government's exercise of power and, as was the prevailing pattern at the time, provided for biennial sessions of the state legislature.

However, during the national elections in the fall of 1866, Radical Republicans and their sympathizers gained control of a majority of seats in the United States Congress and, in the spring of 1867, passed anew Reconstruction Act which was more punitive toward Southern interests than one earlier successfully advocated and implemented by President Andrew Johnson. The new law provided that the governments in existence in the eleven former Confederate states should be abolished. They would subsequently be divided into five districts under the direction of a military commander who, in turn, would appoint a provisional governor for each state. The provisional governor would oversee the operations of the state government until public officials could be elected under the provisions of a new constitution formulated and approved in each state. An especially critical provision of the Reconstruction Act was that pertaining to voter eligibility; in order to participate in the election of delegates to the convention which would draft a new state constitution, in the election to ratify the proposed document, and in the election of public officials following ratification, an individual was required to take an "iron-clad" oath that he had never served or aided the Confederate cause during the Civil War period. When implemented, this voter eligibility requirement had the effect of disenfranchising the bulk of previously active citizens, most of whom were Democrats, and preventing them from participating in state government affairs.

Given the constricted electorate resulting from such a voter eligibility requirement, Republican delegates were elected to the Texas constitutional convention, which proceeded to draft a new constitution which emphasized centralizing power at the seat of state government, as well as annual sessions of the state legislature. This constitution was then ratified in November 1869, and followed by the election of a Radical Republican, E.J. Davis, as Governor, as well as a substantial number of his cohorts to serve in the state legislature. Once in office, Governor Davis was granted substantial new powers by the legislature, including those to operate a state wide police force, declare martial law, and remove local officials. Presumably, Davis made frequent use of these powers to harness and, in some cases, eliminate troublesome opposition to his administration and policies. In addition, although a few more recent analysts have emphasized the role played by the state government in the establishment of a mandatory public education program, the legislature became known, often at Davis' urging, for its liberal spending actions which, in turn, required the passage of several tax measures.

By 1872, the Radical Republicans had lost their majority control of the U.S. Congress. The new, more moderate Republican majority proceeded to pass an amnesty act which included a provision restoring voting rights to most previously disenfranchised Southern residents. Democrats subsequently gained control of the Texas legislature in 1872, followed by the governorship in 1873. A Democratic supported proposal for a constitutional convention was then initiated by the legislature, ratified by the voters, and followed by the election of delegates. For all intents and purposes, Reconstruction in Texas had come to an end.

The constitutional convention, meeting in Austin during the fall of 1875, was dominated by Democrats, many of whom were members of the Grange. The Grange was, for the most part, a farming and ranching movement whose members had recently been experiencing problems associated with a severe economic recession which especially impacted the agricultural community. With Democrats

66

generally displaying their antipathies toward what they perceived to be the constitutional document which spelled out exactly how state government should be organized and operated, as well as what it could and could not do. To assure against the concentration of too much power in the state government, as had occurred under the Radical Republicans, a highly decentralized and dispersed governmental structure was established which included a plural executive branch and a fragmented judiciary, with officials of both branches being popularly elected and serving short terms of office.

In addition to providing for the traditional bicameral legislature and election of its members, the new constitution's legislative article contained the following provision regarding meetings of the legislature: "The legislature shall meet every two years, at such times as may be provided by law and at other times conveyed by the governor. " For the most part, Democrats viewed as having been perpetrated by the annual sessions of the Radical Republican legislature. A legislature which met only once the other year, so the democrats reasoned, was less likely to pass laws which were damaging to the overall public welfare. Provision for biennial legislative sessions was also consistent with the views of the fiscal retrenchment-minded Grangers, since the cost of the legislative operations would be cut in half in relation to that under the previous constitution. A further economic protection was provided by specification in the new constitution of the compensation to be received by lawmakers: $5 per day for 60 days and $2 for subsequent session days. It is interesting to note that legislature under four previous constitutions had been permitted to establish their own compensation by statute; constitutional framers in 1875, however, believed that all future legislatures should need the consent of the public via constitutional amendment when increasing member compensation.

The initial version for Texas' present long, detailed, and statutory-like fundamental character was approved by the voters in mid-February, 1876, and became operative in April of the same year. Overall, the document can be viewed from two broad and, at least to a certain extent, conflicting perspectives. One views the document as involving an inherent irony, in that thereby protecting state citizens from the possible tyranny of government via its provisions for a fragmented governmental structure and restrictions on the governmental exercise of discretionary power, it also has the effect of placing constraints on the quality of social and economic life. The other is that the state's citizens in many respects have a continuing major voice in decision making about what they want the state government to do, since their participation in such decisions has been guaranteed via the constitutional amendment referenda process. It is this process that we now turn our attention to.

Constitutional Revision

Given its long, detailed nature, the Constitution of 1876 has had to be modified, or revised, on numerous occasions over the years as popular views have changed regarding how the state government should be organized and operated, as well as the number and level of programs it should provide. On only one occasion, or in 1975, has anything approaching comprehensive revision been attempted, but this was rejected by those voters who participated in the ratification vote by approximately a 2-1 margin.[2] Instead, since 1847, revision has occurred on a piecemeal basis, with numerous proposed amendments dealing with very specific sections, or paragraphs of sections, being initiated by the legislature and voted upon in referenda. Of 468 separate submissions through 1987, 303 amendments have been approved and added to the Constitution. When submitted, approximately two-thirds of the proposed amendments have received voter approval.

The two-thirds success batting average for amendments overall definitely does not apply to efforts to amend the Constitution to allow the legislature to meet in annual session. As information presented in Table 1 indicates, proposals to do such have been submitted to the electorate on five occasions beginning in 1949 and have failed each time. On only one occasion, however, has the legislature submitted an annual session proposition to the electorate without coupling with other questions, such as pay raise for lawmakers. This occurred in 1969 when voters rejected (45% for, 55% against) an amendment providing for annual sessions, with the second session confined to appropriations matters and emergency measures submitted by the governor. Compensation increases for legislatures have been included with annual session measures on three occasions (1949, 1958, and 1973). In 1975, in association with Texas' first and unsuccessful attempt at comprehensive constitutional reform, an annual legislative sessions provision was included in a proposed revision of the constitution's legislative article, which, in turn was voted on in a "package" proposition which also included revisions of executive branch and separation of powers articles. Except for this 1975 comprehensive revision, all annual session amendments have provided that the main purpose of annual sessions would be for the legislature to pass annual appropriations bills.

Why have attempts at amending the constitution to authorize annual sessions and budgeting failed? Although several explanations for such failures might be postulated, three would appear to be of special significance. The first involves the notion that a significant proportion of Texans continue to distrust their institutions of government. As we noted above, this was the prevailing view at the time that the Constitution of 1876 was drafted and a view that has apparently persisted over the years, although we have no idea at what levels. Recent incidents of alleged scandal, some involving key lawmakers (such as Sharpstown in 1971), have obviously not encouraged the state's citizenry to become any more trustful of Texas governmental institutions and public officials.[3]

A second possible reason for the failure of annual session/budgeting propositions involves the positions taken by key governmental leaders on the question. Generally, when governors have been prone to support such propositions, legislative leaders have been divided or unenthusiastic about them. On the other hand, and this has tended to characterize more recent annual session efforts, when legislative leaders have been united and vigorous in their support, governors have publicly expressed their opposition to annual sessions proposals. For example, Governor Preston Smith opposed the annual session proposition voted on in 1969, arguing that it would dilute the governor's power to influence future agendas of the state legislature via his special session powers. In 1973,

TABLE 1
Proposed Amendments on Legislative Sessions/Pay

Year	Provisions	Action/Vote
1876 Const.	Biennial; No limit on length; $5 per day for 60 days then $2 thereafter.	Passed
1930	Biennial; No limit on length; $10 per day for 120 days, then $5 per day; 30/30/60 split sessions format.	Passed
1949	Annual, including appropriations; No limit on length; Second session restricted to constitutional amendments, appropriations, and other issues by 4/5ths vote; $3,600 annual salary.	Defeated/ 25.0%
1954	Biennial; No limit on length; $25 per day for 120 days, then no pay.	Passed
1958	Annual, including appropriations; first session limited to 120 days spit session format; No limit on second session length; second session restricted to appropriations and emergency matters of governor,$7,500 annual salary, plus per diem for 120 days first session and 60 days second session, with amount determined by law.	Defeated/ 30.7%
1960	Biennial; 140 day limit on session length; $4,800 annual salary, plus $12 expense per diem for first 120 days.	Passed
1969	Annual, including appropriations; first session limited to 120 day split sessions format; 60 day limit on second second session; second session restricted to appropriations and emergency matters of governor.	Defeated/ 44.6%
1973	Annual, including appropriations; first session limited to 180 days; 60 day limit on second session; second session restricted to appropriations and emergency matters of governor; Governor can extend second expense per diem.	Passed/ 43.3%
1975	Comprehensive constitution revision; annual sessions; first session limited to 140 days, with second session limited to 90 days; 15 day veto session when petitioned by 3/5ths of members; compensation to be decided by by special commission.	Defeated
1984	Biennial; 140 day limit on session length: $7,200 annual salary, plus expense per diem at maximum allowable IRS (Est. = $75).	Defeated
1989	Biennial; 140 day limit for session length; legislator salaries to be based on one-half of salary of governor.	Defeated

Governor Dolph Briscoe opposed the annual sessions amendment before the electorate at that time suggesting that it would not only lead to a mere "professional' legislature, but also probably lead to increased state spending and taxes. Briscoe's 1973 opposition was followed by his opposition to the 1975 comprehensive constitutional revision effort.[4] Given his prominence in state political affairs and as a molder of public attitudes and opinions, opposition to annual sessions by Texas chief executives has probably impacted significantly upon the prospects for voter approval at the polls.

A third possible explanation for annual sessions reform failures is related to the tendency for the legislature to couple annual session amendments with other questions, such as legislator pay increases. It is difficult enough to get one relatively controversial issue approved by the voters, or is the line of reasoning goes, without including another controversial issue along with it. Data in Table 1 suggest that there may be some validity to this explanation, since they indicate that the only "pure" annual sessions amendment to be voted on to date (1969) received the highest level of voter support in comparison with all other annual session propositions voted on since 1949.

Generally, where has support for annual sessions tended to come from among Texans? In recent years, most statewide elected officials have been supportive (excluding Governors Smith and Briscoe, of course), as have legislative leaders. In addition, annual session propositions have been favored by the Texas League of Women Voters, state bar officials, and a number of academicians at institutions of higher education, as well as editorial writers for most major newspapers from what we have been able to ascertain. An examination of the county-by-county voting patterns on the annual sessions amendments submitted to the voters in 1949, 1958, and 1973 (1969 results were not available) suggests that support tends to come more from urban counties, as well as those containing a larger portion of Hispanics, Blacks and state university personnel.

The Budgeting Process: Preparation, Authorization, and Execution

As in all American states, the Texas budgetary process tends to fall into three distinct, yet in certain ways overlapping, phases: preparation, authorization, and execution. In this section, we will provide an overview of these phases while at the same time emphasizing two aspects of this process. First we will emphasize those features which tend to differ significantly from ones found in the bulk of American states. Second, and this is our ultimate objective, we intend to emphasize how the biennial budgeting cycle which has been employed in Texas over the years is linked to each phase in the budgetary process.

The first phases in the budget-making process is *budget preparation*. Most generally, budget preparation involves the formulation of (1) a plan for spending state resources during the next budget period and (2) a statement about the projected financial condition of state government at the end of the current budget period.

Budget preparation normally begins with initial planning efforts which occur several months before the formal finalization of a budget document and its submission to the legislative body. Given the biennial budget cycle in Texas, for example, the heads of state agencies, boards, and commissions receive their budget instructions some eighteen to nineteen months prior to the beginning of the first fiscal year of a budget period. Thus, these administrators begin formulating estimates of their agencies' needs for resources which, if approved by the legislature, may be actually expended as much as three and one-half years down the road.

A unique feature of the Texas budget preparation phase deals with its dualistic nature. Prior to 1949, no effective formal budget preparation process to speak of existed in the state. Up to that time, the legislature made its appropriations decisions in a relatively ad hoc manner, of without any overall blueprint, or guideline, available to readily ascertain how its separate spending decisions not only impacted upon each other, but also on available resources. In 1949, the legislature decided to create an agency whose responsibility would be to formulate such a blueprint. But unlike other states (and the national level) where this authority was placed under the direction and control of the chief executive, solons decided to place this agency under their own branch's control via the establishment of a Legislative Budget Board (LBB) consisting of ten key legislative leaders and colleagues. Two years later, or in 1951, the legislature heeded the urgings of Governor Shivers by establishing a separate budget preparation operation within the governor's office; this was implemented at least partially by the transfer of a very weak and inadequately staffed budget section in the relatively autonomous Board of Control to the chief executive's office. The job of this new budget office was to assist the governor in the formulation of his budget request to the legislature. Thus, Texas ended up with a unique dualistic budget preparation and submission system. Since the legislature normally pays more attention to the recommendations of its own budget preparation authority, however, Texas is also generally noted among the American states as being the only state where the legislative branch initiates the budget proposal.

Over the years Texas governors have either publicly or privately expressed their concerns about the dominant role played by the LBB in the state's budget preparation process. One of the most outspoken critics of this arrangement was Governor John Connally, who served as the the the state's chief executive from 1963 to 1969. Throughout his tenure, Connally made no bones about his view that the legislative branch had no business being involved in this phase of the budget process; instead, it should be a function of government assigned exclusively to the executive branch and under the direct control of the governor. To this day, the legislature has ignored such exhortations for change, and legislative supremacy has continued to reign in budget initiation matters in Texas state government.

Although the LBB dominates in the end, it does cooperate with the Governor's Budget Office (GBO) during the initial activities associated with the formulation of a new budget document(s). Most of these cooperative interactions occur on the staff level, and result in a single, or common, set of budget instructions being forwarded to each state agency, board, or commission in the February-March period of even numbered years. Agency budget requests are then forwarded to both the LBB and GBO in July and, in, turn, followed up by a series of joint LBB-GBO hearings with most agencies. Based upon discussions and points-of-view expressed by both LBB and GBO officials and staff members at these hearings, agency directors are responsible for submitting their revised

7 1

estimates of funding needs for the next fiscal biennium which begins in September the following year.

From this point on, the LBB and GBO go their separate ways, with each group formulating its own final budget document. LBB members, along with key staffers, meet on several occasions in order to hammer out a final budget document, with much negotiating and compromising tending to characterize the process. GBO staff members continue to formulate the governor's budget, frequently consulting with the chief executive for advice, recommendations, and directions. Both groups normally put their finishing touches on their budget drafts by mid-December, so that ample time is available for printing and distribution by the time the legislature convenes in mid-January of the following year.

How have the two budget documents differed over the years? Some scholars suggest that their relative spending emphases have tended to vary over the years. They note that during the 1945-1971 period, for example, LBB budget proposals were more conservative, or status quo oriented, than the governor's budget, with lower total expenditure levels and few new program initiatives being recommended. Since the early 1970s on the other hand, the LBB has usually recommended higher expenditures than the governor, as well as several innovations in state programs.[5]

The second phase of the budgeting process involves *budget authorization*. Generally, this means that before an agency, board, or commission can legitimately expend funds for a given program or service, such expenditures must have been approved by a designated authorization authority. In Texas, as well as in other state governments in the U.S; this authority is the legislature, whose authorizations take the form of the passage of appropriation laws. Furthermore, all of these authorizations in Texas are normally consolidated into a single omnibus measure, a procedure followed in slightly less than one-half of the sates.

When the legislature convenes in mid-January, copies of both the LBB and governor's budget are sent to the committees responsible for studying appropriations measures in each chamber: Senate Finance Committee and House Appropriations Committee. The appropriations bill draft which accompanies the LBB budget becomes the working document for both committees, with technical assistance provided by the LBB staff. The Senate Finance Committee proceeds to conduct hearings with the state agency representatives over a 16 week period. In the house, on the other hand, the Appropriations Committee forwards relevant sections of the proposed bill to the substantive standing committees having jurisdiction over given state agencies. A budget subcommittee of each substantive committee then conducts hearings and reports its recommendations to its parent committee. The substantive committee then reports its recommendations for funding levels to the Appropriations Committee, which may hold another round of agency hearings before finalizing its version of the appropriations measure. While many observers suggest that these numerous legislative hearings are rather perfunctionary since they duplicate LBB hearings conducted prior to the session, others point out that agency directors at times have continued to argue that their original budget estimates submitted to the LBB the year before are directly needed. This situation normally does not exist in most states where the governor plays a

72

stronger budget role, since the rules of the game are that agency heads should support the level of funding eventually recommended in his budget proposal.

Via negotiation between leaders of both chambers, one chamber takes the initiative and passes the appropriations bill recommended by its appropriations committee. The bill is then sent to the other chamber, which proceeds to substitute its committee's version of the bill. Limited floor debate occurs in each chamber. Since each chamber insists upon its version of the bill, a conference committee is appointed by the leaders of both chambers. Although this committee is supposed to adjust differences between the two bills before them, it at times will deviate from this practice by adding new items to the appropriations measure. After a period of negotiations, the conference committee reports to each chamber and its recommended funding levels are usually approved with little or no debate.

Appropriations measures approved by the legislature usually provide funding for state agency programs for each of the two fiscal years of the next biennium, which commences on the following September 1 and ends on August 31 two years later. Thus, since one of the final actions of the legislature is to pass the biennial appropriations act as it completes its 140 day session in May, it is authorizing the expenditure of funds which may actually occur some 26 to 27 months later.

Two noteworthy exceptions to the legislature passing a biennial appropriations bill occurred in 1967 and 1969. In 1967, Governor John Connally urged the legislature to send him only a one-year appropriations measure, with the understanding that he would call subsequent special session of the legislature to work on second year appropriations. Generally an opponent of biennial appropriations, Connally argued that the state's present revenue picture was so unsettled that such action was desired. The legislature complied and sent to the governor the state's first annual appropriations bill since the Constitution of 1876 had been ratified. Two years later, the legislature forwarded to Governor Preston Smith a one-year measure, but he vetoed it and called the legislature back into special session to pass a biennial appropriations act, arguing that he preferred the latter. Ironically enough, two years later, in 1971, Smith actually vetoed the second year of a biennial measure and called the legislature into special session in June of 1972 to consider and approve appropriations for the second fiscal year.

As previously emphasized, Texas governors tend to play a weak role in the state's budget decision making process. Their role in budget preparation is especially circumscribed, with the LBB having the upper hand via its ability to determine the key agenda items for the legislature's consideration of budget issues during the course of a regular biennial session. On the other hand, two potentially important tools available to governors to influence legislative decisions are the veto power and the authority to call special sessions of the legislature. The governor's veto power includes his ability to veto specific items in appropriations bills. The implied threat of an item veto can be employed to gain concessions from selected lawmakers in support of the governor's overall budgetary goals. Whatever the situation, a gubernatorial veto of the appropriations bill or items in it is usually final, given the fact that it occurs after the legislature has completed its 140 day session. Thus the legislature is not afforded much opportunity to give serious consideration to override the governor's rejection of a measure or item. Between

1876 and 1968, for example, Texas legislatures managed to override only 25 (or 3 percent) of 936 veto actions taken by governors. In 1979, the legislature did override a local measure which had been vetoed relatively early in the session by Governor Clements. However, the last successful override of a veto prior to that occasion had occurred during the administration of Governor W. Lee O'Daniel in 1939-1941.[6]

The other important tool in the governor's arsenal to influence appropriations decision is that of calling special sessions. Via his skillful use of this power, the Governor can set the legislature's agenda and marshall public interest in support of his program goals, fiscal and otherwise. Governor Preston Smith argued that one of his main reasons for opposing regular annual sessions of the legislature was that he thought they would drastically dilute the significance of special sessions called by the chief executive. Whatever the situation, there is no question that governors have made liberal use of special session calls over the year. From 1876 to 1983, Texas governors called 83 special sessions of the legislature. Only 2 of 26 governors (O'Daniel and Jester) have not called at least one special session. Since 1876, at least 40 percent of these sessions have been called to deal with fiscal matters, such as budget deficits, spending for certain programs, and tax reductions. Table 2 shows the agenda items for 24 sessions called since 1957. Approximately two-thirds of these items fall into the general category of fiscal matters.

Finally, the role of one other key public official in the budget authorization should be duly recognized: the state comptroller. As the result of several treasury deficiencies which occurred during the 1930s, an amendment was passed to the constitution in 1942 mandating that the comptroller must certify that funds are available before the governor is authorized to sigh an appropriations measure. The power of the popularly elected comptroller in this area flows from a corollary responsibility assigned in the same amendment. This provision provides that the comptroller shall make estimates of the amounts of revenues which the state will receive in the next biennium. To our knowledge, Texas is the only state in the U.S. to require this certification procedure, although state comptrollers are often assigned revenue projection responsibilities. Whatever the case, the unique certification requirement certainly enhances the role played by the comptroller in the budget authorization process.

The third and final phase in the budget process is *budget execution*. Budget execution normally involves a system whereby relatively minor alterations can be made in the spending decisions of the legislature when it is not in session. Such changes are usually made in response to unexpected developments, such as an increase in agency's workload, a sudden drop-off in state revenues, etc.

In most states, major budget execution responsibilities are vested in the governor. In Texas, however, such responsibilities until recently were vested in no office or public official. The end result was that Texas had no system for effective budget execution. Unlike in most other states where the legislature meets annually and can itself make at least some adjustments in previously approved spending authorizations, the 140 day biennial sessions of the Texas legislature severely restricts its capacity to play meaningful role in this area.

TABLE 2
Frequency and Agenda of Special Sessions of Texas Legislature, 1957-1988

Governor	Year	Legi-slature	No. of Special Sessions	Agenda Topics
Daniel	1957-58	55th	2	Regulation of Lobbies; Racial Violence
Daniel	1959-60	56th	3	Deficit / Revenues (3)
Daniel	1961-62	57th	3	Deficit / Revenues (2); Teacher Pay
Connally	1963-64	58th	0	
Connally	1965-66	59th	1	Voter Registration
Connally	1967-68	60th	1	Appropriations Act
Smith	1969-70	61st	2	Appropriations Act
Smith	1971-72	62nd	4	Appropriations Act ; Congress Redistricting; Highway Beautification, Insurance Rates /Finance Control
Briscoe	1973-74	63rd	1	Speed law
Briscoe	1975-76	64th	0	
Briscoe	1977-78	65th	2	Tax Reduction: School Financing
Clements	1979-80	66th	0	
Clements	1981-82	67th	3	State Property Tax Repeal/Walter Trust Fund/Congress Redistricting Proposed Tax Code Revision / Medical Practice Act; State Capital Appropriations;Unemployment Compensation Deficit
White	1983-84	68th	2	Brucelosis Control / Unemployment Compensation Administration / Capital Appropriation; Taxation
White	1985-86	69th	3	Indigent Health Care/Aging Department Sunset;Deficit / Revenues (2) / Child Support / Interstate Banking; Community Health Centers / Budget Execution Authority /Payroll/Teacher Retirement /Speed Limit / Election
Clements	1987-88	70th	2	Liability Insurance;Appropriations Act/Water Disposal /Prisons / Education Economic Development /Judicial Conduct /Drunk Driving/ Auto insurance/Child Support/Sexual Abuse/Agricultural Production/ Blood Banks

The legislature at times attempted to assign budget execution responsibilities by statute to certain officials, such as the governor and LBB, but the attorney general ruled that these arrangements constituted a violation of separation of powers doctrine as found in the state constitution. More recent legislative attempts to address this problem have involved the initiation of a constitutional amendment which would, if approved, authorize the establishment of a state finance management committee comprised of the governor and designated legislative leaders. Once established, this committee could be granted by statute the authority to make limited adjustments in state spending -- agency reductions, transfers, and perhaps even either freezes (impoundments) of supplements via a special contingency fund.[7] The electorate however, initially disapproved the establishment of such an interim financial management committee, rejecting the proposition at the polls in both 1980 and 1981.

In 1985, however, voters finally approved a rather vaguely worded constitutional amendment which allowed the legislature to establish some system of budget execution control. At its next regular session in 1987, the legislature passed a measure establishing the framework for such control. The measurer presented a compromise between the legislative leadership and Governor Clements and provided that, when the legislature is not in session, the governor can propose alterations in state agency spending, as long as no agency's appropriation is reduced by more than ten percent or increased by more than five percent. However, all such proposals are subject to the review of the Legislative Budget Board; it can accept, reject, or modify the governor's proposal. Although it remains to be seen exactly how this new budget execution authority will be played out in the face of future fiscal problems or crises confronting the state, it would appear that the legislative branch, via its leadership group, retains a very powerful role in this aspect of the Texas budgetary process.

Elite Attitudes

During the 1984-1985 period, the authors conducted a survey of state government agency heads (excluding higher education and the judiciary) and a random sample of registered lobbyists to ascertain their views regarding the Texas biennial budgeting cycle. Approximately two-thirds of the agency heads (100) and 39 lobbyists responded to a request to fill-out what was essentially a closed-ended questionnaire which tapped various dimensions of the budgeting cycle issue.

A majority of both agency heads and lobbyist groups opposed changing the budget cycle from a biennial to annual basis, arguing that the overall drawbacks of such a change would outweigh any benefits. More specifically, agency heads acknowledged that annual cycle would provide the opportunity for a more accurate assessment of their budgetary needs, as well as facilitate the state's ability to estimate, or forecast, more accurately future revenues. These are two arguments frequently made by proponents of annual budgeting. The agency heads, on the other hand, argued that annual budgeting cycles posed a major drawback for their operations, in that significant additional staff time and resources would be needed for budget preparation purposes. Overall, this negative outweighed the benefits perceived to result from annual budgeting and the agency heads opposed cycle change.

Lobbyists as a group were also cognizant of both advantages and disadvantages of a possible shift to annual budgeting. While agreeing with the agency heads that annual cycles would lead to more accurate revenue forecasts, lobbyists also suggested that annual budgets would strengthen legislative oversight of administrative agencies, as well as facilitate the development of a more informed legislative body on budget matters. Major negatives of annual budgeting frequently cited by lobbyists involved the view that it would lead to full-blown annual sessions and a concomitant increase in their work-load, plus increased state spending and taxes. Generally, these perceived drawbacks outweighed the benefits from annual budgeting and a majority of lobbyists opposed changing the state's budget cycle.

Conclusion

In conclusion, this chapter has analyzed the two-year cycle employed by Texas state government to prepare, authorize, and execute a budget. It has described the historical origins of the state's budgeting system, recent efforts to reform it via constitutional change, as well as the attitudes of two key elite groups (i.e, agency heads and lobbyists) toward changing the budget cycle from a biennial to annual system.

What are the prospects for changing the state's budget cycle? Overall, we conclude that they are not very good. The necessary linkage between annual budgeting and annual legislative session authorizations poses the major hurdle. Traditionally, the prevailing public attitude toward the role of state government and the legislature as an institution has been negative. Furthermore, the recent propensity for lawmakers to couple proposed annual session amendments with increases in their salary, or pay, plus public opposition from the governor's office have hampered annual budgeting efforts. Reservations about annual budgets are also expressed by key elite groups, such as state agency heads and lobbyists. Recent proposals at the national level for the federal government to change to biennial budget cycle, given the difficulty experienced by Congress in approving annual budgets in a timely manner, also provide a general atmosphere not conducive to annual budgeting at the state level.[8]

On the other hand, at least a few factors appear to be operating that probably enhance the prospects for annual sessions and budgeting. Interest in annual budgeting continues to be expressed by several Texas lawmakers (annual sessions and budget measures were approved by the Senate in 1987). If economic conditions continue to vacillate significantly in the state during the decade of the 90's, this should also stimulate interest in and support for changing the budget cycle. Finally, the long-term demographic change in Texas toward urbanization should foster the development of an overall political environment more conducive to state governmental reform and modernization.

Notes

1. This section draws upon the works of W.E. Benton, *Texas Politics: Constraints and Opportunities*. (5th ed), Chicago: Nelson-Hall Publishers, 1984: 44 - 59; J. E. Anderson, et al; *Texas Politics: An introduction*. 5th ed. New York: Harper and Row, 1989: 6-8; B.E. Pettus, et al; *Texas Government Today*. (4th ed.), Chicago: Dorsey Press, 1986: 60-88; and W.M. Bedichek and Neal Tannahill, *Public Policy in Texas*. Glenview, IL: Scott, Foresman and Co; 1982: 17-22.

2. J.C. May, *The Texas Constitutional Revision Experience in the '70's*. Austin: Sterling Swift Publishing Co; 1975 and J.E. Anderson, et al; *op. cit; :* 16-20.

3. Sam Kinch, Jr. and Ben Proctor, *Texas Under a Cloud*. Austin: Jenkins,1972.

4. B.E. Pettus and R.W. Bland, op.cit., 75-76.

5. J.E. Anderson, et al; op.cit., 313.

6. Ibid., 122-123.

7. Interim budget execution authority was favored over the years by the Texas Research League, a group supported primarily by business and industrial interests; see: "Better Budgeting and Monetary Management in Texas," *Texas Research League Bulletin*. February, 1971: 1-10.

8. P.H. Miller and J.K. Rech, "The Biennial Federal Budget: A Proposal for Better Government," *National Contract Management Journal*. Summer, 1984: 1-14; "Biennial Budgeting," U.S.Congressional Budget Office, Staff Working Paper, November, 1987.

6

BUDGET MANAGEMENT: ADMINISTRATION AND PROCEDURES

Kay Hofer

The concept of budget management for the public sector is a relatively recent development. Public budget management, as we know today, evolved from practice developed in England in the wake of the "Glorious Revolution." Prior to that time governments had existed, but budget documents, management and formal allocation processes were not part of the structure of operation. Over time, the documents which were simply a compilation of requests for expenditures became known as budgets.[1]

Management as a concept associated with public documents did not develop until the twentieth century. A public budget today is regarded as a document that reflects policy priorities as defined by the ranking of expenditures for various public goods and services coupled with identification of sources and levels of revenue necessary to finance government activities. Most public budget documents are not, however, comprehensive. Offsetting receipts, earmarked funds, trust accounts, and receipts from quasi-operations may not be included in the appropriation bill. Often these funds constitute a significant portion of total expenditures. Not only does the public budget generally reflect a partial accounting of actual, total government expenditures and revenues, but the budget process is also decentralized and often fragmented. Legislative bodies are the allocating authorities and retain responsibility and control of the structure or organization of the budgeting process and budget management within that structure is most often housed in the executive branch of government. The appropriations that follow may or may not be directly related to the budget request in the form of an administrative document.

Regardless of the fragmentation of the process, budgeting remains the management of available, approved financial resources. If the resources are poorly managed for one area, less is available for another. Although resources are derived from the public at large, there is a theoretical, if not practical, limit to the level of taxation which citizens will bear willingly. As resources are limited, the public manager in the public sector is most often placed in the role of "bean counter" or "financial housekeeper." In recent years, the role of the public financial manager has expanded to include policy planning as well as management of financial control across all levels of government. To some extent, the changes in approaches to budgeting provides some insights as to the focus and role of budget management in the public sector at any point in time. Desired outcomes of budgeting are closely related to format selected for preparation of the document and monitoring the results of these expenditures. This merging of management approaches has resulted in the development of numerous hybrid budgeting systems across the states and in the national government. This chapter now turns to an examination of the budget management in the state of Texas, including an assessment of the impact of constitutional, statutory and procedural changes over time.

The History Of Budget Management In Texas

During the later years of the Progressive reform movement, the State of Texas hired Griffenhagen and Associates to conduct a management audit of the State's financial management and administrative systems. Griffenhagen and Associates was a respected management consulting firm and had completed reviews for fourteen states and a number of municipal governments prior to development of the 1933 Texas Report. This firm was nationally known and specialized in public administration and financial management. Commissioned by the Texas' Joint Legislative Committee on Organization and Economy during 1931, the firm was to prepare a nonpartisan report including recommendations for more effective administrative and financial control of Texas government with primary emphasis on expenditure control. The Griffenhagen report pointed out the role of management, personnel and the organizational structure in financial management. They found the role of management, in general, in the public sector to be limited by constitutional and statutory requirements i.e., successful techniques in the business world could not as easily be applied in the public sector. The structure for budget management in the public sector is determined by constitutions and laws, and such structures are not easily changed with regard to function. Griffenhagen and Associates found that the tension between management and politics remains deeply embedded in state government in particular. The report concluded that

> bad organization often makes the adoption of effective procedures impossible...and managing authorities, even when carefully chosen and well qualified, cannot attain more than moderate degrees of success if the organization through which they function are not designed for effective service and to supply them with the essential elements and agencies of direction and control.[2]

At the time the report was presented to the Texas Governor and Legislature, they found "no provision in the agencies responsible for active management or administration of the financial affairs of the State." The report found the Texas financial management system to be fragmented among independent and multiple state agencies; fiscal accountability was diffused across separate, independent and multiple state agencies; financial authority was further fragmented across the offices of the Treasurer, the Comptroller of Public Accounts, the State Board of Control, and the Governor. The report determined the total absence of sound financial management techniques in Texas with no adequate legal provisions for budgeting, accounting, management, or fiscal control. For the few functions that were provided by the law, Griffenhagen and Associates found the responsibilities for financial management allocated "in such a way as to violate fundamental principles of good organization."[3] They equated agency management of funds after appropriation with management of "individual bank accounts" devoid of any accountability of fiscal responsibility for spending categories and outcomes. Agency budgets were managed as if each account was that of a "separate state."

According to the report, there was no way possible to determine the state of finances in Texas. Total spending and total revenues could not be compiled; no one could determine who was spending how much on what; funds were jealously guarded by numerous independent agencies after appropriation and randomly assigned to appropriations codes on the basis of administrator whim. They found a total absence of fiscal control procedures, planning and a system of incremental budgeting based on "wholly unreliable and inaccurate figures as to the expenditures of past periods."[4] No capital budget existed and no means of financing or expenditures estimates were produced by the state. Additionally, they found that the Comptroller as chief accountant was not required to have any knowledge of accounting. To further compound management problems, the Comptroller was charged with exercising financial management with the existence of a "woefully" inadequate state accounting system. The report found no system to be in existence for accounting for receivables or payables and no mechanism for pre-audit to avoid overextending the appropriated funds. The auditing function was found to violate all principles of sound audit procedures. The audit was an administrative rather than a legislative function with the administrator unable to control the accounting function. The fund structure of the state was disparate and divided in control with no centralized authority for investment. The analysts found that there was no provision in the existing laws for administration of the budget and that budgeting was limited to compiling of agency or departmental requests; such management functions as existed closely resembled those of the national Treasury Department during the early nineteenth century.

The state Board of Control was charged with compiling the estimates of expenditures and preparing the appropriations budget. However, during the period of the report, the State Board of Control consisted of only one individual. Without assistance, this person was solely responsible for preparation of a $55 million budget. He had no staff assistants, not even typists. Although the total state budget during 1931 was $10 million, only half the budget was included in the appropriations budget; the remainder constituted special funds that did not even require legislative review. Worse yet, the study revealed that the State was required to turn to a federal agency, the Census Bureau, for an accurate and comprehensive report of state revenues and expenditures as well as for expenditures arrayed by the various government functions. Griffenhagen and Associates summarized their findings in one rather dismal account. "As fiscal functions are now allocated, there is a hopeless jumble of policy-forming, quasi-legislative, quasi-judicial, accounting, auditing, fiscal reporting, and treasury functions, with responsibility for each one of them almost hopelessly diffused and scattered."[5] In short, the state of Texas' financial management system in the pre-World War II years was dismal.

The report was not so harsh, given the failure of the state to adhere to even the first tenet of sound financial management, as to assume the system had been purposely designed in such a haphazard manner. Griffenhagen and Associates found that the Texas fiscal management system was the result of three primary factors: 1) the limitations of the organizational structure determined by the constitution and state laws; 2) the absence of qualified personnel coupled with inadequate wages which resulted in assignment of fiscal functions to individuals who were capable at the time rather than in any organized or rational manner; and 3) the fear of a strong executive reflected in a fragmented, hopelessly decentralized administrative network with mixed functions for elected as well as appointed officials. With regard to fiscal management, the summary statement reflected a fairly dismal prospect for the future without constitutional reform. Griffenhagen and Associates found that in Texas

> there was nothing even savoring of unity in financial management. There are as many ideas about the financial condition and cost of government in Texas as there are fiscal agencies. Greater confusion, doubt, and uncertainty cannot well be imagined than those which prevail with respect to the budget and the various estimates respecting probable future financial condition.[6]

Given such a dismal assessment, one wonders how the state continued to function over the last fifty or so years. As the constitutional structure has changed very little since the time of the report, we turn first to an examination of the structure currently in place for budget management in Texas.

The Impact Of The Constitution On Budget Management In Texas

Just as the United States' Constitution is a derivative of the reaction to British rule in its attempt to diffuse power and retain primary control of expenditures in the most populous house, so is the Texas Constitution a derivative of both the national constitution and reaction to the form of government experienced during Reconstruction. The current Texas Constitution was approved in 1876, after Reconstruction, and is one of the lengthier documents of the fifty states with enormous detail spelling out the functions of the various individuals who are responsible for the state's taxing, spending and financial management. One does not have to spend a great deal of time analyzing the Texas Constitution to understand that the underlying principle was to diffuse responsibility and prohibit centralization of financial management responsibilities. The Texas Constitution requires officials to give semiannual financial reports to the governor and allows inspection of agency accounts, but the governor is not given the means to assure compliance or to take any action if misappropriation of funds occurs.[7] Diffusion of authority is the key to the Texas Constitution and to budget management in the state. Lack of trust in government, either elected or appointed, is spelled out in the enormous detail and the requirement that most change must occur through specific constitutional amendment.

82

The process of management of the government is so diffused that rather than saying Texas has a weak governor, one might say that Texas has a plural executive when considering budget management or the budget process. Responsibility for management of the state's finances is diffused in a complex framework of checks and crosschecks that include constitutionally-established roles for the Governor, the legislature, the Comptroller of Public Accounts, the Treasurer and statutory roles of the Legislative Audit Committee, the Legislative Budget Board, the State Board of Control and the Sunset Advisory Commission. The purse strings remain tightly held by the legislature, but the legislature is far from trusted. Although the legislature appropriates funds, constitutional restrictions on spending associated with earmarked funds limits legislative decision making to only a portion of the state's total expenditures. The process is further fragmented as appropriated funds cannot be expended without the authority of the Treasurer and the Comptroller of Public Accounts, both of whom are elected and independent of legislative or gubernatorial authority. (Article IV Section 49a and Section 1, Texas Constitution)

Constitutionally, the Governor, the Comptroller of Public Accounts and the Treasurer constitute the budget management team and are specified as part of the "executive department of state." (Article IV Section 1, Texas Constitution) No single agency has control of fiscal administration, and the constitution and statutes protect the independent status of individuals responsible for spending the state's money. Most attempts to alter this independent status for participants constitutionally or by statute have failed. With such a constitutional system in place, the concept of the "executive budget" connected with the national budget reforms is rather meaningless in Texas. While their independent status is protected, administrative discretion of these officers remains restricted by constitutional and statutory definitions of responsibilities. Fiscal control methods which must be followed depend upon the official in question.

To further complicate and diffuse the Texas' budget management process, only a small number of state operating agencies are headed by individual executive officers. Suspicion of executive power resulted in the creation of numerous advisory boards and commissions to head the majority of state operating agencies, almost all of which are independent of the control of the governor both administratively and fiscally. Other than the item veto and enabling powers, the governor has few formal fiscal powers. Enabling power, required for initial approval of federal grant-in-aid programs, too is weakened once the legislature has appropriated funding or passed the necessary legislation, especially if earmarked funds are established for the new programs. In Texas, there are still as many approaches to budget management as there are independent agencies or funds. For all practical purposes, the locus of governmental control of the state's budget is distributed across functions of elected officials having more influence over the budget and budget management than does the governor.

Over the past two decades, states have continued to refine their budget management processes, often in response to changes in the national system. By 1974, forty states had an executive budget management system in place. In contrast to the national trend toward more centralized budget management systems and strengthening of gubernatorial powers, Texas has continued to move even further from an executive budget process during the last decade. By 1989, only Texas and

South Carolina had failed to implement an effective executive budget system. In 1984, a major budget power shift occurred in Mississippi when budget authority was moved to the governor's office from the Commission of Budget and Accounting which had been structured much like the Legislative Budget Board in the state of Texas. The Mississippi legislature created a new Fiscal Management Board (FMB) which is composed of the governor and two of his appointees. Once the state's budget is adopted, the FMB is responsible for implementation and oversight. South Carolina has a budget process that is centered in the State Budget and Control Board composed of the Governor, Treasurer, Comptroller General, Chairman of the Senate Finance Committee, and Chairman of the House Ways and Means Committee.[8]

While Texas according to constitution and statute has a similar budget structure to that of South Carolina, the actual Texas' budget management structure functions primarily as that of a strictly legislative budget with regard to preparation and approval, moving to a plural executive model for implementation and monitoring. In 1989, for the first time since 1951, the Governor's Office of Budget and Planning did not even prepare a separate budget request for consideration by the Texas legislature. The legislature had seldom paid much attention to the Governor's budget even though valuable staff time has been expended in preparation of the document for each legislative session. According to statute, the Governor must prepare a budget request, but, in 1989, the Governor simply endorsed the budget prepared by the Legislative Budget Board for the biennium of 1990-1991. It is too early to determine whether personal influence and trust on the part of the Governor for a key staff person or a simple recognition that was the determining factor in this major departure from precedent and statutory requirements. It is also too early to know if this 1989 precedent will be followed by other governors in the future. The Governor, of course, may exercise the line-item veto. As the budgeting is almost always approved at the very end of legislative session, such vetoes are usually final. Joint agency hearings before the Governor's staff and LBB were retained and used to approve expenditure requests for the 1990-1991 biennium; so, perhaps, preparation of additional executive budget is primarily an exercise in futility. After all, the Texas Constitution has given the legislature the strongest version possible of "purse-strings" control.[9] Within such a political structure, centralized budget management and budget reforms remains difficult to achieve.

Other Factors Influencing Texas Financial Management

Other state agencies or boards have responsibilities for fiscal administration to some degree, but these are not as important as the constitutionally specified offices. These lesser agencies include State Tax Board, the Board to Calculate the Ad Valorem Tax Rate, the Boards of County and District Bond Indebtedness, the Commission on State Revenue Estimates, and the State Highway Department. The various functions of these boards and agencies are not central to the preparation and implementation of the state's operating budget; the responsibilities of most are extremely narrow. For example. the only function of the the Board to Calculate the Ad Valorem Tax Rate is to set the rate when required, and the formula for the rates structure is constitutionally provided. Constitutional limits determine the level and type of allowable state debt. An additional debt limit was added by constitutional amendment in 1978, restricting the rate of growth of state revenues from nonconstitutionally dedicated funds to the estimated rate of growth of the state's economy. (Article III, Section 49 and Article VIII, Section 22, Texas Constitution) Constitutional amendment is required even to issue full faith and credit or general obligation bonds. Texas constitutional provisions have, in effect, established a "pay-as-you-go" system of state finance.

In addition to constitutional structuring of the state's financial management and expenditure system, Attorney General's opinions have also played a significant role in determining the budget structure and responsibilities.[10] Article II, Section 1 of the Texas Constitution specifies that "The powers of the State Government shall be divided among three distinct departments so that no person or group from one department may exercise the power of another department except in the instances herein expressly permitted." This portion of the constitution has been interpreted by Attorney General's opinions over the years as a limit on the budget powers of the legislature as well as the governor. While the governor has some control over budget execution and is by statute designated as the chief budget office of the state, there is no power to transfer appropriated funds from one state agency to another; appropriations may not be impounded or withheld; the rate at which agencies spend funds cannot be regulated; and funds may not be transferred from the line items appropriated within agencies. Once funding has been appropriated, state agencies and departments function as independent fiscal entities with no gubernatorial control. These executive functions are key components of the national budget process and, with the exception of impoundment, are part of acceptable presidential authority for preparation and execution of the national budget. The Texas Attorney General has also held separate supervision of the budget execution process by the governor or the legislature as unconstitutional as well as supervision by a proposed joint legislative/gubernatorial commission.

At the national level of government, the President does have control over budget execution through the Office of Management and Budget (OMB) as well as control over the transfer of funds within agencies, the rate of spending, and some transfer authority across agency lines in the same functional area. Certainly the Texas Governor's lack of power coupled with state's fragmented fiscal management system mitigates against centralized executive financial management or easily located fiscal accountability. When the national government moved to the executive budget process in 1921, Texas had also responded. Preparation of an executive budget was initially lodged in the Board of Control charged with preparing estimates for the state's budget. Subsequently, the governor was designated the Chief Budget Officer in 1931 and given the power to hold hearings. The Board of Control continued to be responsible for preparation of budget estimates even after the Governor was designated as the state's budget officer. Agencies, institutions, departments, and employees of the State are required to submit estimates of appropriations to the Governor. However, the Governor's actual function in fiscal management was not unlike that of the Secretary of the Treasury during Jefferson's administration, a data compiler with control over reports extended only to those of constitutional authority, resulting in compartmentalized responsibility for state expenditure.

Dual Budget Management Systems In Texas

In time, Texas reformed the structure of fiscal management. Faced with a plural executive and a fragmented budget process, the legislature moved towards a centralized executive/legislative or dual system of budget management. In 1949, the Legislative Budget Board (LBB) was created, consolidating legislative budget powers in ten powerful elected officials including the Speaker of the House, the Lt. Governor and heads of key standing committees. Power is effectively centralized in the dual leadership of the Lt. Governor and the Speaker. The Governor's Budget Office was not formally even established until 1951, two years after the LBB was created. Day to day administration of LBB is carried out by a Director who serves at the pleasure of the Board. The Director has no vote but may make recommendations at the request of the Board regarding expenditures. All departments, institutions, and agencies are required to submit estimates and reports relating to appropriations requested by the board in addition to those required by law. The format of the estimates is determined by LBB. LBB is also charged with inspecting properties and accounts before and after estimates have been submitted.

According to current statutes and constitutional provisions, Texas is to maintain a dual budget process – one budget request is to be prepared by LBB; an additional one is to be prepared by the Governor's Division of Operations Analysis commonly known today as the Governor's Budget Office. In practice, LBB's budget estimates have historically carried more weight with the Legislature. Under the dual process, LBB and the Governor's Budget Office (GBO) currently prepare budget requests, using one set of coordinated instructions prepared by LBB. Initially the structuring of budget requests differed in the two branches. Until the early 1970s, LBB concentrated on the traditional preparation of line item budgets, and the governor's office generally relied on a more programmatic approach, thereby compounding any difficulties in monitoring or managing state expenditures. LBB emphasized fiscal control; the Governor's office emphasized planning. Formats varied, and the two budgets were in competition. In general, the LBB budget made lower spending recommendations, and requests for new programs appeared in the governor's budget. Both budgets dealt only with estimating expenditure requirements.[11] State law now requires the two offices to work together in budget preparation including using uniform budget estimate forms, conducting joint public hearings, and exchanging information.

Until the 1990-1991 budget cycle, recommendations were made independently to the legislature by the GBO and LBB after agency hearings. Currently, after analysis of budget requests by the two central budget offices, public hearings on agency requests are conducted by the budget examination staffs of LBB and GBO. Budget requests may be submitted in revised form after the budget hearings and the close of the fiscal year on August 31st. The Internal Board of Review (composed of the LBB Director and senior examiners) examines final recommendations in late fall to ensure consistency with guidelines and uniformity of format. The final document is submitted to the House, Senate, and Governor. Senior budget examiners of LBB work with personnel in all state agencies to prepare budget requests. Normally the recommended budget is completed by the middle of December on even-numbered years, and the draft appropriations bill is prepared and printed by LBB; the staff of LBB then serves as the staff of the House Appropriations and Senate Finance committees in the interim until the session begins and during the session. The LBB staff assists with "mark-up" during agency hearings and preparation of bill drafts that make required program adjustments in agency appropriations. The budget recommendations include estimated sources of revenue broken down by source and funds.

The functions of LBB are actually quite similar to those of OMB at the national level, just weaker with regard to execution control as much of this control is dictated by statute and the constitution. Estimates of required appropriations must be transmitted by LBB to all members of the legislature and the governor within five days of the convening of any regular session of the legislature. Membership on the LBB ceases if a member fails to secure nomination or election to membership in the Legislature for the next succeeding term. This section of the Statute has been reinforced by an Opinion of the Attorney General. (Attorney General's Opinion S-139 (1956.) This statute assures that there will be no "lame duck" budget influence on the part of a member of LBB. In short, LBB assumes many of the functions of budget management that are exercised by OMB at the national level and by other executive agencies at the state level. We turn now to an examination of the changes in Texas budget management that have resulted over time in a system that places such emphasis on legislative budget management/control.

Changes In Budget Formats And Budget Management In Texas

The ability to exercise any type of financial management in Texas is contingent upon the structure within which the process operates. As identified previously, there are three major, but not mutually exclusive, approaches to fiscal management – control (a focus on where and how the money is spent), management (a focus on economy and efficiency), and planning (a focus on decision making process for policy development). Incorporated within the components of financial management are accountability, comprehensiveness, uniform accounting, crosswalking to detailed line-item appropriations, compilations of estimates of expenditures, forecasts of revenues, a system of apportionments/allotments, control of budget format and a specific time frame for fiscal control. For the national government and most state governments, the majority of these functions are located in a central budget office under the direction of the chief executive. The structure of the process in the state of Texas is diffuse; pinpointing responsibility for financial management is difficult. The recognized stages of the public budget process include preparation, approval, execution and audit. With an executive budget process, preparation and execution are concentrated in the executive branch of government in most states and at the national level; approval and audit are generally located in the legislative branch of government. Accountability for execution or management of the approved operating budget generally rests in the executive branch. In Texas, preparation is located in the legislative and, until 1989, in the executive branch; approval is located in the legislative branch; audit is located in the executive and legislative branches; and execution is diffused among plural executive and constitutional offices. Accountability for the operating budget is even more diffused across the fragmented system of numerous independent agencies, commissions, board and special, earmarked funds. With the locus of budget control centralized in the legislature, even the preparation phase of the Texas budget process differs significantly from that of the national government and other states.

Still budget management in Texas today differs considerably from that of prior years. Although the dual process specified by the constitution and statute has been retained, coordination has been improved. In 1973, changes were made in the format of the Texas budget document. A House concurrent resolution was passed calling for program budgeting, and the Senate passed a simple resolution calling for the study of Zero-Base Budgeting and its possible application to the state. A compromise between the two versions resulted in adoption of the Zero Based Program Budgeting System (ZBPBS). In September of 1973, the Governor's Budget Office and LBB were instructed to "undertake a joint effort to design and implement a zero-base, program budgeting system for Texas state government."[12] The ZBPBS budget format incorporates the work load efficiency measures and effectiveness indicators of Performance budgeting and comparison of alternative ways to accomplish goals and objectives and multi-year planning of PPB systems with the evaluation of alternative levels of financing and prioritization for activities. Close examination of new proposals for spending is assured by the zero-base budgeting system. The purpose of the change in budget format was to engage in improved planning, gain better control over the estimated costs of government programs and spotlight duplications of state government programs.

In 1973, the Sixty-third legislature also established the requirement of fiscal notes "identifying the probable costs of any bill or resolution which would authorize or require the expenditure of any state funds for any purposes other than those provided for in the General Appropriations Bill."[13] LBB completed 5,983 fiscal notes during the Regular session of the Legislature in 1987. The purpose of these notes is to project expenditure requirements for five years so that the state does not engage in uncontrolled spending. These required fiscal notes incorporate the multi-year aspects of PPBS. In 1977, Texas' House and Senate rules extended the requirement for fiscal notes to any bills that would have an impact on local government.[14] All expenditures including federal funds are included in the budget, and a single appropriations bill is prepared so that the Texas budget, to some degree, meets the criteria of comprehensiveness of format. House Rule 4, Section 30 requires that the standing committee reviewing the proposed legislative change determine whether a fiscal note is required. If such a note is required, a request is sent to LBB. Committee hearings cannot be held until the fiscal note is attached to a bill or resolution. In addition to the five years of projected expenditures, the fiscal note must also include estimates of personnel costs. Information and data sources must be reported by the Director of the LBB who must sign each fiscal note. The fiscal notes must "remain with the bill or resolution throughout the entire legislative process, including submission to the governor."[15]

A similar system of fiscal notes is also in place at the national level of government. The State and Local Government Cost Estimate Act of 1981 was signed into law by President Reagan in 1981. This legislation requires fiscal notes for all "proposed legislation expected to have an aggregate cost to state and local governments of more than $200 million or is likely to have exceptional fiscal consequences for a geographic region or particular level of government."[16] Executive order 12291 also required federal agencies to submit Regulatory Impact Analysis estimates for regulations that may have an impact of $100 million or more in costs in any level of government. The fiscal notes at the national and state levels are a move towards a more rational budget process. Spending has, in general, been separated from approval of legislation and principles of accountability are violated when those responsible for raising the revenues are not the same individuals as those receiving credit for the change in policies and programs. Mandates also violate the principle of accountability. In recent years, federal mandates have required major fiscal adjustments on the part of many states. Texas faced expansionary budget mandates in the areas of Mental Health and Mental Retardation as well as modification of the prison system. Mandates by another level of government can come at a time when a state cannot easily absorb the costs of the forced expenditures. With fiscal notes in place, those allocating public funds and establishing policies have the opportunity to consider the potential impact of the legislation on funding and the geographic entity which will be required to implement the policy change.

The 1973 legislature also passed a statute requiring the Legislative Budget Board to prepare a performance report for agencies receiving appropriations through the general appropriations act i.e., those receiving nonconstitutionally specified or earmarked funds. LBB makes all of the estimates required for the fiscal notes and the performance report to save duplication of effort on the part of the governor's staff. LBB examines agencies for operational efficiency including such indicators as work-load efficiency data, unit cost measures, and examination of performance against program output standards. This report is furnished to the legislature at the start of each regular session.[17] With the implementation of the zero-base program budgeting system, the performance reports and the fiscal notes, came a reduction in emphasis in the line-item format. Today, more administrative discretion is allowed in preparation of the budget requests. Unlike the national process with the caps of the joint resolutions, there is no specific caps that is required for functional category or agency organizational expenditures. Absolute levels of dollar requests are not specified by either LBB or the Governor's Budget Office. The discretionary management aspects, however, are limited to less than a third of the state's total expenditures, and requests must fall within broad percentage limits or be pre-approved by the Governor's Budget Office and LBB.

In 1977, the Texas Sunset Act was passed, adding the review of operations and functions of state agencies to the state's budget management system. While the Sunset Advisory Commission oversees the reviews, the Lt. Governor and Speaker hold key positions on the Commission, effectively maintaining a concentration of legislative power. Approximately two hundred state agencies and advisory boards are subject to Sunset review. Review is every twelve years, and any agency is automatically abolished unless the legislature votes for its continuance. A number of constitutionally created agencies may not be terminated but are subject to review. Certain agencies such as those of higher education and the courts are not subject to Sunset review. The primary impact of Sunset review appears to be drawing public attention to agency operations.

More than seventy percent of Texas' revenues were earmarked in 1978 and identified as particular funds that can be expanded only for constitutional or statutory-designated purposes.[18] By 1989, that percentage had been decreased to roughly fifty percent of the state's budget significantly enhancing legislative control of general appropriations.[19] The Funds Control Act passed in 1981 has attempted to consolidate and bring all funds under the control of the Treasurer and include such funds in the Comptroller's Annual Fiscal Report. Most loopholes of independent fund accountability were closed by this act; the primary exceptions are funds for higher education which still function as "local funds" within constitutionally mandated accounts. Other local funds such as the Medical Examiner's Board and independent licensing boards are also retained as "local funds" under control of the collecting entity. Special interests connected with these boards have resisted including such funds in the general revenues under the control of the legislature. Such restrictions coupled with the state share or required match for federal programs and for implementation of federal mandates leaves only a small portion of the state's budget available for "discretionary" spending.

Although absolute spending levels for budget requests are not specified, LBB has the statutory authority to specify the format and the details of budget request preparation. The process of budget preparation is extremely detailed and, on the surface, appears to establish spending limits; however, Texas' administrators and budget officers familiar with the process can carve some flexibility out of the process. Each completed agency budget package includes the statement of the mission and legal authority for programs and activities, a five year method of financing table that includes type of funds and type of appropriations (regular, supplemental, or rider), transfers and unexpected balances. Any agency that has had to make use of the Governor's "Deficiency and Emergency Grants" has to make note of the amount of such funds. Program and Activity decision packages are required to include performance (effectiveness) measures at the program level that are quantitative expressions describing the external effect programs have on a particular problem area, and workload measures and unit costs at the activity level.

Details Of Budget Management In Texas

LBB determines the detailed budget preparation requirements which are similar to those of OMB. Preparation by LBB involves: 1) determination of a budget calendar with established deadlines; 2) an agency call or request for budget preparation; 3) a statement of executive policy; 4) general instructions; 5) specific instructions; and 6) examples of documents to be prepared. LBB prepares the detailed instructions for budget submission for state agencies as well the

Governor's Office of Budget and Planning. State agencies in Texas are required to furnish supporting schedules in addition to basic budget materials. These supporting schedules contain the details of the budget justification and provide estimates for changes in agency management, personnel requirements or modifications that are necessary due to inflation and price change. These supporting schedules are in some ways more detailed than the formal budget request. Currently the schedules are required to contain all inter-agency contract receipts, an accounting of all federal funds, appropriation item transfers, special fund analysis, fees, operating expense items, salary rates, and costs of reclassification of full-time employees. This requirement for preparation of detailed schedules is similar to that instituted in the national government. *The Budget Appendix of the United States Budget* contains the detailed schedules of the federal government and is much more specific and comprehensive than the budget request document.[20] The Texas ZBPBS format provides the legislator and the governor with a comparative framework for decision making and incorporates concepts of the OMB Current Services Budget which accounts for mandates, inflation, and increased services demands. The Current Services Budget of the national government provides estimates of the cost of continuing programs at their same level with adjustments for inflation and other uncontrollable factors associated with the cost of service delivery.

Even this detailed format required for presentation of Texas' budget requests does not adequately present legislators with the projected costs of postponing difficult decisions. Analysis is limited to comparison of alternative costs of achieving the specified goals. The budget document reflects a five-year budget time frame (the two previous budget years, current year, and two budget request years). A revised budget which is similar to the joint CBO/OMB fiscal report is filed on October 1 after the close of the current fiscal year. All the second submission does is convert the estimated budget figures of the budget request to amount actually expended at the close of the fiscal year. For the 1989 second operating budget request, the legislator added the requirement that a "cash flow analysis" in a format determined by the State Treasurer be included as a component in the operating budget. The cash flow analysis is one step in the direction of an expenditure monitoring system.

Recently attempts have been also made to improve the State's accounting management functions. As the Chief Accountant for the State as well as the Chief Revenue Collector, the Comptroller is required to provide an accounting of state funds. The Comptroller's official report of the total revenues and expenditures of the state is required by law, however, to be strictly a cash report. Effective budget management is weakened when cash accounting rather than modified accrual accounting is used for such reporting. Modified accrual accounting allows for the compilation of more accurate fiscal reports as encumbrances (legal commitments for expenditures) are recorded when accrued rather than when paid. These encumbrances bear the full faith and credit of the unit of government and must be paid. If encumbrances at year-end are sizeable, agency funds for the next fiscal year may be severely depleted. The failure to record encumbrances leads to a reporting that may be inaccurate with regard to the state's budget. In addition to the Annual Cash Basis Report, an Annual GAAP (Generally Accepted Accounting Procedures) edition of expenditures and revenues has been prepared by the Comptroller for the last two fiscal years. The GAAP report totals expenditures and revenues using modified accrual accounting, and all agency encumbrances are included in the report. While the Annual Cash Report does not distinguish receipts for current income and expenditures from those of other years, the GAAP report makes such a distinction. The Comptroller's Facts Manual provides funds codes for all state funds. These codes have been established and allocated to cost centers that are specifically defined for each appropriation fund. Each state agency or department has an agency code and specific expenditure codes. The Comptroller performs agency oversight by spending quarterly reports of expenditures using these codes to LBB. With the passage of the Interagency Cooperation Act, interagency transfers and contracts as well as warrant expenditures are monitored by the Comptroller.

The appropriations bill is extremely specific, and funds for transfer are identified by code. There are currently more than three hundred separate funds with such codes and individual accounting systems. A committee with input from LBB, the Auditor, and the Governor's office has designed an automated statewide accounting management system that would be in place by 1991. The biennial budget for 1990-1991 implemented the new system of "method of financing" codes conforming with the requirements of Comptroller's Manual of Accounts.[21] The implementation of uniform codes improves assessment of revenues and actual expenditures for the numerous government funds. Once in place, this system will allow encumbrances as well as expenditure monitoring for most of the state's budgetary system. Pre-audits will then be possible; i.e., examination of the accounts at the time a commitment is made, rather than when the warrant for payment is requested. Closer monitoring of budgets will be possible, and risks of deficits occurring before the end of the fiscal year will be lessened. The use of uniform fund codes for reporting and agency operating budgets is a strong, positive step toward the development of an accounting system that will increase the capabilities for professional budgeting in the state.

Currently, the Comptroller's Office encourages, but does not require, a system of modified accrual accounting for agency management. Required reporting and budget monitoring is strictly on a cash basis. Decisions regarding budget monitoring systems are left to executive officers in the various agencies and departments. Each state agency has its own Chief Accountant or Fiscal Officer, and reports of operating expenditures are furnished by these officers to the Comptroller, LBB, the Auditor, or the Governor on a monthly, weekly, or daily basis dependent upon the agency's legal requirements as determined by the Constitution, statute or the specifications of the appropriations bill. Agency transfers across funds can only be undertaken if so instructed by a legislative "rider" to the appropriations bill. Additionally, the state does not utilize an allotment system whereby cash is drawn from accounts in approved amounts at regularly specified, scheduled intervals. Rather, the expenditure process is constitutionally-specified and involves the Comptroller who draws up the warrant and the Treasurer who pays the warrant upon demand. The cash accounting method is cumbersome to administer and does not account for encumbrances that may be in the pipeline. Allotment requests and allocation schedules allow budget managers to examine budget and/or fund status. The data can be used for evaluation of effectiveness, control of expenditures, or planning for future budget cycles. Until such a system is in place in Texas, professional financial management capabilities will be limited to the commitment and desire for effective management fragmented among the state's many fiscal officers.

The fiscal management responsibilities of the Legislative Budget Board have been significantly increased in recent years. The Texas constitution was amended in 1978 to limit the rate of growth from state revenues to the estimated rate of growth of the state's economy. LBB was given the statutory authority the following year to determine and collect "items of information necessary for establishing the constitutional limitation." The items requested must be approved by a committee consisting of the Governor, Lieutenant Governor, Speaker of the House and State Comptroller. The move toward centralized legislative budget management was further extended in 1985 when a constitutional amendment "authorized the Legislature to require prior approval of the expenditure of funds by an agency or the transfer of appropriated funds." The Governor's budget execution authority was also extended by legislation passed in response to this amendment. The accompanying legislation authorizes the Governor to propose impoundments of agency appropriations in the form of spending prohibitions and to propose transfers of agency funds. The proposed change go into effect after publication in the Texas Register, public hearings, and review/approval by the LBB. If the Governor approves the final proposal for change recommended by LBB, it goes into effect. "Total appropriations of an agency for a given fiscal may not be decreased by more than ten percent or increased by more than five percent from the amount set by the Legislature" by this process. As of April, 1988, the Governor had not exercised the authority to change agency appropriations bills, a process authorized by constitutional amendment in 1985.

With the shrinking revenues and increased spending demands of the 1980s, many states developed contingency funds to stabilize expenditures and debt loads during economic downturns. Texas voters passed Proposition 2 during the general election on November 8, 1988, establishing a state "economic stabilization" fund or "rainy day" fund. The fund will be financed by transferring half of any unencumbered state general balances and 75 percent of severance tax revenues, annualized above 1987 levels into a specified account. Such contingency funds are recommended to maintain service levels and to allow a state to function efficiently during periods of revenue decline. In many instances, economic downturns signal a halt in infrastructure development and a decline in state services when they are often needed the most. Ideally, contingency funds should equal the average difference of the error rate in revenue projections, allowing for expected changed in the macroeconomy.[22]

A capital budget system was implemented during the 1987 session to gain control on a statewide basis of costs of repair, renovation, construction and equipment acquisitions. Activity packages of budget request must include capital outlay detail tables for replacement of existing or new items of equipment adjusted by unit cost for the two fiscal years of the budget request. Program packages must either include requests for capital expenditures in the program activity or as a separate capital activity. The weakness of the Texas capital budget system is that capital expenditures financed by constitutionally-approved bonds, those of higher education, and transportation are excluded from general legislative review. The Texas' capital budget as currently implemented is not comprehensive and focuses primarily on construction/renovation projects.

Conclusion

So, how does Texas measure up in the area of budget management? When the criteria for evaluation of budget management are considered, Texas does not meet all of the criteria. With the possible exception of South Carolina, budget management in Texas is perhaps the most fragmented constitutionally of that of any state. The adversary budget process is somewhat weaker and more legislatively-compartmentalized in Texas than in any other state in the nation. With the Governor's endorsement of LBB's budget in the spring of 1989, Texas remained the only state in the nation with a legislative-centralized budget management system. Centralization of budget control is primarily through LBB in contrast to the national level where dual centralization (through CBO and OMB) exists. Dual centralization has the potential to strengthen the adversary process as well as executive management. In Texas, legal accountability remains diffused across elected and appointed officials, and budget management is even more fragmented as this authority is divided among numerous agency and department executives. Budget management is made more difficult within such an organizational structure. The structure has been modified by recent constitutional amendments and statutes to allow budget management and the legislative process to become more cooperative and centralized. Even so, it is clear that budget management includes a plural-executive, fragmented approach. The key participants in financial management remain are the Comptroller, the Lieutenant Governor, the Speaker of the House, the Treasurer, and the Governor with the fiscal power center remaining in the Legislature. Moreover, responsibility for administration of the budget is fragmented and does not allow for clear lines of accountability.

The ZBPBS format of the Texas budget allows for the application of advanced budgeting techniques for consideration of expenditures. Planning, evaluation, and control of public expenditures are components of this budget management system. The components of Performance budgeting, PPBS, and ZBB formats that have been retained in the Texas ZBPBS format are those dealing with projections, coherence and rational choice. Budget management in the state appears to be shifting from one of expenditure control to one of strategic management, including long-range projections, evaluation of alternative means of reaching goals and objectives, and consideration of performance evaluation in conjunction with agency funding. The Budget is composed of program packages supported by cost estimates, data on work load, productivity and effectiveness. Policy analysis is included in the measure of effect of activities on target groups, and resources are considered simultaneously with requests. Specific target amounts that represent reasonable budget needs are allowed, and total expenditures are held within the available revenue levels. The Texas constitution restrictions on debt, especially the growth factor limitation of 1978, forced more careful attention to management and planning in the budgetary process. The format of the budget document is clearly related to desired outcomes, with evaluation an essential component.

Management of budget execution includes projecting, monitoring and controlling expenditures with post-execution audits to determine appropriateness and efficiency of expenditures and, in most cases, evaluation of program effectiveness (outcomes) with regard to attainment of stated goals. The equivalent of post-execution audits are performed through Performance Reports and Sunset Review, rather than through an independent audit process. While Texas still allows the contracting of post-audits (identified as an accountability problem in 1931 by Griffenhagen and Associates), the majority of agencies contract primarily for audits to improve budget management techniques and management information systems. Each agency conducts an annual audit via in-house staff. Those reports are furnished to the State Auditor and to LBB. The state could improve in the area of audit independence.

The budget document is comprehensive with regard to requests that must be submitted to the legislature and funded through the general appropriations process. The budget is not comprehensive with regard to including "all" expenditures of government and subjecting those expenditures to a legislative or administrative prioritization process that presents an accurate view of all government activities and expenditures. The presence of numerous, separate constitutional funds that are free of legislative restrictions mitigates the desired intent of comprehensiveness in budgeting. The presence of constitutionally-dedicated funds assures special treatment for certain activities of state government. Constitutionally-dedicated as well as nondedicated expenditures and revenues are, however, displayed for a five-year time frame which does allow for analysis of changes in activities and costs across time. Under the guidance of the Comptroller, the number of special funds has been reduced significantly, and the budget has moved closer in recent years to meeting the criterion of comprehensiveness. By 1991, the new system is implemented, the move to an adequate system of allocation and budget monitoring should follow proximately. Such a system will provide uniformity of approach even in a system of fragmented management authority. The system of modified accrual accounting as well as allotment systems should be extended to constitutionally-dedicated and nondedicated funds for comprehensiveness expenditure accountability.

Texas is moving to a system of uniform accountability and implementation of a system that will allow pre-audits of agency expenditures in the future. In monitoring public budgets and funds, a system of modified accrual accounting in which encumbrances are recorded when they are made is essential as the full faith and credit of the government is involved in contracting and purchasing. Cash accounting methods cannot be utilized effectively in budget monitoring during the execution stage as these do not take the encumbrances into account. Systems of competitive bids and the government contracting process required by law assure that a considerable time lag may occur in the public sector between the time an order is placed and the check is actually written. Close monitoring of the outlays in relation to the appropriations is necessary to prevent budget overruns. Although the Comptroller currently monitors outlays on a quarterly basis, for the most part, monitoring remains on a cash basis until the end of the fiscal year. The move to the modified accrual system of accounting in 1991 will greatly enhance budget management in Texas.

While Texas has recently initiated a capital budget process, moving the state in a positive direction, not all requests for capital expenditures are subject to legislative review. The separation of requests for capital expenditures into an identifiable category of agency operating budget is a step in the right direction; however, for the Texas' capital budget process to be effective, all capital expenditures should be included in a comprehensive budget. Although not politically popular, requests of higher education, transportation, and special projects funded by constitutionally approved bond issues should vie with other proposed capital expenditures in the legislative process. The establishment of a "rainy day" fund for periods of economic downturn should assist budgetmakers in avoiding cuts in services and infrastructure maintenance that can increase expenditures at a latter date. This system coupled with a comprehensive capital budget would greatly enhance long-range planning ability for Texas budgetmakers.

Budget management for the public sector is difficult to define as the management of financial resources involves subjective judgement, application of generally accepted government accounting techniques, evaluation of alternative means of achieving goals, allocation of scarce resources, performance evaluation and monitoring of legal compliance. For example, techniques of financial management may be applied but must be weighed against social and other unmeasurable costs or benefits. Budget maximizing which involves identification of activities that can be performed at less cost, evaluation of priorities for spending relative to costs, and evaluation of the reallocation of funds through budget adjustment is more difficult to achieve in the public than in the private sector. The current national budget does not include rewards for frugality. The system is structured informally in such a manner that failure to spend all appropriated funds is often rewarded with further cuts in funding. This process may lead to last-minute expenditures for unnecessary items such as office equipment and a flurry of last-minute travel. State budget follows much the same pattern -- the norm is to request increased funding or a percentage increase to the agency base. However, Texas does not require that unexpended funds be returned to the state treasury. Unexpended funds lapse to the fund of origin unless the Comptroller authorizes their carryover into the next fiscal year. Unexpended funds must also be reported in an agency's budget request to LBB and the Governor's Budget Office. Such carryovers must be authorized in the next fiscal year's appropriations act. The trend to add incrementally to the base may decline in the future as the gap between the need for expenditures and available revenue widens and as budget management becomes more professional.

"An unfortunate byproduct of the debate over approaches to budgeting is the stress upon format and procedures. One begins to believe that good government results from good public budgeting and that good budgeting exists if the correct procedures and formats are followed."[23] This assessment of public budget management by Lynch is reminiscent of the 1933 Griffenhagen report which equated problems of Texas budget management to the structure and the absence of appropriate budget procedures. There have been few changes in the Texas structure, but budget management today certainly comes closer to meeting professionally-recognized criteria for effective, efficient public budgeting. The changes in Texas budget management have occurred for the most part within the 1876 constitutional framework, adjusted primarily by changing responsibilities and coordination of the offices responsible for financial management. The outmoded constitutional structures have been unable to prevent budget innovation and change. The Texas budgetary process may actually come closer to recognition of the need to incorporate politics into the management process than the budget system in place at the national level. As the majority of significant changes in the Texas budgetary process are related to constitutional amendment and statutes passed to established procedures associated with such amendments, the process at a minimum remains more clearly defined than that of the national government. Constitutional accountability for fiscal administration remains fragmented in Texas, but responsibility for budget management is becoming increasingly centralized in the Legislature. Key elected officials such as the Speaker and the Lt. Governor continue to have more influence on budget outcomes than does the Governor. The Lt. Governor may well be the most powerful individual involved in the budget process.

Clearly, the Texas budget management system presents a viable alternative to the long-touted executive budget process. While power is centralized in the Legislature, these individuals are elected, not appointed as are officials in OMB. Texas has one of the lowest per capita debt levels of any state ($317.40 in 1988); only Arizona, Iowa, and Kansas have lower levels. Only two states had lower per capita taxes than the state of Texas in 1989, and the state does not have an income tax, corporate income tax, tax on food, or state property tax. The majority of the state tax all of the foregoing. In past years, fiscal analysts focused on the regressivity or progressivity of effective tax rates; the focus has now turned to total tax levels regardless of source or effective rates. In an era of increasingly scarce resources, the emphasis has turned to holding the line on taxing and spending while providing needed and desired services. It would appear that the Texas budget process has been able to hold the line on taxing and spending; whether the level and type of service provided has met needed or desired levels remains an issue that must be answered through the political process. Clearly, the outcome of the Texas' budget process is one supported by the majority of voters in the state. While such an outcome does not presume a budget management system without flaw or one that satisfies all residents of the state, the results of recent improvements may allow for significant change and adaptation in future programs before the taxing and debt levels similar to that of other states and the national government is reached. The increased effectiveness and efficiency of Texas' budget management may result in enough cost savings to assist in offsetting growing requests for increased expenditures. With the close of the 1988 fiscal year, the state was once operating in the "black." Projections of the State Comptroller's office are that the current trends reflected in state budget totals will continue. The recent changes in budget management on the part of the Comptroller also indicate that such a forecast is more likely to be accurate than those of the past. The changes in budget management in recent years have enhanced the capacity of Texas' fiscal officers to correct the problems of the present and to improve planning for the future.

Notes

1. T.D. Lynch, *Public Budgeting in America.* Englewood Cliffs, New Jersey: Prentice Hall, Inc., 1979.

2. Griffenhagen and Associates, *The Government of the State of Texas Part-1 -- Organization and General Administration.* Austin, Texas: A.C. Baldwin and Sons, 1933.

3. Ibid., 6

4. Ibid.

5. Griffenhagen and Associates, *The Government of the State of Texas Part-2 -- Financial Administration: The Fiscal Agencies* Austin, Texas: Von Boeckmann-Jones Co., 1933.

6. Ibid., 5

7. Clifton McCleskey et. al., *The Government and Politics of Texas.* Boston: Little, Brown and Co., 1978.

8. *The Book of the States 1988-89 Edition.* Lexington, Kentucky: The Council of State Governments, 1988.

9. B.E. Pettus and R.W. Bland, *Texas Government Today.* Chicago: The Dorsey Press, 1986.

10. Stuart MacCorkle, Dick Smith and J.C. May, *Texas Government.* New York: McGraw-Hill, 1974. See also, E.S. Redford, *The Texas Constitution: Its Impact on the Administration.* Houston, Texas: Institute for Urban Studies, 1973.

11. Legislative Budget Board, "The Budgetary Process in Texas," LBO:2/16/88: Austin, Texas, 1988.

12. Legislative Budget Board, "Responsibilities of the Legislative Budget Board and Staff in the Appropriation Process in Texas," LBO-BP/1: Austin Texas, May, 1988.

13. Ibid.

14. Ibid.

15. LBO: 2/16/88, op. cit.

16. R.D. Whitman and R.H. Bezdek, "Federal Reimbursement for Mandates on State and Local Governments," *Public Budgeting and Finance.* Spring, 1989: 47-62.

17. MacCorkle, op. cit.

18. W.E. Maxwell and Ernest Crain, *Texas Politics Today.* New York: McGraw-Hill, 1974.

19. *Texas Annual Financial Report Cash Basis -- For the Year Ended August 31, 1988.* Austin, Texas: Comptroller of Public Accounts, 1988.

20. Bruce Johnson, "The OMB Budget Examiner and The Congressional Budget Process," *Public Budgeting and Finance.* Spring, 1989: 5-15.

21. Legislative Budget Board, "The Budgetary Process in Texas," LBO:3/29/88: Austin, Texas, 1988.

22. J.L. Mikesell, *Fiscal Administration Analysis and Applications for the Public Sector.* Chicago: The Dorsey Press, 1986. See also, J.D. Vasche and Brad Williams, "Optimal Governmental Budgeting Contingency Reserve Funds," *Public Budgeting and Finance.* Spring, 1987.

23. Lynch, op. cit., 27.

7

ZERO-BASE BUDGETING IN TEXAS

Aman Khan

Governments in recent years have shown a great deal of interest in budget reforms by adopting a wide variety of management tools and approaches. Most of these reforms have been driven by the need to achieve economy, efficiency, and improvement, or what is commonly regarded as "better management."[1] In budgetary parlance, they refer to such areas of concern as strengthening administrative processes, achieving effective financial controls, ensuring legislative accountability and, more importantly, improving the public's understanding of the budget.

As in all reforms, budget reforms go through periodic changes and transformations. The course of reforms and their success or failure reflect, to a large extent, the economic and political environment in which budgets have to operate and the problems that are germane in transforming the strategies of reform into routine budget activities. This chapter discusses one of the most significant budget reforms in Texas, the factors that led to its implementation, and its implications for the future.

Development Of The ZBB System

The development of Texas budgeting toward a more progressive system in recent years began in the seventies when the governor's budget recommendations to the 62nd Legislature called for a budget process away from traditional practices. Following the reform movement that was sweeping the nation at the time, the recommendations emphasized the need for a system that would pay greater attention to programmatic needs, priorities, and results.[2] It was reinforced by a cost conversion and program workload schedule, developed two years earlier by the state, similar to a crosswalk relationship between program and object of expenditure costs. Prior to that, no formalized system existed in the state to clearly associate organizational activities or cost centers around operational goals and objectives.[3] As a result, it was difficult to produce analytical measures and other data with which the government could establish control, and determine efficiency and effectiveness of various programs.

In May 1973, the 63rd Legislature passed House Bill 169 to establish a system of audits and evaluation designed to provide for a comprehensive and continuing review of programs and operations of each state agency, department, and commission.[4] The Legislative Budget Board (LBB) was designed as the body to perform this function and to prepare for each regular session of the Legislature a *performance report* based on an evaluation of the program effectiveness and operating efficiency as well as legal responsibilities as measured by workload, costs, efficiency measures, and program output standards. The report was also required to provide recommendations for improving the management and delivery of state programs and services.

Shortly after the enactment of the bill, the 63rd Legislature approved a House concurrent resolution calling for program budgeting and the Senate passed a simple resolution requesting the Legislative Budget Board to study the concept of zero-base budgeting (ZBB) with a view to implement it as an aid in the budget recommendation and decision making process. A compromise was reached and in September of that year, Governor Dolph Briscoe, Lt. Governor Bill Hobby, and Legislative Budget Board Director Thomas Keel directed their staff to undertake a joint effort to design a *zero-base program budgeting* system for Texas state government to be implemented for the 1976-77 biennium.[5] In a memorandum to the legislative and executive staff a month later, the Governor and the Lieutenant Governor described the new system as

> a management process that must be ingrained into the way an agency runs its operations and makes its decisions. Zero-base budgeting must therefore become an agency process, not merely some budget forms to be filled out for the Budget Offices.[6]

According to the new system, all programs and expenditures must be reevaluated or reexamined every two years (since the state operates on a biennial budget) in terms of workload and other efficiency measures to determine their priorities for alternative levels of funding. The reexamination would allow each program, old or new, to be justified in its entirety each time a new budget is formulated, thus providing the Legislature and the governor with better control of resources needed to accomplish desired goals and objectives. This marked a major departure from the budget practices of the state which traditionally focused on incremental changes from a previous year.

Zero-base budgeting, as an operational tool, was first introduced in the U.S. Department of Agriculture in 1964. It was used, though without much success, by the agency as a means to justify its program needs, expenditure requests, and cost structure.[7] Several years later, Peter Phyrr revitalized interest in ZBB by successfully implementing it in Texas Instruments as a method of controlling the overhead costs.[8] Impressed with its success, the then Governor of Georgia, Jimmy Carter, invited Mr. Phyrr to help him implement it in the state and in 1976, when he became the President, required its adoption by the federal government.[9] Today, more than two dozen states and a host of local governments, along with numerous private and quasi-public organizations, use ZBB or some variations of it.

The Basic Operating Elements of ZBB

Zero-base budgeting has been variously defined. In the most literal sense, however, it implies constructing "a budget without any reference to what has gone before, based on a fundamental reappraisal of purposes, methods, and resources."[10] It makes no assumption about the past and every operation is questioned, scrutinized, and justified on the basis of its own merit (costs and benefits). Conceptually, it involves a "bottom up" approach where managers at all levels of decision making participate in the budget process by systematically deciding how activities and resources of a government should be allocated to accomplish its goals and objectives.

An important characteristic of zero-base budgeting that distinguishes it from all other budget systems is its flexibility. It does not require a rigid structure, or procedure, and can be tailored to fit each government's unique needs and circumstances. Although the specifics may differ, the steps involving a ZBB process remain basically the same. They are: (1) the development of a program structure; (2) the development of decision packages; and (3) the ranking of these packages in some priority order.

Development of a Program Structure

The program structure serves as the basic starting point for budget development. Its purpose is to systematically identify all agency operations designed to meet various problems, needs, and demands.[11] In addition, a program structure identifies program costs, recognizes managerial responsibility for budget development, and preserves organizational identity by acknowledging those instrumental in achieving its goals and objectives.[12] These characteristics provide a useful framework within which data can be organized to help key decision-makers in the executive and legislative branches in the preparation, review, appropriation, and finally, the execution of the budget.

The development of a program structure in the state is a joint responsibility of the legislative and executive budget staff as well as of the agencies themselves. The program structure consists of three principal elements, namely functional category, program, and activity.[13] A *Functional Category* is the highest element of the program structure and is external to agency operations. It includes all programs and activities of state agencies and institutions. Currently, there are eight such functional categories in the state. They are: (1) education, (2) transportation, (3) health and human services, (4) public safety, (5) regulations, (6) natural resources, (7) general government, and (8) employee benefits. Table 1 presents a sample program structure for the Department of Public Health.

TABLE 1
A Sample Program Structure for the Department of Public Health

Functional Category	Program	Activity
Health and Human Services	[A] Personal Health Services	1. Kidney Health Care 2. Chronic Disease Screening 3. Cancer and Heart
	[B] Tuberculosis Services	1. Administration 2. Inpatient Services 3. Outpatient Services
	[C] Laboratories	1. Administration 2. Field Services 3. Capital Construction
	[D] Vital Statistics	1. Vital Records 2. Statistical Services

Source: Compiled from Detailed Instructions for Preparing and Submitting Requests for Legislative Appropriations. Austin, TX: GOBP and LBO. March 1990.

Each functional category is divided into a number of programs which, in turn, are divided into a number of activities. The *programs* are constituted on the basis of needs of an agency. Program needs are derived from legislative intent, past records as well as from specific groups of individuals which have been identified as having the need. The third and final element of the program structure is the activity. *Activities* include those operations which implement programs. Most programs are complex enough to warrant several activities for their operation. An activity usually corresponds to an organizational unit, called *decision unit*, such as Kidney Health Care, Outpatient Services, or Vital Records so that they can be measured in terms of output or workload.

Although zero-base budgeting can be designed within the framework of a traditional object classification system, it is more readily adaptable to a program budgeting structure. This is due to the fact that decision packages are by their very nature oriented toward governmental functions and activities rather than specific budgetary line items. Peter Phyrr believed that the two systems are complementary and, if properly integrated, both could work together to provide a thorough budgeting tool.[14] The program structure is important to all agencies because requests for appropriations are justified at the program and activity level.

Development of Decision Packages

A decision package provides justification for and describes the various programs and activities of a program structure. It is an important building block of

102

the ZBB process since decision packages are prepared for each program and associated activities. Each agency prepares program as well as activity decision packages. Formulating a decision package requires, as a first step, that an agency determine appropriate objectives for each program and related activities. Objectives are quantitative statements of the amount of work a program or activity will need in order to achieve critical administrative goals. There are many different and mutually exclusive ways of determining an objective, but only the best is selected. Once a choice regarding the objectives of a program or activity has been made, several different levels of effort, called *funding*, are described. Each level of funding expresses an incremental cost and benefit, built upon a base that provides support for other levels. By providing different levels of funding, management can avoid elimination of a program or activity by choosing a lower level of funding.

Four levels of funding are currently used by the state.[15] *Level 1*, regarded as the "minimum level effort," specifies a level below which a program or activity is no longer considered viable, or effective. For the 1992-93 biennium, this level is required not to exceed 90 percent of the 1991 budgeted level of funding for a program. What constitutes this minimum and how large the increment should be can vary from year to year, depending upon program needs and demands. Considered as "current services level," *level 2* represents funding at 100 percent of last year's budgeted level. Funding cannot exceed this level unless major changes take place in the program or activities, such as projected changes in school enrollment, entitlements, retirement system costs, workers' compensation, and so on. *Level 3*, or "intermediate level," generally reflects the projected level of available revenue, and the anticipated statewide level of funding. Currently, it stands at 107 percent of the previous year's level. Finally, *level 4*, or the "most desired level," represents an agency's full request in order to provide all projected programs and activities. It is used only in those circumstances where the total request for a program exceeds those prescribed in level 3. These decision packages together constitute the total budget request for an agency.

After the various levels of funding have been identified, the managers evaluate the marginal benefits provided by these levels for each program or activity. The decision packages are then prepared to provide a more thorough description of these programs and activities. Each decision package consists of three parts: Part I describes the objectives of a program or activity, summarizes how they operate, defines and estimates the need indicators, and highlights the workload (for activities) and performance measures (for programs). Part II discusses the various levels of effort (funding) for a program or activity, and Part III provides a budget detail by appropriate objects of expense. Both program and activity decision packages use the same structure for presenting information on various elements.

Tables 2, 3, and 4 illustrate how the process of developing a decision package is operationalized in the state. The decision unit that is described is the Outpatient Activity of the Tuberculosis Services Program. The activity has two principal objectives: (1) to examine approximately 16,300 persons with newly developed or suspected cases of tuberculosis; and (2) to provide prescribed therapy through approximately 9,400 clinic sessions annually (Table 2). It is expected that through these objectives, the program would be able to ensure adequate treatment of known cases and provide preventive care to persons at high risk of developing tuberculosis.

103

TABLE 2
An Activity Decision Package: Part I
Objectives, Description, Need Indicators, and Workloads

Agency: Department of Health   Program: Tuberculosis Services

---

Activity: Outpatient Services

Activity Objective:

[1] To examine approximately 16,300 persons with newly developed or suspected cases of tuberculosis;
[2] To provide prescribed therapy through approximately 9,400 clinic sessions annually for new active tuberculosis cases.

Activity Description:

Through this activity, facilities and operations have been established throughout the state for finding cases of tuberculosis, ensuring adequate treatment of known cases, and providing preventive treatment to persons at high risk of developing tuberculosis.

Need Indicators:	FY 1990	FY 1991	FY 1992	FY 1993
[1] No. of persons seeking therapy	9,925	9,750	9,600	9,600
[2] No. of high risk persons in TX	25,250	26,172	27,000	27,500

Workload Measures:

[1] Number of contacts examined; [2] Number of clinic sessions held; and [3] Number of hours of treatment provided to new active cases.

Source: Compiled from Detailed Instructions for Preparing and Submitting Requests for Legislative Appropriations. Austin, TX: GOBP and LBO. March 1990: 39.

Table 3 presents a partial description of the various levels of effort or funding for this activity, discussed earlier. Note that the descriptions are incremental and focus mostly on the methods, actions, and operations needed to perform the services at these levels. Each level explains only those operations that are added at that level and does not restate operations of the preceding levels. In other words, they are not cumulative. Each level also describes the advantages and disadvantages of providing the service at that level.

Table 4 further illustrates the decision package in terms of various objects of expense, workload measures, and methods of financing. The expense schedule includes information on various expenditure items, such as salaries and wages, materials and supplies, utility and travel, and capital outlay. These expenses represent the total dollar cost of the various outpatient services at different levels of funding. For instance, at Level 1, also known as *decision package* 1 of 4

TABLE 3
An Activity Decision Package: Part II
A Partial Description of Levels of Effort

Agency: Department of Health   Program: Tuberculosis Services

---

Activity: Outpatient Services

At Level 1:

This level of funding would allow the operation of approximately 265 outpatient clinics throughout the state to find cases of tuberculosis, ensure adequate treatment of known cases, and provide treatment to persons at high risk of developing tuberculosis. ... Approximately 95 nursing positions, 20 community service aides, and 9 x-ray technicians would provide the direct care to those individuals requiring outpatient services. [Etc].

At Level 2:

At this level of funding, an additional 40 outpatient clinics, or a total of 305 (265+40), would be operated throughout the state resulting in an increase of 10 percent new contacts $[((14,708-13,368)/13,368)x100]$ to be examined and 14 percent in the number of clinic sessions $[((8,460-7,445)/7,445)x100]$ held for new active cases, when compared to Level 1. ... Eighteen nursing positions would be added with emphasis being placed on services in East Texas. [Etc].

At Level 3:

The addition of approximately 10 positions at this level of funding along with $100,000 in contracts with private physicians would result in a significant reduction in the amount of resources necessary in inpatient services activity. Hospital stays would be reduced from an average of 42 days per patient to 35 days on a statewide basis. ... Also, at this level, greater emphasis will be placed on patient collection. [Etc].

At Level 4:

Funding at this level will be used to contract with private physicians in 30 West Texas counties in 1992 and 15 additional counties in 1993. ... Also, at this level of funding, equipment will be replaced at the South Texas region and a new x-ray unit will be purchased for the El Paso area. The current unit is 15 years old and requires annual maintenance costs of over $2,000 per year. [Etc].

Source: Detailed Instructions... GOBP and LBO. March 1990: 40.

(since there are four such levels), the package would examine 13,368 cases and hold 7,445 clinic sessions at a cost of $5,034,500, which is about 10 percent below the current services level.

TABLE 4
An Activity Decision Package: Part III
Budget Detail (In $000)

Agency: Department of Health			Program: Tuberculosis Services		

Activity: Outpatient Services					

Object of Expense	Budgeted 1991	Level 1 1992	Level 2 1992	Level 3 1992	Level 4 1992
Salaries/Classified	4,063.8	3,707.7	469.1	274.5	-
Longevity Pay	30.1	32.2	2.1	1.0	-
Professional Fees	512.2	475.5	31.0	106.2	475.0
Consumable Supplies	468.5	447.3	35.3	5.6	-
Utilities and Travel	186.1	171.2	20.2	13.9	-
Capital Outlay	14.3	9.4	5.0	4.0	-
Etc......................					
Total This Level:	x	x	581.4	429.7	496.0
Cumulative Total:	5,515.7	5,034.5	5,615.9	6,045.6	6,541.6
No. of Positions:	x	x	19.4	9.8	0.0
Cumulative Total:	193.6	175.2	194.6	204.4	204.4

Workload Measures:

N of Contacts Exmd.	14,600	13,368	14,708	15,550	16,475
N of Clinic Sessions Held	8,374	7,445	8,460	8,950	9,395
N of Treatment Hours (New Active Cases)	4,950	4,550	4,950	5,250	5,975

Method of Financing:

General Revenue	4,999.0	4,578.6	525.9	408.2	470.8
Federal Funds	303.9	254.9	37.0	-	-
Patient Collections	212.8	201.0	18.5	21.5	25.2
Total This Level:	x	x	581.4	429.7	496.0
Cumulative Total:	5,515.7	5,034.5	5,615.9	6,045.6	6,541.6

Source: Detailed Instructions... GOBP and LBO. March 1990: 41.

At Level 2, and for an additional $581,400, the package could examine an additional 1,340 cases and run 1,015 more sessions. At Level 3, and for another $429,700, it could examine 842 more cases and provide 490 additional sessions. Total funding requests for this level would be $6,045,600 ($5,034,500+$581,400+$429,700) resulting in 15,550 (13,368+1,340+842) cases examined and 8,950 (7,445+1,015+490) sessions held. Finally, at Level 4, and for an additional $496,000, the package could examine an additional 925 cases and hold 440 additional sessions. Total funding request for this level would be

$6,541,600 ($5,034,500+$581,400+$429,700+$496,000) for a cumulative total of 16,475 cases and 9,395 sessions. Funding for these activities would come from general revenue, federal income support, and patient collections.

In addition to the above, the decision package also provides detail budgetary information on personal services and capital outlay. Personal services include various exempt and classified salaries as well as different categories of wages. The capital outlay details each item by the level of activity in which it is requested. It includes options for both new and replacement items. Requests for a capital item is generally based on a "unit cost" approach.

Ranking Decision Packages

The final element in the ZBB process includes a ranking of the decision packages in priority order. High priority packages rank at the top, low priority packages at the bottom. Table 5 presents an activity priority listing for the Tuberculosis Services program. In addition to ranking the various activities in descending order of importance, the table also provides information on budget requests for the biennium years, including their cumulative totals. As the table shows, decision package 1 of 4 of *administration* ranks first, followed by decision package 1 of 2 of *inpatient services*, and decision package 1 of 4 of *outpatient services*, and so on. These rankings are finally used to evaluate and determine the funding levels for each activity in the program.

TABLE 5
Activity Priority Table: Program Level

Agency: Department of Public Health   Program: Tuberculosis Services

R A N K *	L e v e l	C o d e *	Activity Name (Package)	Budg- eted 1991 ($000)	Reques- ted 1992 ($000)	Cumul- ative 1992 ($000)	Reques- ted 1993 ($000)	Cumul- ative 1993 ($000)
1	1	01	Administration 1-4	1,145	1,008	1,008	1,008	1,008
2	1	02	Inpatient Services 1-2	6,527	5,556	6,564	5,561	6,569
3	1	03	Outpatient Services 1-4	5,169	5,034	11,598	5,034	11,603
4	2	02	Inpatient Services 2-2	....	676	12,274	689	12,292
5	2	03	Outpatient Services 2-4	....	581	12,855	595	12,887
6	2	01	Administration 2-4	....	99	12,954	88	12,975
7	3	03	Outpatient Services 3-4	....	430	13,384	430	13,405
8	3	03	Outpatient Services 4-4	....	496	13,880	506	13,911
9	4	01	Administration 3-4	....	102	13,982	102	14,013
10	4	01	Administration 4-4	....	53	14,035	53	14,066
			TOTAL	12,841	14,035	....	14,066	....

Source: Detailed Instruction... GOBP and LBO. March 1990: 47.

A similar priority table is prepared at the agency level to display all activities in relative sequence of importance to the agency's mission. Unlike the activity priority table at the program level, the agency priority table is much more comprehensive and is used in the same manner for evaluation and determination of funding at that level. The judgments used in ranking of agency priorities are essentially those used in ranking priorities at the individual program levels, but from an agency perspective.

The ranking of decision packages throughout the entire budget process involves a careful and thorough analysis. It becomes complex as the list of packages becomes long and far too detailed. At the agency level, where the manager has the added responsibility of consolidating the packages, the complexity can increase severalfold. Nevertheless, the process does give the manager and other decision-makers at each level some control over the substantive mix of programs and activities, which is crucial to the functioning of a ZBB process.

Consolidation of the ZBB Process

In summary, the ZBB process in the state follows six basic steps: (1) the chief administrative officer, board members, agency administrators, and various program managers conduct needs assessment and prepare planning guidelines; (2) activity managers prepare activity decision packages; (3) program managers rank activity decision packages for each program on the activity priority table; (4) program managers prepare program decision packages; (5) agency managers rank activity decision packages for all programs on the agency priority table; and (6) agency managers prepare the agency decision packages. Figure 1 illustrates this consolidation process.

The sequence is modified somewhat as managers at different levels communicate with one another in refining the packages so as to determine their consistency within agency guidelines, available data, etc. The following presents a brief description of the significant milestones in the ZBB process:

January-June	:	Agencies develop budgets, set policy and goals, and make staffing decisions.
June-July	:	Agencies submit the first budget requests.
July-September	:	Budget hearings with LBB and GOBP take place.
October	:	Agencies submit the second budget requests.
December	:	Comptroller submits revenue estimates. LBB develops and adopts funding recommendations. Board staff presents analysis for program evaluation.
January	:	Governor makes budget recommendations. LBB recommended Appropriations Bill is introduced.
January-May	:	Agencies present priorities. Committees determine funding levels. Both houses approve the budget.

PROGRAM STRUCTURE

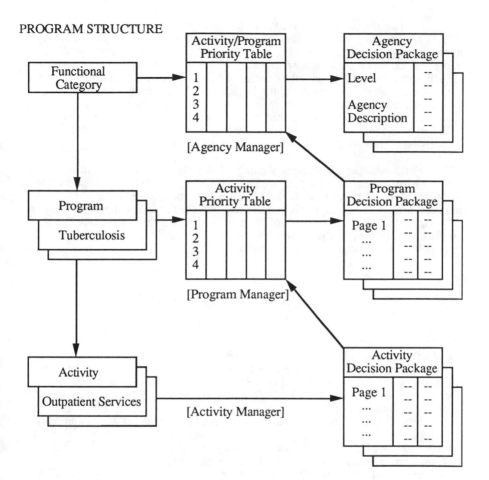

Figure 1. Decision Package Ranking and Consolidation Process. (Illustrated)

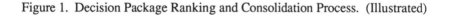

May	:	Comptroller certifies fund availability.
June	:	Governor signs Appropriations Bill.
September 1	:	Fiscal Year begins.

Once the agency process is completed, the component packages and tables are assembled along with the administrator's general statement and any supporting material. The documents are then sent to the legislative and executive budget offices for further analysis, where the staff of the two offices holds joint public hearings, with agencies defending their requests as well as making public any additional comments concerning those requests. At this point, the two offices, GOBP and LBO, independently develop their recommendations, which, after consideration by the Governor and the Legislative Budget Board, are submitted to the Legislature when it convenes in January of each odd-numbered year. "The LBB recommendations are introduced in both houses as the General Appropriations Bill and provide a base from which the Legislature enacts the bill for final submission to the Comptroller and the Governor."[16]

Following the Governor's signing of the Appropriations Bill, agencies begin to implement the adopted budget. Unless expressly given permission through rider and other means, the agencies are not allowed to transfer funds between programs or line items and are responsible for following appropriation authorizations. The Comptroller's office monitors expenditures to ensure that they conform with appropriated items, as do budget examiners for background in developing future budget recommendations.

Experience from the ZBB Process

Texas is one of the earlier states to adopt a zero-base budget in the country. More than fifteen years have passed since it was formally introduced. Despite some initial difficulties, the system has done well to have survived that long. Much of its success can be attributed to the PBS and a performance structure that facilitates its operation. The benefits derived from this process are numerous. For instance, it brings open unarticulated assumptions and forces all participants to focus on the importance of choices as the key elements in budget making. It furnishes the management with the information necessary to determine whether the current funding level is justified or whether a lower or higher funding level would provide a greater overall program benefits. It seeks to provide the management with a vehicle to identify possible areas of reduction if the executive budget recommendations are decreased by the Legislature's appropriations. It also serves as a useful apparatus in determining budget items to be vetoed by the Governor, if necessary.

On a more specific level, both the agencies and the budget staff derive some benefit from this process. The description of programs and activities, by varying levels of funding, provides new insight for both agency and staff personnel. At the same time, the volume of paperwork and the coordination between a large number of participants limit the amount of time that could be devoted to a more thorough budget analysis. This is clearly evident from the 1,392 programs and 3,866 activities that make up the system, covering 302 agencies, including universities and junior colleges; the workload is onerous. Unfortunately, this is a problem common to all ZBB processes and Texas is not immune from it.

The ranking of various decision packages in priority order remains a frustrating experience with most agencies. Although each agency is expected to prioritize its programs and activities on the basis of clearly defined criteria, political and other considerations often make it difficult to do so. The state Railroad Commission's recent effort to prioritize "rail safety" over "economic" needs, is a good example. The Commission's decision was based in part on legislative interest and, in part, on the need to impress the public with its effort to control the number of rail accidents. The presence of other factors, such as legal constraints, earmarked, or court-mandated programs make it even more difficult for the top management to consolidate the decision packages for final ranking and adoption.

A common concern with ZBB, one that seems to be just as relevant for the state system, is the rationale for incremental levels of funding. There is no clear evidence that justifies the cut-off points established for these levels. The use of percentage allocations seems arbitrary and one of convenience rather than anything else.

Of particular significance is the notion that ZBB provides budget decision-makers with a rational way to reduce and control budget growth, which is not necessarily true. For the past few years, the state budgets have been increasing at a moderate pace (although not as fast as during the hey days of oil boom), while the growth in state revenue has considerably slowed down due in part to declining oil prices and a slagging financial and real estate market. The prospects now loom for a budget shortfall in the 1992-93 biennium and it is unlikely that ZBB process would provide much in the way of accomplishing significant savings in this regard.

However, the prospects for ZBB, as a process well into the future, seems secured in Texas. A number of measures have been taken in recent years to augment its application in state budgeting. For instance, the Legislative Budget Board has recently introduced an automated data processing system for use by the budget examiners and program analysts to check the accuracy of budgetary data as well as to have easy access to this information. This not only saves time but also helps the decision-makers make better use of the available information.

A *fiscal note* procedure System which was introduced in 1973 to ensure that the government does not engage in uncontrolled spendings has since been updated to automatically track the staff assigned responsibility for writing the fiscal note. The system allows LBO to track "on-line" the note processing from the moment a request for a fiscal note is received by the office to its completion and return to a legislative committee.

One area, where opportunities exist for much more improvement, is the research on measurement data. In order to improve the quality and reliability of the budget requests, agencies and program analysts need to look for better measurement data by which to evaluate them. Both performance data and needs assessment data need further improvement if they are to be reliable instruments by which to make budgetary decisions, and to measure the performance of activities and programs once they have been funded.

Conclusion

The Texas experience with zero-base budgeting is not unique. Problems faced during the early years are similar to those experienced in other states, such as Georgia, New Mexico, and New Jersey.[17] Many of the problems were the result of the change in budgeting system and have been corrected over the years, while others remain. One of the reasons why the system has continued to improve is the cooperation between GOBP and LBO in realizing the benefits of ZBB. This is a key element in any budgeting system and will continue to provide incentives for further improvement in the state.

Notes

1. A. Wildavsky, "Political Implications of Budgetary Reform," *Public Administration Review*. Volume 21, Spring 1986: 183-190.
2. R. Jordan, *Performance Evaluation in a Legislative Budget Framework*. Paper Presented at the Southern Regional Conference of the National Association of the State Budget Officers, June 14, 1974: 1.
3. Ibid.
4. Legislative Budget Board, "Responsibilities of the Legislative Budget and Staff in the Appropriation Process in Texas." Austin, TX: LBO-BP/1 (Revised Edition), May 1988.
5. Ibid.
6. Office of the Lieutenant Governor, Memorandum on "Implementation of Zero-Base Budgeting." Austin, TX: October 26, 1973.
7. M.H. Granof and D.A. Kinsel, "Zero-Based Budgeting: Modest Proposal for Reform," *Federal Accountant*. Volume 23, December 1974: 50-56.
8. T.D. Lynch, *Public Budgeting in America*. Englewood-Cliffs, NJ: Prentice-Hall, 1990: 51-53.
9. P.A. Phyrr, *Zero-Base Budgeting: A Practical Tool for Evaluating Expenses*. New York, NY: John Wiley and Sons, 1973.
10. G.M. Taylor, "Introduction to Zero-Base Budgeting," *The Bureaucrat*. Volume 6, Spring 1977: 33.
11. T.M. Keel and C.D. Travis, "Joint Guidelines for Agency Internal Program Structure Determination." Austin, TX: LBB Memorandum to State Departments, Agencies, and Institutions, November 5, 1973: 24.
12. Legislative Budget Board, "Performance Report to the 64th Legislature." Austin, TX: LBB Report, 1975: 3.
13. Governor's Office of Budget and Planning and the Legislative Budget Office, *Detailed Instructions for Preparing and Submitting Requests for Legislative Appropriations*. Austin, TX: GOBP and LBO, April 1990: 1-2.
14. P.A. Phyrr, "The Zero-Base Approach to Government Budgeting," *Public Administration Review*. Volume 37, January/February 1977: 1-8.
15. GOBP and LBO, *Detailed Instructions*. ... op-cit., 5.

16. G.M. Rymal, *Zero-Base Budget Implementation in Texas*. Austin, TX: LBJ School of Public Affairs. The University of Texas at Austin. June 1975: 11.

17. F.J. Draper and B.T. Pitsvada, "ZBB-Looking Back After Ten Years," in A. Schick [ed] *Perspective on Budgeting*. Washington, DC: ASPA, 1987: 101-115.

8

REVENUE ESTIMATING: METHODS AND RESULTS

Bob Bullock and John P. Moore

Determining how much revenue will be available in the coming years is at the heart of all budget-making activities. In Texas, the responsibility of estimating revenue lies with the Comptroller of Public Accounts. When the Comptroller releases a revenue estimate, public attention usually focuses on just one number. Texans and their legislators want to know how much money the State will have over the next two-year budget period, or biennium.

Like the tip of an iceberg, however, this one number is only the most visible part of a much larger effort. The revenue estimate requires the Comptroller to predict the strength of the national and state economies for up to three years in advance.

The estimate requires forecasts to be made about everything from inflation and interest rates to the rate of economic growth and the price of oil in international markets. The Comptroller's staff must then use this information to make individual forecasts for more than a thousand sources of state income, ranging from sales and other tax Collections to agency sales of used equipment.

The Revenue Estimate: A Constitutional Responsibility

Article III, Section 49a of the Texas Constitution requires the Comptroller to submit to the Governor and the Legislature an "itemized estimate of anticipated revenue based on the laws then in effect" at the beginning of each regular legislative session, each special session, at at other times when there are "probable changes" in the revenue outlook.

The revenue estimate is legally binding. According to Article III, Section 49a of the State Constitution:

114

No bill containing an appropriation shall be considered as passed or be sent to the Governor for consideration until and unless the Comptroller of Public Accounts endorses his certificate thereon showing that the amounts appropriated is within the amount estimated to be available in the affected funds.

Thus, if the Legislature wishes to spend more money than that estimated to be available, it must find new revenue sources to enable the Comptroller to certify the budget.[1] The basic concept underlying this "pay as you go" provision is simple. The Comptroller determines how much money the state will have to spend and the Legislature, except under extraordinary circumstances, is bound by law to live within this means.[2]

The Revenue Estimate: Resources

The Comptroller's staff economists and financial experts -- directed by the Deputy Comptroller for Legislative Affairs and Revenue Estimating -- are at the heart of the revenue estimating process. They monitor the economy and state revenues on a monthly, daily, and sometimes hourly basis, and are in constant contact with industry experts in key sectors of the state economy. The economists are assisted by an array of modern technological devices to help them analyze the wealth of economic data pouring into their offices every day.

The Comptroller employs the services of major national economic services, such as the WEFA Group and Data Resources Incorporated (DRI), to keep track of the national economy. The Comptroller's State of Texas Econometric Model (STEM) attempts to simulate the complex interrelationships that drive the Texas economy and use this information to predict future developments. Econometric models are also used to forecast revenues for several major tax sources, including the sales, motor fuels, motor vehicles and franchise taxes.

Although econometric models are invaluable, they cannot provide all the answers. No model, for instance, could have predicted the stock market crash of October, 1987. Because of this, the Comptroller's Office supplements economic modeling with other monitoring techniques. For example, in order to gauge business expectations, the Comptroller goes straight to the source by surveying 250 top taxpayers in the state's major industries every quarter. The Comptroller's staff also measures the health of the employment markets by preparing a monthly index of help-wanted advertising, and compiles a monthly stock market index and leading economic indicators index for the state.

Finally, all economic forecasts are reviewed by the Comptroller's Economic Advisory Committee -- a group of highly respected experts representing a wide range of Texas industries.

In all, revenue estimating is part science and part art. Econometric models and other statistical devices appear to provide precise answers, but these must be tempered with a healthy dose of human judgement in order to insure their accuracy. The Comptroller's 99.5 percent accuracy rate over the past six years proves he has devised a system that works.

The Revenue Estimate: The Process

The revenue estimating process is a four-part procedure, involving: 1) economic/population forecasting; 2) individual revenue estimates; 3) compilation; and 4) review and publication. At times, more than 20 economists and revenue analysts on the Comptroller's staff, as well as senior agency personnel in several divisions, are involved in the project.

Economic/Population Forecast

The revenue estimating process begins with the state economic forecast produced by the Comptroller's micro-computer based State of Texas Econometric Model (STEM). STEM was originally purchased in 1979 from Chase Econometrics, Inc. (now part of WEFA), one of the world's foremost economic data and forecasting services. The model was completely rebuilt and expanded in the spring of 1986 to better reflect the changing Texas economy.

STEM is a modified "export-base" model based on three basic assumptions about the state economy (Figure 1). These assumptions are:

• First, what happens in Texas depends on events in the national and world economies. For example, if the price of oil changes, the Texas oil and gas industry and the overall state economy will be affected. Similarly, if the national economy falls into a deep recession, Texas will almost certainly follow.

• Second, the Texas economy includes a number of export oriented industries that produce for national and worldwide markets. The Texas agriculture industry, for example, produces beef and cotton that are the state's "economic base," and include agriculture, oil and gas, manufacturing and federal government installations, such as military bases.

• Third, a large portion of the state's economy, such as trade and services industries, supports these export industries. For example, if the state's manufacturing industries are prospering, they will spend more of accounting, consulting, and other support services. Thus the economic health of these "domestic," or support, industries depends on the condition of the export industries.

116

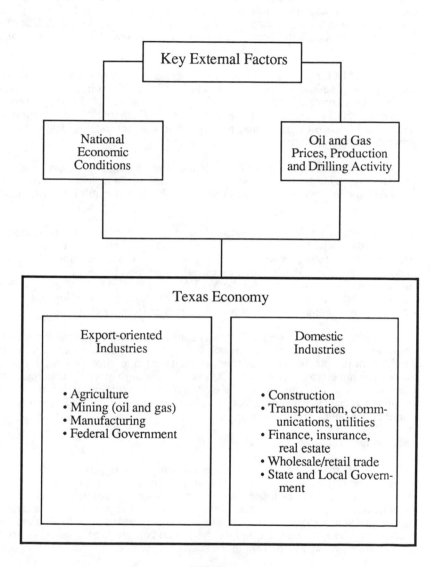

FIGURE 1
General Structure of the State of Texas
Econometric Model

Today, STEM contains approximately 130 equations and forecasts a wide range of variables, including gross product and employment by industry, personal income by sources, disposable income, single and multi-family housing starts, nonresidential and nonbuilding construction, retail sales by industry, labor force and unemployment, bank deposits, agriculture cash recipients and new car and truck registrations.

STEM's forecasts are updated in the spring and fall of each year and extend for 20 years. The industry detail used in the model is shown in Table 1. A related model -- the Comptroller's State Population Analysis Model (C-SPAM) -- produces annual population forecasts by age and sex. Each year, the population is determined by adding births and net migration and subtracting deaths from the previous year's population.

STEM and C-SPAM are linked by population data and the two models run interactively. STEM produces forecasts of net migration which are then fed into the C-SPAM model, while C-SPAM predicts the birth and death forecasts used by STEM.

In producing the state economic forecasts, assumptions must be made about key external factors affecting the Texas economy, such as national economic growth and the future trends of energy prices. Forecasts of national economic variables, including GNP growth, industrial production by industry, inflation and interest rates are obtained from the WEFA group. Forecasts of energy-related variables, including oil and gas prices, production, and drilling activity are developed by Comptroller staff in consultation with industry contacts.

Many private economic forecasts consist of series of alternative scenarios about an economy's future progress. By law, however, the Comptroller may produce only one official revenue estimate at one time, so only one and accompanying economic forecast is issued. But during especially uncertain times, Stem is used to analyze the effects on alternative assumptions for some major economic variables, such as differing scenarios for oil prices or Federal Reserve interest rates policy on the Texas economy.

Individual Revenue Estimates

When the economic forecast is completed, it is provided to a staff of revenue analysts, each of whom is responsible for one or more revenue sources. Although the revenue estimate includes more than a thousand sources of state income, attention usually focuses on the 70 key revenue sources that account for most of the state's money. For example, the six largest tax sources -- sales, motor fuels, motor vehicle, franchise and natural gas and oil production taxes -- normally account for more than 85 percent of the state's tax income.

Each analyst is responsible for producing a best estimate of revenues based on individual revenue models, actual revenue performance, legislative changes andinformation from industry contacts. From time to time, the Comptroller also conducts special surveys when information is needed on a particular revenue-related issue. Recent examples have included a survey of automobile dealers on the

TABLE 1
Industry Detail Maintained in the State of Texas Econometric Model

----

Agriculture
Mining (Oil and Gas)
    • Nonduables
        Food Processing
        Textiles
        Apparel
        Paper
        Printing and Publishing
        Chemicals
        Petroleum
        Leather
        Other Nondurables (Tobacco, Rubber, and Plastics)
    • Durables
        Lumber and Wood Products
        Furniture and Fixtures
        Stone, Clay, and Glass
        Primary Metals
        Fabricated Metals
        Oil-Field Machinery
        Other Nonelectrical Machinery
        Electronics
        Aerospace
        Other Transportation Equipment
        Instruments
        Miscellaneous Manufacturing
Transportation and Public Utilities
    • Transportation
    • Communications
    • Public Utilities
Finance, Insurance, and Real Estate
Trade
    • Wholesale
    • Retail
Services
    • Business and Repair
    • Health
    • Other Services
Government
    • State
    • Local
    • Federal

Source: Bob Bullock, Comptroller of Public Accounts.

prospects for new car sales and a survey of retailers on the outlook for Christmas sales.

Analysts also often contact other Comptroller personnel and officials in other agencies for information useful in producing their forecasts. For example, the sales and franchise tax analysts usually contact the Comptroller's audit division for data to estimate revenues from audit collections. And the State Insurance Board usually supplies industry information for the insurance tax estimate.

Some revenue sources lend themselves well to extensive economic modeling, and in these cases the revenue estimate is largely the product of an econometric forecast. The sales tax model, for example, contains over 40 equations explaining taxable sales by industry. Figure 2 shows the key structural relationships between variables forecasted by STEM and major tax revenues.

Estimates for some revenue sources, on the other hand, are heavily reliant on noneconomic factors. The franchise tax estimate, for example, is greatly affected by legal decisions in the courts. Forecasts of oil and natural gas production tax revenues are largely determined by expected OPEC behavior and interactions on world petroleum markets. Revenue estimates for minor revenue sources that do not demand individual attention are generated by a "Standard Forecast Report," which uses various statistical techniques to make projections based on historical data.

Compilation

The individual estimates of state revenue sources are next reviewed by the Comptroller's senior economists and revenue estimating staff for consistency with historical trends, other revenue estimates, and the economic forecast.

The individual forecasts are then compiled into an overall estimate of available state revenues. Each revenue source is allocated to one or more of the 240 active state funds according to state law. Motor vehicle tax revenues, for example, are allocated to General Revenue (75 percent) and the Foundation School Fund (25 percent) based on provisions in the State Constitution and state law.

Review and Publication

The final step in the revenue-estimating process involves review of the estimate by top Comptroller officials -- principally by the deputy comptroller responsible for revenue estimating -- and publication of the final document.

All revenue estimates are personally reviewed by the Comptroller himself because of the vital importance of the figures to the operations of the state government. After the estimate receives the Comptroller's final approval, it is prepared for public distribution. State finances are complex, but Comptroller staff take pains to make the revenue estimate as clear and understandable as possible for the public and the Legislature.

A revenue estimate document can take any form ranging from a two- or three-page write-up to a full-scale bound publication. The most elaborate

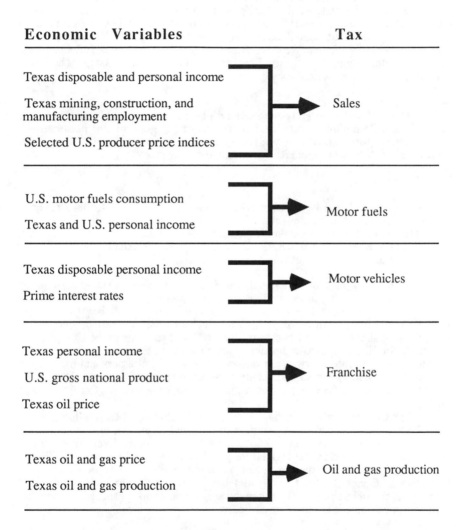

Economic Variables	Tax
Texas disposable and personal income Texas mining, construction, and manufacturing employment Selected U.S. producer price indices	Sales
U.S. motor fuels consumption Texas and U.S. personal income	Motor fuels
Texas disposable personal income Prime interest rates	Motor vehicles
Texas personal income U.S. gross national product Texas oil price	Franchise
Texas oil and gas price Texas oil and gas production	Oil and gas production

FIGURE 2
Key Structural Relationships Between Economic Variables
and Major Tax Revenues

publication is usually the *Biennial Revenue Estimate* (BRE) prepared at the beginning of each regular legislative session.

The revenue estimate is a product of its times and its look and message usually reflects the state of the Texas economy when it is issued. The 1987 *Biennial Revenue Estimate* published during the depths of the 1986-87 oil induced statewide recession, for example, began with the gloomy words "Texas is short on money." The 1989 *Biennial Revenue Estimate* , on the other hand, reflects a state economy on the rebound. The narrative opens with the upbeat message "The Texas economy is in recovery and the state government's revenue outlook is better than it has been in years."

The 1989 BRE recently won second place in the National Association of Government Communicators Blue Pencil Award for government publications. Table 2 shows forecasts of the state revenues for state budget years 1990 and 91, by source, from the Comptroller's November 1989 revenue estimate.

Fiscal Notes

When the Texas Legislature comes to Austin, the Comptroller's revenue estimating workload increases dramatically. As noted earlier, if the Legislature wishes to spend more money than the Comptroller estimates is currently available, it must find new revenue sources. And the Comptroller is usually responsible for putting the numbers on various revenue proposals.

In fact, any piece of state legislation affecting revenue or spending requires a "fiscal note" indicating its probable impact on state finances, whether positive or negative, over the next five years.[3] The fiscal note process begins with the Legislative Budget Board (LBB), which receives a formal request for an estimate from the Legislature. The LBB passes many of these requests to the Comptroller, especially for bills with a major impact on state finances. Estimates are required for a wide range of proposals, from the state revenue impact of a personal income tax to the effect of adding barber and beauty services to the sales tax base. During the 1989 regular session, the Comptroller prepared a total of nearly 700 fiscal notes.

The Comptroller's Office has to complete its estimate on each bill in time for the LBB to pass it along to the appropriate committee hearing that bill. In fact, a bill cannot get a committee hearing without an attached fiscal note. Every time a bill is significantly amended in the legislative process -- when it is introduced in the committee, heard in the House or Senate, or sent to conference -- a new fiscal note is prepared. Generally, the Comptroller has only 72 hours to review a bill and estimate its financial impact. But when the session heats up -- especially at the end -- this response time is cut to 48 or 24 hours.

The fiscal note estimating process is similar to that for a fullfledged revenue estimate. Individual analysts are asked to produce a best estimate of the problem impact of the legislation on state finances based on the current economic forecast and revenue estimate, taxpayers files, available and industry data, trade associations, agency contacts, and taxpayer surveys. In some cases, legal opinions on law that could affect the proposal's fiscal impact are also required. For a major

122

TABLE 2
State Revenue by Source (Funds 1-849)

Tax Collections	Revenue in Millions				Percent change from prior years			
	1988	1989	1990 (est.)	1991 (est.)	1988	1989	1990	1991
Sales Tax	$6,242.9	$6,914.7	$7,292.6	$7,742.3	35.2	10.8	5.5	6.2
Oil Production and Regulation Taxes	499.9	501.5	455.7	462.9	-6.2	0.3	-9.1	1.6
Natural Gas Production Tax	555.6	666.5	585.0	686.0	-13.8	19.9	-12.2	17.3
Motor Fuels Taxes	1,473.8	1,500.6	1,569.5	1558.9	15.8	1.8	4.6	-0.7
Cigarette and Tobacco Taxes	417.0	428.4	404.3	436.5	12.4	2.7	-5.6	8.0
Motor Vehicle Sales and Rental	947.1	1,015.2	1,054.1	1,111.8	18.0	7.2	3.8	5.5
Corporation Franchise Taxes	932.6	680.1	635.4	529.2	6.7	-27.1	-6.6	-16.7
Alcoholic Beverage Taxes	315.5	319.6	322.1	321.0	-3.1	1.3	0.8	-0.3
Insurance Occupation Taxes	545.8	441.6	397.8	423.5	29.0	-19.1	-9.9	6.5
Inheritance Tax	108.4	104.9	104.9	106.0	-4.7	-3.3	0.0	1.1
Hotel-Motel Tax	90.0	105.6	110.9	116.5	44.0	17.4	5.0	5.0
Utility Taxes	185.3	189.2	203.8	223.0	-0.3	2.1	7.7	9.4
Other Taxes	49.6	37.2	25.3	26.1	23.8	-25.1	-31.9	3.1
Total Tax Collections	$12,363.7	$12,905.0	$13,161.3	$13,743.7	20.4	4.4	2.0	4.4
Revenue by Recipient Type								
Tax Collections	$12,363.7	$12,905.0	$13,161.3	$13,743.7	20.4	4.4	2.0	4.4
Business Professional Fees	179.1	178.8	230.7	244.3	37.5	-0.2	29.0	5.9
Noncommercial Permits and Fees	1,003.1	1,021.7	1,029.1	1,045.5	3.9	1.9	0.7	1.6
Violations, Fines and Penalties	91.3	97.0	96.6	97.5	15.7	6.2	-0.5	0.9
State Service Fees	166.9	169.1	173.6	177.5	12.9	1.3	2.7	2.2
Sales, Rental and Repayment	208.6	149.1	127.5	138.0	94.7	-28.5	-14.5	8.2
Grants and Donations	0.9	1.3	0.8	0.6	-7.6	41.5	-37.7	-24.7
Federal Receipts	4,425.3	4,890.1	5,307.4	5,711.7	10.6	10.5	8.5	7.6
Interests and Dividends	1,169.0	1,221.8	1,112.4	1,130.9	7.9	4.5	-9.0	1.7
Land Income	280.8	279.5	285.5	320.5	2.6	-0.5	2.2	12.3
Other Receipts	354.6	440.4	353.7	353.6	-33.1	24.2	-19.7	0.0
Total Revenue	$20,243.2	$21,353.8	$21,878.6	$22,963.7	15.1	5.5	2.5	5.0

Source: Bob Bullock, Comptroller of Public Accounts, November 1989 Certification Estimate

omnibus tax bill that makes dozens of changes in the state's tax code, as many as 15 to 20 analysts may work on the bill's fiscal note.

Many proposals require estimating the impact of changes on existing tax rates -- for example, the gains from raising the sales tax rate from 6 to 6.5 percent. Preparing such an estimate is less straightforward than it might appear. The estimate cannot rely on a simple projection based on existing revenues from the tax, because higher tax rates increase the price of products and reduce their consumption, as customers cut back on purchases, find untaxed substitutes and restructure their transactions to avoid the tax. In addition, all estimates must be adjusted for implementation and collection lags, taxpayer coverage, sale for resale provisions, existing contracts, and other legal provisions that could alter the fiscal impact.

Some estimates offer particularly complex problems. For example, the Comptroller once was asked to estimate the impact of a one dollar surtax for credit card purchases in excess of $100. Unfortunately, the Comptroller's staff was unable to obtain figures on the number of transactions that would be covered by the tax. Some companies were unable to say how many affected transactions they had in Texas. Others flatly refused to cooperate. In this case, the Comptroller was finally forced to say that the fiscal impact of the proposal could not be estimated.

All fiscal notes contain detailed write-ups describing the revenue effects of the proposals and methodology used to obtain the figures. Like full revenue estimates, all fiscal notes are reviewed by the Deputy Comptroller for Legislative Affairs and Revenue Estimating for methodological soundness, reasonableness, and consistency with other estimates before they are released.

Conclusion

Revenue estimating is a complex and intricate process linking data, computers, and people. All revenue estimates are part art and part science. Computer models are used in all aspects of the process, but human judgement always determines the final figures. As evidenced by an ever-increasing accuracy rate (the latest forecast was off by only $8.7 million out of a total three-year projection of $36.7 billion), it appears that the Comptroller has found the right combination.

People often ask what the Comptroller considers in putting together a revenue estimate. The answer -- in all honesty -- is nearly EVERYTHING.

So one may now ask: "where is Texas heading?" Well, the Comptroller's current economic forecast and revenue estimate indicates that the moderate growth that has been occurring since the beginning of 1987 will continue. Employment will continue to break new records, the state's population will continue to climb as net in-migration turns positive, and state revenue will continue to grow.

Notes

1. In theory, the Legislature can over-ride the Comptroller's certification and send an appropriations bill straight to the Governor with a four-fifths vote in each House, but this has not occurred since the current State Constitution was adopted in 1945.

2. The state's "pay-as-you-go" provision prevents the state from deliberately spending beyond its means. It is possible, however, for the state to run an unintentional deficit if revenues fall below expectations, as occurred when the oil prices collapsed and the state economy fell into recession in 1986-87.

3. Fiscal notes also include the administrative costs to the state of implementing the legislation.

9

FORECASTING TEXAS ECONOMY IN THE 1990s

M. Ray Perryman

In a broad sense, a model is any abbreviated representation of observed facts or phenomena. In economics, however, models represent more defined aspects of a chosen situation, and can therefore be formulated mathematically. Thus, economic modeling suggests the testing of probable hypotheses that yields statistical inferences for a designated set of data. Given selected input and a group of variables forming a scenario, a model will produce output that, with judgement, can "forecast" a possible reality.

Economic models cannot quiet all the fears associated with forecasting, but they can lay to rest many uncertainties. In the 1930s, students of J.M. Keynes used models to help envision his complex, dynamic theories. It was a short step for economists to go from modeling business cycle theory to modeling the real world.

In the 1990s, academics and practitioners in both public and private sectors use models to help understand information in order to make decisions. For instance, companies making decisions for expanding locations must consider factors such as energy and labor supplies. A forecasting model can help identify present and potential infrastructure support. One such model is the Econometric Model of the State of Texas, an extensive matrix of data maintained by Perryman Consultants, Inc.

Model Background

This model essentially revolves around the prediction of total output, employment, and income within the State of Texas. Total Output, as represented by real Gross State Product (GSP) is defined as the value of all final goods and services produced in the State during a specified time (expressed in terms of inflation adjusted dollars). GSP is, then, the regional equivalent of Gross National Product (GNP). No government agency maintains consistent data on state output; therefore, the series is developed with underlying information from the output of all producing sectors. The sum of these individual measures is, thus, the aggregate state output. The Texas model used in this chapter's subsequent forecast uses ten categories of GSP:

1. Agriculture (agricultural services, forestry, and fisheries)
2. Mining (petroleum and natural gas extraction)
3. Construction
4. Energy
5. Non-Durable Manufacturing
6. Wholesale and Retail Trading
7. Finance, Insurance, and Real Estate
8. Transportation, Communication, and Public Utilities
9. Services
10. Government

In this model, total personal income in Texas is explained through the use of equations that incorporate results for employment, wage rates, and the major non-wage components of income. Person-hours of employment in each sector are multiplied by their corresponding wage rates, yielding estimates of wages and salaries by industry. The sum of these values provides a prediction for total labor income. Total labor income is then combined with forecasts of other aspects of personal income (such as contributions to social insurance and government transfer payments) for a final forecast estimate. In addition to output and income determination, the model predicts numerous other key aggregates and demographic factors, with the balance of the process devoted to individual sector of the economy. Summaries of several major sectors follow.

Manufacturing

The three basic manufacturing variables which the model estimates are outputs, employment, and wages. In addition, sufficient data exists to generate equations for output, employment, and new capital expenditures in many specific industries in the Manufacturing sector. Areas with significant production in Texas include 1) food and like products, 2) textile mill products, 3) apparel and other textile products, 4) lumber and wood products, 5) furniture and fixtures, 6) paper and allied products, 7) printing and publishing, 8) chemicals and allied products, 9) petroleum and coal products, 10) rubber and various plastic products, 11) stone, clay, and glass products, 12) primary metal products, 13) fabricated metal products, 14) nonelectric machinery, 15) electric and electronic equipment, 16) transportation equipment, and 17) instruments and related products.

The data for manufacturing in Texas is kept by the Census Bureau and is only available on an annual basis, and then with a three-year lag. As a result, forecasting into the future for these industrial sectors is extremely tenuous. Nevertheless, significant insights into the interrelationships among the Texas manufacturing sections are revealed. Furthermore, the model anticipates the behavior of individual durable and non-durable industries under alternative conditions and as assessment of the linkage between national and state production.

Agriculture

Within the Texas model, the agricultural sector is used to predict cash receipts from the marketing of major livestock and crop products. Straightforward estimates may be generated for sales of poultry and eggs, dairy products, meat animals, feed crops, cotton crops, and vegetables. Predictions for sales for over fifty individual products, such as cattle and calves, hogs, and sorghum are more complex.

One quality of an accurate forecasting model is its ability to account for correlations among individual production categories, such as "substitutes" (corn and sorghum) and "complements" (corn and hogs). A dynamic time relationship exists between the prices and quantities of various goods, due in part to the time lags between the decision to produce a farm product and the actual harvest of it. The Texas model is designed to reflect these correlations in a reasonable and realistic manner, staying consistent with established historical patterns. The State has long ranked among the top three nationally in total farm output, so the model recognizes the importance of agriculture to the state economy while incorporating the volatility of numerous non-economic factors (such as weather).

Energy

Energy related products, especially petroleum and gas, play a dominant role in both the internal economic performance of Texas and its national and global relationships. Therefore, products that are energy related are thoroughly integrated into each major sector. The following list defines the areas of obvious linkage:

1. Energy inputs from a data base maintained by the Census Bureau are an important part of production in the manufacturing industries.

2. The extraction of petroleum and natural gas dominates the total output of the mining sector in Texas. Therefore, these products play a major role in determining gross product and employment in mining.

3. Several disaggregated industries within manufacturing are related to energy production processing, such as petroleum refining and chemical production.

4. Energy constitutes both significant input and output in the regulated industries (transportation, communication, and public utilities).

5. The government revenue base is dependent upon energy production and consumption. For example, gasoline taxes, public utility taxes, road use taxes, extraction revenues (severance taxes), and major portions of the general retail sales tax are largely determined by energy market phenomena.

Finance

The financial sector, as the key component of the State's economic performance, is analyzed within the model in great detail. Specifically, the model provides forecasts for each of the major items on the aggregate balance sheet for Texas: principal loan and investment categories, primary holdings of demand and time deposits, borrowing and lending in the federal funds market, and borrowings from the Federal Reserve. The model is constructed to account for both the direct and indirect effects of Federal Reserve policy within the Texas and national financial sectors.

In addition to estimating commercial bank behavior, the model also simulates the behavior of both savings and loans and credit unions.

Retail Sales

The Economic model for the State of Texas offers an extensive analysis of quarterly and annual retail sales behavior. Simulations permit general analysis of durable and non-durable sales on a quarterly basis and a more detailed breakdown by store group on an annual basis, including categories such as food, eating and drinking, general merchandise, drugs, automobiles, and furniture.

Government

The amount of revenue from various tax and non-tax sources is critical to planning the financial expenditures of the State. The model can provide basic projections of key revenue sources while permitting simulation of the revenue impacts of changes in the tax structure. Moreover, the government sector interacts with other sectors within the model in order to provide projections of the impact of overall state business conditions upon the government revenue base.

The value of a systematic framework such as the Econometric Model of the State of Texas is its predictive ability to consistently evaluate the impacts of national, state, and local factors on related variables. The flexibility of this particular model allows both 1) the evaluation of alternative economic scenarios and 2) detailed examination of the performance of sub-regions within the State.

Texas Forecast

Despite the uncertainties and pitfalls inherent to long-term forecasts, a few basic patterns will inevitably be of vital importance in determining the level of future economic activity over an extended time horizon. The number of workers and their productivity are virtually the sole driving forces in defining "potential" expansion statewide. Productivity, in turn, depends on a combination of natural resource base, training, and ability to create and implement new technologies. Demand conditions, which receive enormous attention in short-term projections, merely define deviations from potential levels of production. All these factors are reflected in the present outlook to the maximum extent possible given current information.

This knowledge offers annual projections for a variety of indicators of the Texas economy over the period through 2010. Throughout the report, the latest available data revisions are employed. The long-term version of the Econometric Model of the State of Texas has been completely reformulated and expanded in an effort to fully reflect the current knowledge base regarding the state economy.

Projections of overall national and international activity, primarily derived from the models of Wharton Econometric Forecasting Associates, Inc. (WEFA), are incorporated into this assessment. Obviously, the path of the external economy will have a substantial and sustained effect on overall performance in Texas.

Texas must continually strive for greater diversification of its production complex in order to achieve optimal levels of prosperity and insulation from external shocks. Without question, however, the price of oil in world markets will continue to be a crucial function in defining the future of the state. Hence, it is imperative to examine the projected patterns in overall activity under alternative oil price conditions. The next section in this chapter addresses the long-term outlook for the national economy, thus serving as a backdrop for an analysis of Texas. The following three sections then offer descriptions of detailed outlooks under Baseline, Low Oil Price, and High Oil Price conditions, respectively. These forecasts are obtained from the long-term version of the Econometric Model of the State of Texas.

The Long-Term Outlook for the Economy of the United States

Many relevant factors will shape the domestic business environment over the course of the next two decades. The most noteworthy changes that are likely to occur lie in the demographic composition of the country and the labor force. As the "baby-boom" generation matures and enters the latter phases of the life cycle, a major shortage of workers will characterize the economy of the United States. In fact, this pattern is already occurring in many parts of the nation and in numerous occupational categories. The results are structural declines in the unemployment rate and increases in labor force participation by the working-age population. In particular, the demand for labor will enhance the reward structure in a manner which is likely to bring many additional female workers into the economy. As an illustration of the dramatic demographic shifts occurring, the group of individuals between the ages of 20 and 24 peaked in 1982 and will see a reduction of more than 4 million persons by 1997.

One of the consequences of the changing patterns in the population is, of course, the incentive to adopt labor-saving technology which substitutes automated capital for workers. Given the rate at which such modernization can realistically be expected to occur, however, there will not be sufficient new investments to sustain the growth experienced during the long expansion of the 1980s. Consequently, the long-term forecast for domestic business activity calls for positive expansion, but at a pace somewhat lower than that observed in recent years.

With regard to specific details, projections for real gross national product indicate a rate of expansion of about 2.5% per year over the remainder of this century. This pace compares to an average compounded rate of 4.0% per annum over the past five years of substantial economic recovery and prosperity. During the first decade of the twenty-first century, the yearly increases will slow to about 2.3%, again reflecting primarily lower potential production as a result of demographic movements. With regard to the composition of output, domestic demand will expand somewhat more slowly than overall output, resulting in a greater relative dependence on exports to absorb national production.

Consequently, the balance of trade will experience noticeable improvement during the latter portion of the forecast horizon.

Overall, the Industrial Production Index is projected to advance at an annual rate of about 2.6% during the 1990s and 2.4% over the years from 2000 through 2010. Income will expand in real (inflation-adjusted) terms of about 2.1% over the forecast horizon. Consumer and output prices rise by about 4.5 to 5% per annum. The various producer price indices will, as in the current decade, increase at a somewhat slower rate.

Population growth, which exceeded 1.0% per annum during the past decade, will slaw to only about 0.9% per year during the next decade and 0.75 over the latter phases of the forecast horizon. The rate of household formation will be somewhat higher, however, resulting in work force expansion of slightly more than 1% per year over the next two decades. Employment will advance at a pace of about 1.2% per year, thus putting downward pressure on the unemployment rate.

Following the current cyclical fluctuations in interest rates, a long-term downward trend is projected. In essence, lower rates of inflation are a primary determining factor in this projection. By 2010, it is expected that rates will be approximately 2 percentage points below current yields in short-term instruments and 2.5 percentage points below current yields in more extended maturities.

In essence, the national economy will experience long-term growth at rates below those experienced in recent years. Although cyclical fluctuations will no doubt occur in response to numerous factors as the next two decades progress, the overall trend will be driven by demographic and productivity constraints. In many respects, the projected situation is conducive to improvement in several key aspects of the overall position of the United States in a global economic environment.

The "Baseline" Long-Term Outlook for the Texas Economy

The Baseline forecast for the Texas economy over the next two decades follows the basic national economic assumptions discussed in the preceding section and the short-term oil market conditions that assume West Texas Intermediate Crude oil prices will generally fluctuate in the $17-$21 barrel range over the next two years, with increases at rates slightly above overall inflation beyond that point. The long-term pattern of petroleum consumption will increasingly move towards foreign production, as domestic fields age and their production levels continue to decline. Under the economic and oil market conditions employed in this Baseline scenario, the recovery which has surfaced in Texas during the past several quarters is sustained and, in fact, accelerated through 1991. Beyond that point, long-term expansion is projected to occur at rates well above those expected for the nation as a whole.

In large measure, the greater relative prosperity of Texas again stems from demographic and resource factors. Texas has a younger population and will experience labor force expansion at rates well above those for the nation as a whole. Thus, as the shortage of labor surfaces and intensifies throughout the country, the state will gain a competitive advantage in attracting new and expanded business opportunities. Moreover, Texas will continue to benefit from major new

131

developments which encourage the implementation of new technologies in a variety of industries. Finally, little doubt exists that the natural resource base of the state will continue to be an important element in defining overall economic potential.

Some of the major findings to surface from a Baseline forecast are briefly summarized below:

- Nominal Gross State Product increases at a compounded annual rate of 7.4% over the period from 1988 through 2010. When adjusted for anticipated inflation among the categories of goods and services produced within the state, this pace translates into growth in real output of 2.8% per annum. This pace is well above the 2.4% yearly increases that we are expecting for the nation as a whole during a comparable time horizon.

- Personal Income advances by about 7.3% per year, with gains in overall real purchasing power totaling 2.6%.

- Total non-agricultural Employment within the state rises to almost 9.4 million workers. The rate of increase projected in the Baseline outlook is approximately 1.6% per year on a compounded basis. This growth in jobs is sufficient to reduce the Unemployment Rate in Texas from present levels to less than 4.5% by the conclusion of the forecast period.

- The Population of Texas is expected to grow at a yearly rate of almost 1.3%. This pace is well in excess of that anticipated for the United States and reflects modest levels of migration into the state over the forecast horizon.

- Productivity within Texas is projected to improve at an annual rate of 1.2%, which is comparable to that forecasted for the nation as a whole.

- The Consumer Price Index for Texas, which is measured as the average of the indices for the Dallas and Houston metropolitan areas, rises at a a 4.6% yearly pace given the Baseline forecast.

- Spurred by gains in Income, Population, and Employment, Retail Sales are projected to improve at a compounded annual rate of 7.3%.

- The residential real estate market within Texas enjoys a modest recovery during the remainder of this century, stabilizing at a range of about 80,000 to 85,000 Housing Permits per year during the period from 2000 to 2010. This level is, of course, less than one-third of the peak which occurred during the early 1980s.

- The Texas Regional Business Cycle Index, a measure of the sensitivity to overall external conditions, experiences modest rises throughout the forecast horizon. One of the primary factors shaping the state economy in the future is, thus, its greater dependence on the course of national and international conditions.

- Gains on a per capita basis are observed in real Income, Output, and Sales during the forecast horizon. Consequently, we expect the living standards of Texas to be significantly enhanced over the next two decades.

- The Mining sector of the state economy, which is dominated by oil and gas extraction, experiences a peak in 2001 and sees a gradual pattern of output reductions beyond that point. Over the entire forecast horizon, its compounded annual growth rate is only 0.3%.

- The greatest relative gains within the economy occur within Services (3.8%) and Finance, Insurance, and Real Estate (3.2%). The increases in the financial industries reflect, to a great extent, a recovery from recent depressed conditions as the aggregate economy is enhanced and the glut of commercial, industrial, residential and retail space within the state is absorbed.

- Both Durable (3.0%) and Nondurable (2.9%) Manufacturing enjoy healthy gains during the forecast period.

- Wholesale and Retail Trade advances by 2.9% per year, while the Regulated Industries (Transportation, Communications, and Public Utilities) grow by 3% on an annual basis.

- The Construction sector advances by only 2.1% per annum, with Agriculture improving by 2.3% per year.

In brief, the results from the Baseline forecast reveal that the Texas economy should experience sustained growth over the next two decades, although the expansion will not approach the levels attained during the "oil boom" of the 1970s. On the whole, the performance will exceed that of the nation as a whole.

A "Low Oil Price" Outlook for the Texas Economy

Short-term assumptions in the Low Oil Price outlook reflect a continuation of excessive production among OPEC nations and a corresponding response by other producers. These forces combine to push prices into the $13-$17 barrel range. Such a pattern would obviously reduce exploration, adversely impact manufacturing, and decrease the overall base of state exports and spending. Beyond the next few years, this outlook assumes that real prices remain virtually constant i.e., that the price of oil parallels overall inflation in the economy.

The primary conclusions obtained from simulation of the Econometric Model of the State of Texas under Low Oil Price conditions are described as follows:

- Under Low Oil Price conditions, Nominal Gross State Product advances by 6.5% per year, with real gains of less than 2.4% per annum being observed. This level of expansion is well below that which the national economy would experience under these assumptions.

133

- Personal Income in Texas grows by 6.4% per year in this scenario, with inflation-adjusted annual increases in purchasing power of only 2.1% being sustained.

- The rise in Employment slows to only 1.4% per annum, with about 400,000 fewer workers being supported within the state by the conclusion of the forecast period.

- The Unemployment Rate under these conditions falls to only 4.9% per year, despite aggregate increases in the work force which are comparable to (only slightly above) those in the nation as a whole under these conditions.

- The rate of growth in Population slows to less than 1.1% per year under Low Oil Price assumptions, thus indicating virtually no net migration into the state over an extended time horizon.

- Output per worker advances by only 0.9% under these conditions.

- Reduced petroleum prices and a weaker economy obviously bring lower inflation. The Texas Consumer Price Index expands at a compounded annual rate of about 4.2% in this scenario.

- Lower consumer confidence, smaller increases in income, and a smaller work force would reduce the growth rate in Retail Sales to only about 6.4% per year.

- While the residential market would make a modest recovery from its recent trough, overall Housing Permits would average only slightly more than 70,000 units per year during the latter phases of the forecast horizon.

- The gains in Real Income, Sales, and Gross State Product on a per capita basis are extremely sluggish under these conditions.

- With the exception of Agriculture, all sectors of the Texas economy exhibit lower growth rates under these conditions than under Baseline assumptions.

- The Mining sector experiences a net decline in output of about 0.4% per year over the forecast horizon in an environment characterized by sluggish oil prices.

- The growth in Manufacturing falls substantially, with Durables seeing a rise of only 2.2% per annum and Nondurables gaining at a 2.3% pace.

- The Service sector advances at a 3.4% pace under this scenario, with Trade increasing by 2.6% per year, and Finance, Insurance, and Real Estate by only 2.7%.

- The recovery in Construction is retarded significantly by lower oil prices, with output expansion of only 1.7% per year being observed.

134

- Growth in the Regulated Industries slows to about 2.7% per year, while Agriculture sees its expansionary path increase to a 2.5% level.

Obviously, the fortunes of Texas are adversely affected to a significant degree by Low Oil Prices conditions. Billions of dollars in output and income are lost over an extended time horizons, and job growth is reduced substantially.

A "High Oil Price" Outlook for the Texas Economy

In a more optimistic forecast regarding business conditions in Texas, we assume that the speculations, delivery problems, and other supply reductions that have surfaced in recent months are sustained over a period of six to eight quarters in which the price of oil rises to the $21-$24 per barrel range. Beyond that point, it is presumed that overall petroleum costs rise in excess of anticipated inflation by 2-3 percentage points. Hence, rises typically would occur in the 7.0% to 8.0% range over an extended time horizon. Obviously, a High Oil Price scenario of this nature brings accelerated prosperity to the state economy and helps virtually every sector to achieve a more robust overall performance. This strength in the underlying asset base also enables us to further benefit from the demographic advantages which characterize the state over the next two decades.

Some of the principal conclusions derived from the High Oil Prices forecast for the Texas economy are summarized below:

- Nominal output in Texas expands at a compounded annual rate of only slightly less than 8.0% per year under these conditions. Once adjusted for inflation, real Gross State Product, the standard barometer for judging economic performance, advances at a yearly pace of 3.2%. This rate of growth would be far greater than would be experienced by the national economy in a climate dominated by relative rapid increases in energy costs.

- Personal Income advances by 7.9% per year under these conditions, with real gains of 2.8% per annum being projected.

- The Unemployment Rate falls to only 4.1% under these conditions, with overall Employment advancing by more than 1.8% per annum.

- The Population expansion of Texas occurs at a rate of almost 1.5% per year under these conditions, as a more prosperous overall economy brings additional migration of workers to the state.

- Productivity advances by more than 1.3% per annum under these conditions. Obviously, higher oil prices bring a greater incentive to invest in new capital equipment within the state economy.

- Rising oil prices and more robust aggregate demand bring higher prices. In particular, the Texas Consumer Price Index is predicted to rise by almost 5.0% per year in a high oil price environment.

- The additional Population increase spurred by greater business activity would bring somewhat higher demands for new housing. In particular,

135

Permits would establish an equilibrium value slightly above 90,000 units per year under these conditions.

- Retail Sales advances by about 7.9% per year under High Oil Prices assumptions, thus reflecting a more vibrant economy and enhanced consumer confidence.

- Substantial gains are exhibited on a real per capita basis in all measures of Individual Economic Welfare within the state.

- Virtually all industries (other than Agriculture) enjoy net benefits from higher oil prices.

- While the Mineral extraction industry continues to experience the effects of aging fields and rising production costs, the sector achieves overall growth of 0.8% per year under High Oil Prices conditions. The peak level of aggregate output occurs in 2003 under these conditions.

- The recovery and long-term activity in the Construction industry are stimulated to some extent by higher oil prices, with a composite rate of increase in output of 2.4% per year being forecasted.

- Manufacturing exhibits substantial gains in output within an environment characterized by rising oil prices. In particular, Durable goods production advances at a 3.4% yearly pace, with Nondurables growing by 3.3% per year.

- Output in the Service Sector continues to lead the expansion, with annual gains of 4.2% being observed.

- Wholesale and Retail Trade advances by 3.2% per annum under these conditions, with the Financial sector enjoying rises in aggregate production at a 3.6% pace.

- The Regulated Industries generate a growth rate of 3.3% in the High Oil Price scenario, while output in Agriculture and related sectors falls to only 2.1% per year.

In sum, although anticipated diversification efforts will expand the economic base of Texas in the future, and oil production will continue its long-term secular decline, it is nonetheless apparent that Texas would benefit substantially from an economy characterized by higher oil prices.

Conclusion

The preceding projections are offered under three alternative scenarios over the period through 2010. Demographic factors heavily favor the Texas economy in

136

the coming two decades. Specifically, labor force issues are rising to position of paramount importance in defining future growth, and Texas enjoys significant advantages in many respects. On the other hand, the potential expansion patterns can only be realized if the State successfully meets the education and training needs of the new technological age. Given its demographic base, natural resources, and extensive ongoing diversification efforts, Texas should experience sustained growth over the next two decades.

While the Texas "oil boom" is unlikely to he revisited, use of The Econometric Model of the State of Texas offers reliable support for state expansion at a pace above that of the nation as a whole. Hence, the econometric models are ideal instruments for providing relevant forecasts in a reasonable and realistic fashion.

10

CAPITAL BUDGETING AND INFRASTRUCTURE DEVELOPMENT

Kay Hofer

In a broad sense, capital budgeting is a decision-making system that allows for planning of major acquisitions and expenditures in such a manner that adequate structures and long-term assets are provided while deficits and exceptional debt levels are avoided. Capital expenditures are considered to be assets that produce benefits over an extended period of time and involve the outlay of substantial sums of money. Although definitions of capital assets vary across governments, most often these definitions include physical infrastructure acquisition and maintenance (buildings, highways, bridges, waste treatment facilities, airports, major computer systems, and renovation). The useful life of such projects extends far beyond the normal fiscal year, and long-term financing is generally required for capital projects due to the expense involved.

According to Hush and Peroff, "a capital budget is characterized by the extent to which capital spending is presented, enacted and analyzed separately from other spending."[1] But capital budgeting is much more than a separate budget. Capital budgeting incorporates budget, debt, and revenue management over time. John L. Mikesell gives four major reasons for capital budgeting. Capital budgeting can be implemented: 1) to improve the equity of financing of nonrecurring projects and provide projects that are needed and required; 2) to stabilize tax rates and relate the costs to the service life of the project; 3) to avoid the mistakes that are often made in public infrastructure construction which remains for years after a project is completed and may be impossible or expensive to correct; and 4) to apply management to the application of limited financial resources. Mikesell points out that these reasons for having a separate capital budget are far more important and pertinent to state and local government than to the federal government.[2] Capital budget are especially necessary if the fiscal demands are great in relation to the tax base. Because of the high levels of debt associated with most state capital expenditures, only the annual costs of the capital projects can be included in a single fiscal year operating budget without a disastrous skewing of financial capability and spending patterns.

This chapter traces the history and development of capital budgeting in the state of Texas and evaluates its interrelationships with planning, debt management and other practices.

138

The Development Of Capital Budgeting In Texas

The application of capital budgeting techniques to management of a state's finances has been encouraged since the Progressive reform movement of the early 1900s. When Griffenhagen and Associates was hired by the State of Texas to perform an administrative audit of the state's financial management system in 1931, the nationally recognized management consulting firm found the following with regard to Texas financial management and capital budgeting. There was no unified fiscal system or unity of planning in the forms of comprehensive budget in place. They found that the "fiscal laws were voluminous, detailed, complex but wholly inadequate" and that "the costs of government could not be measured from year to year." The report found no distinction among various fiscal functions to be recognized or provided for in the Texas' system. Each state agency was allowed to determine its spending needs which varied according to the ideas of management.[3] Griffenhagen and Associates recommended that the "biennial budget estimates relating to permanent improvements be an integral part of a long-range financial program embodying a comprehensive building program."[4] These agencies prepared their budget requests, including capital expenditures projects with no regard for activities of other agencies and with no attempt at integration. The patchwork financial management system reflected the complete absence of capital planning. While budget preparation was relegated to the Board of control, that board was not responsible for analysis of proposed building of properties, acquisition of equipment, or acquisition/modification/repair of facilities. Moreover, the Board of Control made no effort to account for the property values of state properties. Budgeting in general, and capital budgeting by legislative fiat consisted of compiling estimates, holding hearings, preparation of a budget document and appropriation of funds for capital projects as well as general expenditures. In short, budgeting did not constitute financial administration or include planning for capital acquisitions.

Griffenhagen and Associates recommended "complete segregation of the ordinary recurring expenses, extraordinary expenses, and capital outlays of each unit, in the budget report and in consolidated statements of expenses of the government as a whole."[5] They further recommended that expenditures for capital outlay include the total amount and specify the fiscal years and amount of expenditures for each year. In 1931 the examiners found that "some attention appears to be devoted to major repairs and other extraordinary expenses and capital outlays, but even the work on this phase of budget making falls far short of the minimum standard essential for good financial administration."[6] Griffenhagen and Associates distinguished between financial management and document preparation. For a state to have a sound financial management system in place, capital budgeting was essential. Financial planning from the viewpoint of this firm involved long-range planning, control of finances, and quality of administrative management. In addition, the general structure of the state including policies and practices needed to be organized in an effective and efficient manner. Efficient and economical financial administration of a state government involves "coordinating, supervising, and directing the fiscal affairs of the State and the fiscal procedures to ensure the carrying into effect of a definite financial policy and adherence to a definite financial plan."[7] A major concern expressed in the report in relation to the failure of Texas to plan for capital projects was the deferral of capital outlays and repair expenditures in the short-term due to failure of planning and analysis; this budget approach resulted in increased expenditures at later dates that were related to the delay period.

Until 1989, little had changed since the time of the Griffenhagen report with regard to capital budgeting in Texas. Only through an in-depth analysis of each year's appropriations bill could the total budget of the state be compiled. The State's spending for capital projects was interspersed throughout the appropriations bill on an agency-specific basis. No statewide comprehensive evaluation or ranking of requests for capital construction or other capital acquisitions was undertaken at any stage of the budget process on a formal basis. In 1989, Texas began to take the first steps towards creation of a capital budgeting system. First, all appropriations for capital projects financed by special and general funds were compiled in a separate appropriations article – Article VII. The total amount of state capital appropriations authorized was $704,972,361 for the 1990-91 biennium. Those capital projects financed from general funds amounted to $218,201,413 or 31 percent of total statewide capital expenditures. Capital expenditures financed by federal funds amounted to $34,042,569 or 4.8 percent of total capital expenditures for the same period. Funding for capital projects in higher education and transportation amounted to 45.6 percent (fiscal year 1990) and 53.3 percent (fiscal year 1991) of the state's total capital expenditures. A balance of $372,922,319 remained for other capital expenditures for the biennium. Article VII does not differentiate between capital spending for construction and for other items such as equipment and maintenance.[8] Exact levels of spending for various types of capital assets, are interspersed throughout the appropriations bill as has been the pattern over the years. For example, in the 1986 appropriations bill the Texas Department of Mental Health and Mental Retardation in item 14 was awarded $3,058,200 for construction improvements; item 15 awarded $90,132 transferred from Maintenance and Construction to Facilities Planning and Construction; item 21 appropriated $2,500,000 from the General Revenue Fund for 1987 fiscal year for life safety code construction improvements; item 8 awarded unobligated balances from 1979, 1981, and 1983 form the Department of Mental Health and Mental Retardation Construction Program for the same purposes. For the Texas Department of Health item 25 appropriated $1,768,000 fir the construction of a hazardous materials testing laboratory during 1987-1988.[9] It is apparent that the inclusion of capital acquisitions as exercised even until 1988 by the State of Texas did not constitute capital budgeting as identified by general principles of financial management. The long-range plans of the state do, however, include a more comprehensive form of capital budgeting.

The 1989 change in the Texas capital budgeting process also included the requirement of the preparation of separate agency requests for capital expenditures. As part of the 1990-1991 budget cycle, capital construction and nonconstruction capital expenditures had to be identifiable as a component of each agency's budget request. Agencies were instructed by the Legislative Budget Board (LBB) and the Governor's Budget Office (GBO) to prepare the request for capital construction expenditures within the Zero-Base Program budget format in one of two ways: 1) a capital construction program decision package or 2) a capital construction activity decision package. The program package compiled all requests for capital construction into one program unit while the activity capital construction decision packages compiled and prioritized capital requests on an activity-specific basis. Capital expenditures are required to be further broken down into two basis types – construction and nonconstruction, identified by specific budget codes for easy electronic compilation. Code 5002 identifies all construction related to capital expenditures, including buildings, land acquisition and improvements. Code 5001 includes all other capital outlays excluding construction, i.e., machines, equipment and nonconsumable supplies. Capital construction is requested in the separate decision packages while other capital outlay requested remain interspersed with agency operating budget requests denoted from other expenditures only by the code and item description. Development of a comprehensive budget process in Texas is only in the initial information gathering stages. The change in the budget format and codes will provide the necessary information to allow development of a process to classify state government construction requests on a statewide basis. Each capital construction project is required by the new system to utilize a classification system mandated by the Legislative Budget Board and the Governor's Office of Budget and Planning. Each project is to be placed in the category cost closely identified with the principle purpose to which the cost can be attributed. In the future, projects will be considered for funding as they relate to the merit of other projects and the factors of categorization. The new classification system for categorization of Texas capital construction projects is presented in Table 1. Although the categories each have a specific code for identification of the type of capital construction, the codes are not in order of priority. Prioritization will occur during the allocation process as the capital-construction projects requested each budget cycles are evaluated against other requests. The LBB/GBO instructions clearly indicate that the numerical codes assigned should not be misinterpreted as a priority ranking for possible funding.

In order to further facilitate planning for capital infrastructure development, all state agencies are now required to complete a "Future Capital Construction Form" identifying projects that are planned for the future as well as those currently requested. In addition, each program or activity capital decision package must include a detailed schedule for each project that includes a project justification, alternatives considered, and the project category identification. The project justification is required to provide the anticipated use of the project and the particular needs that will be satisfied. The alternatives section is to include a discussion of alternatives considered and why these alternatives considered were rejected. Agencies will then rank requests for capital construction projects against all others in the agency. In the final process, agency requests will be evaluated and ranked against each other statewide. Agencies are also required to provide a separate summary of all current (1989) capital construction, repair and renovation projects in progress. The summary is required to include the percentage of project completion and the expected completion date as well as the current estimated cost of construction and a project status report indicating current stage of project planning. This information is vital to the development of a long-range capital plan.

The state cannot plan for further development without knowing the current status of capital projects and funding associated with those projects. Methods for financing are to be included for each capital construction project. A capital construction individual project detailed schedule is also required for all proposed constructions projects. This detailed schedule includes the estimated construction commencement date and the estimated costs for site acquisition, utility extensions,

141

TABLE 1
Capital Project Classification Categories: State of Texas

Category 1: Hazard

Projects to eliminate definite and immediate health and safety hazards. This category is to be used to classify projects aimed at eliminating hazardous conditions that should not exist in a publicly used facility both in terms of hazards to individuals and to protect equipment and other facilities. The category includes projects to eliminate structural, electrical, and fire hazards.

Category 2: Project Completion

Projects to complete construction of facilities begun through funding provided with prior appropriations. This category is to be used to classify projects which cannot be completed and the purpose and planned use cannot be realized without additional funding.

Category 3: Major Repair-Cost Savings

Projects to improve facilities in such a manner as to reduce operating costs or to remedy conditions which are causing, or which have the potential for causing damage or deterioration to the facility. This category is to be used to classify projects including energy or utility conservation measures, preventive maintenance projects, roof repair, and other similar projects.

Category 4: Major Repair-Upgrading Conversion

Projects to upgrade existing facilities or to convert existing facilities to new use. This category is to be used to classify projects which will improve functional and/or efficient use or to convert obsolete structures to meet current standards or to renovate structures for more efficient space utilization.

Category 5: New Construction – Overcrowding and Growth

Projects aimed at eliminating crowded conditions that are unquestionably unacceptable according to generally accepted standards. This category may also be used to classify projects to increase that existing capacity will not adequately serve anticipated population needs in a manner consistent with current or generally accepted standards.

Category 6: New Construction – New or Expanded Programs

Projects necessary to provide facilities required to implement a new program or service or to expand existing programs or services where such expansion is contingent on approval by the Legislature or other governing authority, or where program or service expansion is contingent on funding the project.

Category 7: Eliminate Architectural Barriers

Projects to eliminate current architectural barriers to the handicapped.

142

Category 8: Other Construction

This category is reserved for projects that do not conform to criteria specified in other project classifications. This category includes but is not limited to landscaping, grounds lighting, aesthetic improvements to buildings, and razing or demolition of buildings.

Category 9: Routine Construction, Repair, and Rehabilitation

This category is reserved only for those projects that cannot be identified of a project specific basis at the time the budget request is submitted and should only be used in the event one of the eight above categories is not appropriate. Examples may include: a) funds appropriated for routine maintenance and repair where specific projects are not determined in advance, or b) funds appropriated from a dedicated revenue source for construction projects to be selected from alternatives, where the final decision or use has not been made or is subjected to change.

Source: Legislative Budget Board, 1988.

construction-related costs, survey and architect/engineer fees and estimated costs of furniture and equipment for the facility. The groundwork is in place for development of a comprehensive capital budget for the state. With this new process in place, a complete assessment of capital spending should be possible during future budget cycles. The information will be in place for planning and development of future capital spending.

At the current time, even the Comptroller's Annual Fiscal Cost Report does not include a complete assessment of capital spending for the state. This report has, however, been the only means of determining approximate total capital expenditures for the state. The report for fiscal year 1988 does state that "improvements to state facilities such as highways and parks increased 13.4 percent in fiscal 1988 – jumping from $2.7 billion in fiscal 1987 to $3.0 billion in fiscal 1988."[10] The report further shows an increase in expenditures for payment of debt of 155 percent between 1984 and 1988 year end. The payment of public debt has increased to 2.2 percent of net expenditures for the state in 1988 compared to 1.2 percent in 1984. The report does show a major improvement in the general management of long-term debt, however, as the payment of public debt was 7.0 percent of meet state cash expenditure in 1986. The Comptroller's cash report indicates a total net expenditure of $1,293,128,356 for fiscal year 1984 for capital outlays for highways, land and buildings, and other capital projects compared to $2,519,061,230 in 1988. The capital outlay portion of cash expenditures for fiscal year 1988 amounted to 13.0 percent of the net state cash expenditures.

While the report provides some information on capital spending for the state, many of the same questions that existed in 1931 remain unanswered. What is the long-term outlook for capital spending in the state? How is the debt retirement interrelated for the various types of general obligation bonds over the next twenty years? Which function have received the most in the way of capital funding? How has the ratio of general obligation to revenue bonds changed over the past ten years? The cash report is certainly any thing but comprehensive. As required by the Constitution and statute, the Comptroller's report is strictly on a cash basis. That report does not identify the encumbrances that exists with regard to capital projects or the total long-term debt interrelationships. Moreover, the expenditures and revenues for one year are not differentiated from those of previous years. In short, we have very little idea of the state of capital budgeting in Texas if this report is the only means of analyzing such expenditures.

The Essence And Purpose Of Capital Budgeting

Capital budgeting involves planning over a definitive period of time, generally ten years at a minimum, with arraying of expenditures for debt retirement and capital outlays displayed according to time of debt retirement and priority for financing. The capital budget should include an assessment of expected changes in the macroeconomy as such change is related to the ability to finance general obligation bonds, the cost of capital, and the availability of capital. In addition, socio-demographic estimates should be closely tied to the capital plan. The demographic estimates or forecasts can be used to project client-need for facilities and projected needs for infrastructure change dependent upon the changing composition and size of a population. Socio-economic indicators can be used to measure perceived social needs and associated costs as well as problem correction. For example, national demographic projections indicate that the elderly will become a more significant portion of the population reaching levels of close to 20 percent of the population by the year 2000. Financial analysis also indicates that expenditures for medicaid and nursing home reimbursement is one of the most rapidly increasing categories of national and state expenditure. This data combined would indicate a need for additional and different facilities in place by the year 2000 than those currently in place in 1989. The impact of demographic change can be measured, and the state can plan for the necessary facilities without facing a high risk of deficit situation in the late 1990s. If revenue growth is not keeping pace with drastic last-minute tax enactment or change, cash requirements for the state can be based on known expenditures with a capital budget in place.[11]

The essence of capital budgeting is a format that allows selection and ranking of proposed capital projects from a number of projects and alternatives presented. The format should also include the schedule for completion of the projects, a debt-retirement schedule and impact analysis that includes the source of funding and projected maintenance/operating cost changes over time. Enhancing the decision making process is the essence of capital budgeting. The capital budget establishes a mechanism for consideration of major projects. If capital budget includes integration with socioeconomic analysis, costly mistakes can be avoided. Considerable lag may exist from the planning to completion stages of capital projects, and no one wants to see a major public project financed that will be obsolete before it is completed. Taxpayers object to such mistakes. To remain effective, capital budgets should also be a part of a continuous cycle of reappraisal and reevaluation. As project costs and demand for the project changes, priorities

144

should be reevaluated. Failing to change the prioritization or projects in the face of change may result in unneeded projects. The reranking is essential due to the tendency of older projects to remain at the highest ranking levels. In many cases, the old projects are not reevaluated in light of new proposals.[12]

In addition to these advantages, capital budgeting allows for the application of business techniques to public expenditures in a manner that can save expenditures in the future and and allow realistic and useful evaluation of alternatives. While depreciation is not generally utilized by public organizations in accounting management, the concept is very useful in capital budgeting. The depreciation of a capital facility should roughly equal the period of debt retirement. In evaluating proposals for capital expenditures, especially those financed with general obligation bonds, choices can be made that do not get the state involved in costly building projects that will not last the life of the debt required to finance that project. Such information may also be utilized to determine the financing mechanism for long-term debt. For example, sinking funds that are roughly equivalent to the depreciation period may be established to spread the cost of the repayment of the debt over the life of the bonds. Demands on the annual budget will then be made in an orderly fashion. Additionally, financing needs can be correlated with revenue that is expected. Moreover, business techniques such as present value analysis allow a greater measure of empirical analysis to be involved in the decision making process when considering the alternatives of rebuilding versus renovation and repair. While such cash based measures cannot be the only criteria for evaluation of capital projects, to exclude these measures increased the risk of costly mistakes.

Steiss defines a capital facility as any project having a long life (usually 15–20 years), involving a large investment of resources, nonrecurring and yielding a fixed asset.[13] The long-life of such capital assets and facilities requires comprehensive planning. With a "pay-as-you-go" system of capital budgeting, a state is actually using a system of incremental budgeting. Incremental budgeting does not consolidate requests for capital expenditures so that prioritization of expenditures can occur based on economic, social, and other indicators. Rather, the best predictor of expenditures most often becomes previous budgets and expenditures. The mistakes that are made without such a capital budgeting system in place often lasts longer than the fifteen or more years of the life of the asset as costs are uncontrolled and debt mounts in an unanticipated manner. The tab that has been building over a number of years may suddenly come due. With capital budgeting in place, requests for capital expenditures can be arrayed, examined, and evaluated against each other to determine the most pressing need. Decision making is enhanced as some projects may be financed while others are abandoned. When expected costs and total costs of capital budgets are accumulated in one document, such costs often exceed projected revenues. Capital budgeting, therefore, enhances the risk control and reduces the uncertainty of ability to provide for change in the infrastructure and avoid deficits. Crisis can be averted.[14]

Capital Budgets: The Interrelationships Of Planning And Debt Management

Without a capital budget, a comprehensive framework for planning and management of long-term debt doesn't exist. Included in most state capital budgets are costs for buildings, construction, major maintenance or repair, and purchases of major equipment. While capital budgeting may not be essential at the national level due to the expensive tax base and lack of restrictions on debt, few states can afford the luxury of such approaches to management of capital financing for maintenance and development of the infrastructure. The majority of states have a constitutional limit on the allowable debt level. Texas, for example, has two limits on the debt level: 1) The 1876 Texas Constitution limits the level and type of debt to $200,000 in the aggregate for casual deficiencies of revenue to pay existing debt and to finance activities connected with war, insurrection or invasion.[15] 2) In 1978, a constitutional amendment was passed that limited the rate of growth of state revenues from nonconstitutionally dedicated funds to the estimated rate of growth of the state's economy.[16] The amendment also specified that appropriations could not exceed revenues as specified in Article III, Section 49a; this section of the constitution required the Comptroller of Public Accounts to certify that revenues exist on a fund-specific basis to finance requested expenditures. Added as an amendment to the constitution in 1942, Section 49a provided for the issuance, sale, and retirement of serial bonds to retire existing debt accumulated during the Great Depression and World War II. This amendment serves to further limit debt the state may accumulate and implicitly requires more careful budgeting to manage the state's financial commitments and protect the infrastructure.

These constitutional provisions also implicitly prohibited the issuance of full faith and credit bonds except through additional constitutional amendment to finance capital projects and established a "pay-as-you-go" system of state finance. The Texas Constitution authorizes the state to issue three types of bonds – General Obligation backed by the full faith and credit of the state, Permanent University Fund Bonds, and Higher Educational Constitutional Bonds. Only nine categories of "full faith and credit" bonds are constitutionally authorized – Veterans Land Bonds, Veterans Housing Assistance Bonds, Farm and Ranch Security Bonds, and Texas Public Finance Authority General Obligation Bonds. Texas Public Finance Authority General Obligation Bonds are sold to finance the acquisition, construction or equipping of new state facilities or major repair of existing facilities; these bonds amounted to $285.4 million in fiscal year 1988, and all bond funds were self-sufficient regarding debt service during 1988. Texas has also recently authorized the issuance of $500,000,000 Supercollider Bonds to finance eligible projects connected with the high-energy research facility; none of the Supercollider Bonds had been issued at the end of fiscal year 1988.[17]

Capital spending for higher education has long been separated from the funding for other capital projects in Texas. The Texas Constitution provides for a Permanent University Fund for the establishment and maintenance of the University of Texas and for Texas A & M systems. A colleges and Universities Construction Fund provides for the capital construction of other state institutions of higher education. Up to $100 million in appropriations from the money coming into the state treasury not otherwise appropriated by the constitution is available for the purpose of land acquisition, building construction, building equipment, permanent improvements, major repairs of buildings and acquisition of capital equipment for state institutions not part of the University of Texas and Texas A & M systems. This 1984 constitutional amendment provided that funds be allocated among the various universities every tenth fiscal year with readjustments in the allocation allowed every fifth year from September 1, 1985 forward. Legislative contributions to this higher education fund continue until such time as the principal totals $2 billion as certified by the Comptroller of Public Accounts. When the principle, which can never be spent, reaches $2 billion, the dedicated funding through appropriation ceases. A growth factor to assure future solvency was also figured into the fund as the amendment requires that 10 percent of the earned interest and income accruing from the fund be added to the principal each year after the fund reaches $2 billion. Interest payable on bonds for capital building must be paid out of the remainder of the interest earned prior to funding additional new projects.

In general, the state systems and institutions of higher education are not allowed to receive additional funds from the general revenue for capital projects. Only by supra majority vote of two-thirds of the legislature may any other revenue be committed from the general funds for capital improvements or projects that are above and beyond funds received from the permanent fund. These funds are structured so that expenditures may not exceed debt that can be securely financed through the earned interest of the funds. These constitutional provision established a form of capital budgeting for higher education.[18] Capital funding for highway maintenance and construction is also constitutionally provided with revenues from motor vehicle licensing and fuel earmarked for the highway fund.[19] Funding for capital projects in higher education and transportation amounted to 45.6 percent (fiscal year 1990) and 53.3 percent (fiscal year 1991) of the state's total capital expenditures. The constitutional provisions for higher education, transportation and other fund-specific capital projects do not, however, constitute capital budgeting in the context of a management decision-making system.[20]

Capital projects in Texas other than those financed through constitutionally-allowed bond issue vie for funding with all other programs funded by state general revenues. Almost all state and local governments finance costly building projects through bonds or loans. The interest rates that must be paid on these borrowed funds is determined by the bond ratings associated with the entity issuing the bonds. Creditworthiness ratings are based on debt policy, debt structure, debt burden, and debt history. Hence, the cost of capital projects is related to general financial management and soundness of a government. Good financial management lowers fiscal risk ratings and reduces the costs of major construction and renovation. Long-range capital planning allows those managing the resources of a state to project expenditures and determine the impact on the state's general expenditures and expected financial conditions in future years. As the costs of major capital improvements has increased, states have also accumulated increased debt levels. The annual rate of growth of state and local government debt has averaged 8.7 percent a year since the early 1970s; almost 95 percent of the debt of state on local governments is long-term.[21]

The debt of a state may be "full faith and credit" or backed by the tax base of the government or nonguaranteed (limited liability, generally based on revenue bonds). Such debts as are accumulated limit the flexibility of future budgets as the required amount of funding must be retained to retire the debt plus interest. Capital expansion generally occurs and is correlated with economic growth. If a unit of government is financing capital projects on a "pay-as-you-go" basis from current operating expense, a higher level of risk is associated with the state's financial future. Debt financing, on the other hand, includes known and fixed costs. When bonds are issued, the interest rate of cost of borrowing the funds is specified. When costs are known, future commitments of state revenues can be planned thereby avoiding an overcommitment of resources. Politically, long-term debt is popular as legislators can promise and deliver a facility or improvements that are desired now and leave future legislatures to figure out how to finance the debt as it accumulates over time and in no planned order. While long-term financing is appropriate from an equity of benefit/cost perspective, the potential for abuse does exist. The Texas Constitution requires a pay-as-you-go approach at the current time for capital projects that are not covered by constitutionally provided long-term debt bond issues. Additional bond issues are only through constitutional amendment. Texas like most states departs significantly in management of capital financing from the capital budgeting process as it has been defined in classic management specifications.

In 1988, Hush and Peroff[22] surveyed all fifty states to determine the procedures, definitions and techniques of capital budgeting used. They attempted to identify state applications of capital budgeting arrayed against the criterion of a capital budget as separately presented and appropriations for capital expenditures as well as financing mechanisms. In 1989, Texas was one of eight states that had no evidence of capital budgeting in the allocation/appropriations process. In analyzing all fifty states with regard to the practice of capital budgeting and the level or type of borrowing to finance capital projects, Hush and Peroff found that capital budgeting varied widely in application across the fifty states in regard to legislative management, coverage of the capital budget and how states financed capital projects. In general, the authors found that most states that have capital budgets exclude capital items such as transportation and higher education form their budgets as the bulk of these capital expenditures are financed through earmarked funds and special grants. "The major exclusion is usually for highways, which in 1985 accounted for $17.5 billion or 58 percent of total state capital spending."[23] Texas does not depart from the general pattern across the states.

States obtain much of the funding for capital projects from the federal government. Federal funds in the form of direct expenditures accounted for almost fourteen percent of state capital spending in 1986. An additional significant portion of state and local capital expenditures are financed by federal grants. Most of these direct expenditures and federal grants finance highways, sewage treatment plants, Corps of Engineers projects, power administrations and state infrastructure projects. In spite of the high level of federal spending, states retain a major responsibility for schools, water supply, higher education, state buildings, sewage projects and highways. The bulk of state capital expenditures are for highways and higher education. With such a large portion of state budgets devoted to capital expenditures, it is difficult to imagine a state functioning effectively from a financial management perspective without a separate capital budget.

Other Considerations Associated With Capital Budgeting

Without a capital budget in place, planning for mandates from another level of government also becomes difficult. For example, the state of Texas experienced much higher spending levels in the fiscal year 1988 due to court ordered improvements to the state's prison and mental health systems.[24] Mandates impose conditions that must be met backed by law. Although the State and Local Government Cost Estimate Act requiring the preparation of fiscal notes that would estimate the impact of programs on state and local governments, if such impact was expected to be more than $200 million was signed into law by President Reagan in 1981, such legislation does not prohibit policy changes that may have a major financial impact on state and local government. Fiscal notes only require that estimates of the costs be included with the proposed legislation. In recent years, the federal government has cut state grants for infrastructure programs while the increasing the level of regulations imposed. Regulations may impose costly capital expenditures on states as federal standards that are mandated must be met. Executive Order 12291 required federal government agencies to submit a Regulatory Impact Analysis (RIA) to OMB for any regulation that may impact the economy by $100 million or more or may impose substantial costs on states and local governments.[25]

Mandates may also be imposed on state governments by "partial preemption." Partial preemption involves establishing a standard such as the Clean Air Act Amendments of 1970 which required a certain standard but left the funding and enforcement up to the states. In some cases, states were faced with development of costly mass transit systems to try to meet air quality standards. During the 1980s states experienced the increase in federal mandates with little or no funding associated. Federal mandates were also generally imposed without consideration of the special financial circumstances of a particular jurisdiction. Capital budgeting can increase the capability of states to provide the federal government with a more accurate picture of their current financial status due to long-term financial commitments. Long-term debt commitments bearing the full faith and credit of the government must be met prior to allocation of general revenues in all states. Claims on state funding in the form of mandates may change the financial outlook dramatically. Since revenue sharing has been eliminated, the costs of mandates and the long-term fiscal requirements for state infrastructure improvement and associated costs have increased in importance. These activities coupled with the decrease in federal grants in aid since 1981 have increased the necessity of capital budgeting. In 1986, for example, the Asbestos Hazard Emergency Response Act provided $25 million annually to school districts to administer the asbestos control and removal plans of public schools. These funds accompanied the mandate to remove the asbestos; the funds, however, only covered actual administration in the form of oversight and planning. "The Environment Protection Agency has estimated the cost of cleanup to school districts at $3 billion,"[26] and states, at the current time, are not expected to receive additional federal funds. Such costs associated with the asbestos removal will have to be absorbed by increased state general revenues of increased local property taxes. As state and local costs of implementation of federal mandates are not compiled or considered by any one individual or agency at the federal level, states will need to compile the necessary data of cost impact and use that data to achieve input at the federal level. A state capital budget can provide an essential picture of long-term debt levels as vital input into the mandate process.

Conclusion

Capital budgets vary in design across the states. The structure of the capital budget system is not as important as the definition of items to be included and the format for display of the budget. The items to be included should in the form of mutually exclusive categories of expenditures. For example, some capital budgets establish a dollar limit for inclusion of items. The definitions of the categories for inclusion on the Texas capital budget implicitly identify the capital outlay detail table for equipment is to be included in activity decision packages. This capital outlay detail table includes replacement and new items of equipment based on unit cost and number of items needed interspersed among other operating expenditures. Other state capital budget formats include acquisitions, such as office equipment replacement and replacement of vehicles within the total planning document. In the majority of states, agencies submit their requests for total capital expenditures as part of the operating budget request. The requests for funding for capital projects are reviewed by the governor and the legislature and final recommendations are made to the legislature. The requests for capital expenditures are generally reviewed on an agency-specific basis and not on the basis of a total capital plan for a state. In general, states show capital expenditures in three ways: 1) as a separate section of the budget, 2) integrated with agency spending, and 3) as a separate budget. Currently, Texas integrates capital expenditures with agency spending.[27] The new capital budget process in Texas will result in the integration of nonconstruction capital assets into agency budgets and a separate statewide capital construction budgeting plan.

When capital spending requests are integrated into requests for agency spending, these projects compete with other operating items funded by general revenues. Such a system often relegates capital funding to what is left over after the required operating budget is in place. During a downturn in the economy when revenues decrease, such methods of determining capital expenditures may delay a project that is needed and result in increased costs at a later date. For example, payment of public debt in Texas increased from $224,503,082 in 1985 to $1,298,471,827 during fiscal year 1986 or 7.0 percent of net state expenditures. This increase represented a 478.4 percent increase over debt repayment in 1985 as a percentage change of net cash expenditures. The general downturn in the macro economy resulted in a changed outlook for the state and a shortfall in revenues that was expressed in cutbacks in funding for numerous state functions during fiscal year 1987. Grants to highway maintenance, grants to political subdivisions, mental health, and natural resources experienced significantly decreased expenditures during 1987. Bond indebtedness that was outstanding increased by $321,430,000 between 1987 and 1988 for general obligation bonds. Most of the funding cuts were directed to a slow down or postponing of the development of the state infrastructure.[28]

When capital expenditures are financed from special funds such as those of the Texas Permanent University Fund, the Highway Trust Fund, and other constitutionally earmarked funds, these capital projects are protected from competition with other funds in the assessment of total statewide needs for capital projects. Although the governor can veto appropriations lines, he cannot veto lines that are part of "local funds" expenditures under the acts that allow independence of financial planning for the Texas higher education system. The majority of states that do have capital budgets exclude certain funds from those budgets; in most cases, the exclusion includes capital projects for highways and higher education – the two most significant and costly state expenditures. Such exclusions are politically popular but do prevent the development of a comprehensive capital budget for a state. The majority of states with capital budgets include purchases of major equipment, land acquisition, construction, and major maintenance in the separate capital budget. Some states include only projects that are debt-financed in their capital budgets. Such an approach as the latter, does not allow for significant planning that is a vital part of capital budgeting. To be truly comprehensive, the capital budget should include machinery, construction, debt and revenue planning.

Capital budgeting provides an essential link to a total assessment of a state's budget. Capital budgeting allows for a breakout of expenditures on the basis of those committed and considered "uncontrollable" such as for entitlements or other federal programs and mandates, those that involve the full faith and credit of the state such long-term debt financing, those that involve essential public services, and the remainder of the revenues available for "discretionary" spending. When this data is available for the State of Texas, it would seem probable that a major portion of the state's expenditures will be identified as "uncontrollable" in much the same manner as for the national government. Uncontrollable expenditures of the national government are currently estimated at over 80 percent of total expenditures. The smaller the pool of discretionary funds available, the more necessary capital budgeting and long-term planning becomes for management of a state's finances. The common denominator of all government programs is cost; and that cost must be managed within available revenues.

Notes

1. L.W. Hush and Kathleen Peroff, "The Variety of State Capital Budgets: A Survey," *Public Budgeting & Finance*. Summer, 1988: 67-69.
2. J.K. Mikesell, *Fiscal Administration Analysis and Applications for the Public Sector*, 2nd edition. Chicago: The Dorsey Press, 1986: See especially Chapters 1 and 5.
3. Griffenhagen and Associates, *The Government of the State of Texas Part II – Financial Administration: The Fiscal Agencies*. Austin, Texas: Von Boeckmann-Jones Co., 1933: 47-77.

4. Ibid., 67.

5. Ibid.

6. Griffenhagen and Associates, *The Government of the State of Texas General Summary Part I – Organization and General Administration:* Austin, Texas: A.C. Baldwin & Sons, 1933: 6.

7. Ibid, 5.

8. Article VII, 1990-1991 Appropriations Bill, State of Texas.

9. Appropriations Bill, State of Texas 1986.

10. Bob Bullock, *Annual Financial Report Cash Basis for the Year Ended August 31, 1988.* Austin, Texas: Comptroller of Public Accounts, 1988: 10.

11. A.W. Steiss, *Financial Management in Public Organizations.* Belmont, California: Wadsworth, 1989.

12. *Fiscal Administration.* Op. cit.

13. Steiss, op. cit.

14. *Fiscal Administration*, op. cit.; *Financial Management In Public Organizations*, op. cit.; and "The Variety of State Budgets: A Survey," op. cit.

15. Texas Constitution, Article III, Section 49.

16. Texas Constitution, Article VIII, Section 22.

17. Bob Bullock, *Texas Annual Financial Report Cash Basis for the Year Ended August 31, 1988.* Austin, Texas: Comptroller of Public Accounts, 1988.

18. Texas Constitution, Article VII, Sections 17 and 18.

19. Texas Constitution, Article VIII, Sections 7a and 9.

20. *Comptroller's Annual Cash Report*, op. cit.

21. Mikesell, Fiscal Administration, op. cit., 435.

22. Hush and Peroff, "The Variety of State Capital Budgets," op. cit.

23. Ibid., 68.

24. *Comptroller's Annual Financial Report Cash Basis*, op. cit.

25. R.D. Whitman and R.H. Bezdek, "Federal Reimbursement for Mandates on State and Local Governments," *Public Budgeting & Finance.* Spring, 1988: 47-62.

26. J.E. Kee, "Assessing the costs of Federal Mandates on State and Local Government," *Public Budgeting and Finance.* Spring, 1989: 108.

27. Hush and Peroff, "The Variety of State Budgets," op. cit.

28. *Comptrollers Annual Financial Report Cash Basis*, op. cit.

11

EVALUATION, PRODUCTIVITY, AND THE STATE BUDGET PROCESS

Jerry Perkins and Thomas Finke

The three elements of this chapter title are closely related. The budget process allocates scarce resources among numerous agencies and programs. The basis for allocation can depend in part on how effectively public programs achieve their objectives, measuring effectiveness has both evaluative and productivity dimensions. In terms of evaluation, decision-makers are interested in whether the program works. Does the programmatic activity produce the committed objectives? Do the costs bear some fruit in terms of benefits? Productivity assessments seek to ascertain how efficiently available resources are converted into the goods and services delivered by public agencies. Can these goods and services be provided more economically?

The budgetary process is influenced by many forces. Much of the traditional scholarship on budgeting suggests that budgetary outcomes are heavily influenced by a variety of considerations, a thesis which maintains that the balance of political forces and the limitations on human capacity to calculate or create an inclination to make marginal adjustments to past budget decisions apart from the economic efficiency of such efforts.[1] Evaluation and productivity standards, by contrast, are not concerned with the past. Both are rooted in rational assessment of program outcomes and are mainly focused on the future. Do the programs work? Should we continually fund them considering their costs and benefits? How can the efficiency and effectiveness of programs be improved?

In the past fifty years, there has been much emphasis on "rationalizing" the budgetary process. The budget is considered by many to be the most unified and comprehensive decision-making mechanism available in most state governments. Thus, scholars have pointed out how measures of productivity,[2] and the use of evaluation activities[3] might assist in budgetary decision-making. Grizzle[4] links all elements by suggesting that funding decisions cannot be economically rational without productivity and performance information.

Most states have instituted rational components into their budgetary procedures. This chapter outlines the process in Texas, highlighting the structures and procedures mandated by law. While the budgetary process exists both in the legislative and executive branches of Texas government, the focus here is on the role of the Legislative Budget Board and its Program Evaluation Section.

Legislative Budget Board

A ten member Legislative Budget Board (LBB) was created by law in 1949 for the purpose of developing recommendations for legislative appropriations to all state government agencies. The membership of the board was also established by statute. Automatic members of the board includes; Chairman-Lieutenant Governor, Vice-Chairman/Speaker of the House. Other standing members of the Board include; the Chairman of the House Appropriations Committee, House Ways and Means Committee, Senate Finance Committee, and the Senate State Affairs Committee. Two additional members each from the House and Senate are selected by the Chairman and Vice-Chairman to fulfill the ten member requirement. The service branches within the LBB are headed by the Legislative Budget Director, who is appointed by the Board.

The purpose of the Legislative Budget Board is to systematically evaluate the operations of all state government agencies and prepare a set of budget recommendations for these agencies. In 1973, by concurrent resolution of the 63rd Texas Legislature, the LBB was given the responsibility of designing and implementing a zero-based program budgeting system for the state government. ZBB and Program budgeting are both rational attempts to control budgets. ZBB is a process which identifies all substantive aspects of agency operations, initiates alternative levels of financing each separate activity within the agency, by using performance indicators, project the expected outcome of each alternative level, and indicates the agency's priority level for funding the programs. Program budgeting, which is one of the most discussed form of budgetary reforms, had attempted to change the nature and form for developing budget requests. Program budgeting requires a supplementary breakdown of expenditures by program and their components, e.g., sub-programs and activities. It is widely utilized by all forms of government, local, state, national, and many foreign nations.

The system was started to provide the Governor and the Legislature with more comprehensive information on funding levels required to implement and fulfill state policy objectives. To achieve this, the LBB was charged with "establishing a system of performance audits and evaluations designed to provide a comprehensive and continuing review of programs and operations of each state agency, commission, and institutions. In September of 1973, the Legislature authorized the establishment of the Program Evaluation Section within the Legislative Budget Office.[5]

Program Evaluation In Texas

The purpose of the Program Evaluation Section is to provide the LBB and the Legislature useful usable information on the programs and operations of all state agencies in terms of compliance with statutory requirements, operational efficiency, and effectiveness. This information is garnered from two years of intensive work by the Evaluation Section's program analysts and culminates in a biennial performance report (Texas operates on a biennial budget cycle). The workload of the Evaluation Section fluctuates as its functions are tied to the legislative process, e.g., special legislative projects, new agency reviews, board and commission meetings, etc. However, the work usually follows a predictable pattern.

The Program Evaluation Section has the responsibility to:[6]

1. Establish program output measures that can be used to analyze program efficiency and performance of each state governmental entity.

2. Explicitly state the statutory function of each entity through a review of all relevant and pertinent legislation.

3. Analyze, on a continuing basis, the operational efficiency of state agency operations and program performance through the use of: unit-cost measurement data; workload efficiency data; and program output data.

4. Create and disseminate to the Legislature a performance report (program productivity evaluation report).

5. Guarantee proper performance standards are upheld to provide for effective program evaluations by ensuring that analysts possess good working knowledge of the principals and practices of state agency financial and accounting operations; statistical methods; and the objectives and policies of program evaluation procedures.

In addition to above functions, the program evaluation staff provides assistance to various legislative committees as needed, such as: conducting special studies and preparing reports, assisting state agencies in selecting appropriate program performance reports, and maintaining liaison with the various state fiscal agencies.

In preparing the evaluations, and subsequent performance reports, the Program Evaluation staff uses a four stage development plan. This includes: Stage One – surveying the agency, Stage Two – developing the work plan, Stage Three – conducting the evaluation, and Stage Four – writing the performance report.

Stage One : This phase involves a thorough review of all relevant documents, e.g., the enabling statutes, all subsequent and current legislation, financial, and organizational documents, which allows the analyst to become completely familiar with the agency. An in depth consultation of the Legislative Budget Office (LBO) staff and committee staff members who have had a prior contact with the agency, is another important element of the process. A comprehensive background review of the agency and operations is also accomplished in the early stages of the evaluation.

Stage Two : Once the agency survey had been completed, the analyst must begin preparation of one of the most essential elements of the evaluation process, the work plan. This consists of selecting or narrowing the area(s) to evaluate, identifying the critical tasks and issues of the areas to be evaluated, developing and testing hypotheses pertinent to the area(s) under evaluation, and to determine the appropriate work steps and time necessary to perform the work.

Stage Three : The implementation and application of the evaluative work plan and hypothesis tests, identified in the second stage, are accomplished in Stage Three. In addition, throughout the implementation phase, the analyst is to constantly analyze and adjust the implementation process and work plan for reliability, continually question the accuracy of the information to fully examine available situation alternatives as well as additional hypotheses and tests generated during this stage. Using the information just described, the evaluator is able to develop plausible recommendations and proceed to the fourth stage, writing the performance report.

Stage Four : Stage Four comprises the actual writing and presenting of the biennial *Performance Report to the Legislature*.[7] This report, though also given in oral presentation to the LBB, is presented in short, concise form since it is the primary method used to communicate the evaluation findings to the LBB..Three procedures are used to disseminate the information in the Report. First, a draft report is prepared from the information derived from the previous three stages. Second, various interested parties review the subject matter of the draft report. Third, the final report is submitted to the legislative policy-makers.

Conclusion

In Texas, as in other states, the actual linkage between evaluation, productivity and the budget process remains tenuous in practice, even though the formal policies are in place. In their 1985 study on centralized productivity improvement efforts in state governments, Poister et al[8] point out that while the term "productivity" has many interpretations, it can best be described as an attempt to "improve the relationship between the resources consumed and the quantity and quality of the services provided." A 1978 General Accounting Office survey showed that although most state and local governments recognized the need for productivity improvements (PIs), there were few comprehensive productivity improvement programs in operations. Likewise the study also stressed that since the six years following the GAO survey, many state governments have attempted to implement productivity improvement programs. However, their study concludes that in the long-term, most states failed to demonstrate improvement programs. In the past, many Texas Legislatures have recognized the need to link productivity measures to budget allocation decisions, yet until now no formal mechanism has been utilized.

Premchand[9] notes that two factors, managerial and environmental, often hampered the integration of productivity within the budget process. Managerial problems are often complicated by the lack of acceptable mechanisms to measure governmental activities, and the fact that the measurement of productivity was not part of the budget process. Likewise, environmental factors such as uncertain economic forecasts, inflation, and stagflation hampered productivity and budgeting improvements. In the case of Texas, it has been suggested that the latter could possibly help explain the lack of formal use of productivity measures in the budget process. For decades, the Texas economy was heavily infused with oil money. During the "boom days" when revenues were plentiful, few people were overly concerned about productivity and economic efficiency.

According to a LBB source, the concept of integrating productivity incentives into the budget process in Texas has been debated, but a final decision from the Legislature has yet to be reached. At present, the Performance Report to the Legislature provides the methodology by which the State of Texas uses to evaluate the operating efficiency and program effectiveness of each state agency. The Texas Legislature relies heavily on the recommendations presented in the Performance Report, according to the LBB.

From the standpoint of improving the efficiency and effectiveness of service delivery for social programs, and reducing the cost of government, the linking or "paralleling" of the budget process to productivity measures/efforts could be a vital public management tool, especially in times of cutback management.

Notes

1. A. Wildavsky, "The Political Economy of Efficiency: Cost-Benefit Analysis, Systems Analysis, and Program Budgeting," in A.C. Hyde and J.M. Sunfritz (eds.), *Government Budgeting*. Oak Park, Ill: Moore Publishing Company, 1978: 170-190.

2. T.P. Lauth, "Budgeting and Productivity in State Government," *Public Productivity Review*. No. 42, 1987:21-31.

3. C.H. Weiss, *Evaluation Research*. New Jersey: Prentice-Hall, Inc. 1972.

4. G. Grizzle, "Does Budget Format Govern Budget Outcome?" *Public Budgeting and Finance*. Volume 6, No. 1, 1986: 60-70.

5. Legislative Budget Board, "Responsibilities of the Legislative Budget Board and Staff in the Appropriations Process in Texas." Austin, TX: LBO-BP/1, May 1988: 1-10

6. Legislative Budget Board, "Program Evaluation Manual." Austin, 1988.

7. Legislative Budget Board, "Summary of Program Evaluation Recommendations," *Staff Report*. Austin, 1986.

8. A. Premchand, "Government Budgeting and Production," *Public Productivity Review*. No. 41, 1987:9-19.

9. T.P. Lauth, "Performance Evaluation in the Georgia Budgetary Process," *Public Budgeting and Finance*. Volume 5, No. 1, 1985: 68-82.

12

BUDGETING FOR PRIVATE, NONPROFIT ORGANIZATIONS

Siegrun F. Fox

Budgeting is not a very popular topic in private, nonprofit corporations. There never is enough money to meet the myriad of pressing needs, and the search for revenues takes up a substantial amount of time. But to find new income sources and use the funds in the most optimal way, good financial planning is important. The budget should be written in a way that it serves as a planning tool for the next fiscal year, provides the basis for long term, strategic considerations, and simultaneously functions as an operational control device for management and the board of directors during the current fiscal year.[1] The budget document should not be mistaken with financial statements. The former is a financial proposal, covering anticipated revenues and expenditures, while the latter is an accounting tool, describing actual income and outlays. Nonprofits are free to select their own fiscal year. It can coincide with the calendar year or some other cycle, but usually agencies select a period that best matches the rhythm of their programs.

In considering the budget for nonprofit corporations in the state of Texas, several sources are useful to consult. One source is the Texas Nonprofit Corporation Act, a second one consists of the allocation guidelines of United Way agencies, and a third one is the actual practice of third sector entities. General information can be obtained from handbooks and manuals on nonprofit organizations. In addition to the ones cited elsewhere in this chapter, a number of significant works currently exist on the subject.[2] The following analysis looks at the financial planning of small to medium-sized nonprofit corporations in the human service field, leaving out educational institutions, hospitals, facilities of the fine arts, and associations.

The Texas Nonprofit Corporation Act

Nonprofit, cooperative, religious, and charitable activities fall under the Texas Nonprofit Corporation Act (Vernon's Ann. Rev. Civ. Stat. Tex. Art. 1396). While the Act is quite specific in the organizational and personnel features of third

159

sector entities, it provides only limited guidance on the budget. According to the Act, all financial transactions, including all incomes and expenditures, have to be recorded in accordance with generally accepted accounting practices (GAAP), and the board of directors must prepare an annual report of the financial activities of the corporation for the preceding year. In other words, organizations are free to structure the budget or the financial planning document for the next year any way they want to, but have to use accepted accounting standards with respect to their current and past financial activities.

Budget Requirements Of United Ways

The majority of nonprofit human services agencies receive funding from United Way, and therefore have to follow its guidelines in budgetary matters. These requirements vary from city to city because United Way is a decentralized organization, with each local United Way issuing its own policies. Common features can, however, be observed since the policies are based on recommendations issued by the national office of the United Way of America and also developed in consultation with other local United Way entities.[3]

The budget process of United Way, in general, is simple. Each year, usually in Spring, United Way asks previously funded agencies to file preliminary budget requests for the ensuing year. After proper review, United Way asks for the final budget request, generally in Fall. The budget document should list all anticipated expenditure items, divided into operating expenses and capital equipment. Furthermore, the packet should contain a description of the proposed services. Additional supporting documentation may include information on other programs provided by the applicant together with statements of assets and liabilities. Occasionally, a site visit precedes the final approval of the budget.[4]

For new applicants, the process starts earlier in the year and is more extensive, since it includes a request for admission. United Ways around Texas have detailed guidelines with which prospective organizations have to comply. One important requirement is tax-exempt status under federal and state law. Other admission criteria include a clearly documented human need that the agency proposes to address with its services and widespread community support, which can be substantiated by the number of volunteers and past financial contributions. The applicant organization also needs to demonstrate its ability to operate in an effective and financially responsible way.

Being a United Way agency has several advantages. An important one is, of course, the financial support. Table 1 shows the amount that United Way campaigns were able to raise around the state of Texas in 1988. Another advantage is the administrative and financial advice that United Ways give to their member agencies to ensure effective operations and proper accounting of all receipts and disbursements.[5]

TABLE 1
Funds Raised By United Ways In Texas, 1988
(Areas That Raised At Least $500,000)

City/County	Population of Campaign Coverage Area	Amount Raised in Dollars
Abilene	112,400	1,499,600
Amarillo	168,600	2,512,900
Angleton/Brazoria County	205,200	2,953,200
Austin	565,500	5,530,800
Baytown	72,600	959,300
Beaumont/N. Jefferson County	135,400	2,218,000
Brownsville	77,400	504,300
Bryan/Brazos County	108,400	537,800
Corpus Christi/Coastal Bend	463,200	3,852,800
Dallas/Metropolitan Area	1,837,300	38,182,600
Denton	146,600	793,900
El Paso/El Paso County	570,000	4,850,100
Fort Worth/Tarrant County	1,118,400	21,283,500
Galveston	69,300	701,400
Houston/Texas Gulf Coast	3,106,900	50,760,400
Laredo	113,400	525,000
Lubbock	184,500	3,092,900
Midland	116,100	2,257,300
Odessa	134,300	814,700
Orange/Orange County	83,100	704,400
San Angelo/Tom Green County	98,100	1,562,200
San Antonio/Bexar County	1,161,600	19,246,400
Sherman/Grayson County	68,600	1,282,500
Temple	50,600	615,000
Texarkana	65,800	810,700
Texas City	135,000	924,200
Tyler	156,100	1,350,300
Victoria	77,100	541,000
Waco/McLennan County	183,000	1,972,200
Wichita Falls	121,400	1,719,200

Source: United Way of America, *1990 International Directory.* Alexandria, VA: United Way of America, 1989.

It needs to be mentioned, however, that United Way affiliation can also have potential drawbacks. Supported agencies can be discouraged or even prohibited from holding their own fundraisers apart from United Way efforts to avoid dilution of the concept of a "united way" or one annual fund raising drive. But other funding sources are available to nonprofit organizations, and the following section summarizes them.

Revenues

The nature of third sector entities makes a shortage of income one of their common trademarks. The reason for establishing a private, nonprofit corporation often is the demand for a certain social service that neither the public sector can meet because of inadequate taxpayer support nor the proprietary sector because the persons in need do not have the money to pay for it in full. Nonprofit agencies can offer the services by relying on a variety of funding sources.

Despite the limited means of many service recipients, an important source is fee for service. It can be assessed in full from those clients who can pay for it and on a sliding scale from other customers. Membership fees and donations should also be considered. Well established organizations may be be able to attract endowments, which provide steady interest income. Another revenue source can be government grants and contracts. Table 2 lists major federal programs in the human service field and amounts of funding available. A complete listing of all federal grant and contract programs is published annually in the *Catalog of Federal Domestic Assistance*. Private foundations are also good sources for grant money. Detailed information is available from the *Foundation Grants Index*, which is published by the Foundation Center in New York in bimonthly issues and in annual volumes. The *Annual Register of Grant Support* is another comprehensive and authoritative source on grant support programs of government agencies, public and private foundations, and corporations.

The substantial amount of money that United Way collects in Texas for distribution to human service agencies was already mentioned above. In some communities the distribution is based on the principle of deficit funding. Under this arrangement, United Way agrees to pay the difference between the cost of a certain service and the revenues from other income sources.[6] Deficit funding is useful because it ensures steady service. Member agencies can plan the approximate number of people they want to serve and write the budget proposal accordingly, with the knowledge that money shortfalls will be covered by United Way. Some United Ways also provide venture grants to encourage new services.

Success in attracting all sorts of revenues depends to a great extent on the initiative of the management and the board of directors. An entrepreneurial attitude is appropriate in locating possible income sources. The agency can also try to have directors appointed to the board who have ties to potential contributors. But the search for revenues should not be all consuming. Foundations, individual benefactors, and government agencies may attach so many reporting requirements and other strings to a grant that it is possible that costs outweigh its possible benefits.

TABLE 2
Federal Grants and Contracts Programs
(Selection of HHS Programs for which Nonprofits are Eligible to Apply)*

Program Number	Title of Program	Appropriations in Dollars FY 1988	FY 1990 (estimate)
13.137	Minority Community Health Coalition Demonstration	1,400,000	1,400,000
13.144	Drug and Alcohol Abuse-High Risk Youth Demonstration Grants	23,400,000	19,918,000
13.151	Project Grants For Health Services to the Homeless	14,232,390	63,600,000
13.600	Administration for Children, Youth and Families-Head Start	1,206,145,000	1,485,000,000
13.623	Administration for Children, Youth, and Families-Runaways and Homeless Youth	26,087,000	26,923,000
13.647	Social Services Research and Demonstration	3,533,00	3,550,000
13.668	Special Programs for the Aging-Title IV	23,926,000	24,173,000
13.670	Administration for Children, Youth and Families-Child Abuse and Neglect	13,304,000	13,647,500
13.671	Family Violence Prevention and Services	8,138,000	8,219,000
13.995	Adolescent Family Life-Demonstration Projects	6,585,000	6,247,000

* Additional federal grants and contracts monies are made available to states for distribution to nonprofits. Interested organizations should contact the respective state agencies, which are listed in the annual edition of the Texas Almanac.

Source: Executive Office of the President, *1989 Catalog of Federal Domestic Assistance*. Washington, DC: Government Printing Office, 1989.

Expenditures

Nonprofit agencies, like government entities, start the budget process with a list of programs that they would like to offer in the next fiscal year. This is followed by the calculation of costs and a search for possible revenues. Reiteration and adaptation are common. Program goals are proposed, expenses are estimated, anticipated revenues are considered, and goals are adjusted to reflect more realistic income scenarios.

The first step in estimating expenses is to define the proposed activities and their likely costs. Personnel expenses tend to be the highest ones and to keep them down, the use of volunteers should be considered. Costs for goods and services can also sometimes be contained by inviting donated material and labor.

Some nonprofit efforts are so essential that minimal provisions are preferred to no service at all. This is, for instance, the case with shelters for battered women and children. To be safe, the terrorized persons are willing to sleep on bare mattresses on the floor. As the beneficial nature of the service is more widely recognized in the community, more money may be forthcoming and a more pleasant service environment can be created.

In considering the budget, it stands to reason that established agencies have a better understanding of the financial possibilities and limits than new ones. Start-ups are advised to be flexible and to keep very good books so that discrepancies between estimates of revenues and expenditures can be caught quickly and budget plans adjusted accordingly. Actually, a well thought-out budget document is important for good financial and program management in any organization. The next section discusses some of the control aspects of budgeting for nonprofit organizations.

Program Budgets And Other Financial Controls

Since nonprofits lack the bottom line discipline of for-profit firms, they have to be managed well to satisfy clients and patrons.[7] For small nonprofits that offer only a few services, the basic line-item budget and fiscal status reports are good managerial control devices. Table 3 shows a simple example of a fiscal report. It lets administrators immediately know which accounts are underspent, overspent, or on target. Larger agencies are advised to divide their activities into programs and write a separate budget for each unit to improve accountability. The line-item budget is, however, limited as a plan for the future, since it focuses on expenditure items and not on the objectives. To overcome this shortcoming, various other budget approaches have been recommended in recent years.

164

TABLE 3
Fiscal Report: First Quarter, FY 1991

Item	Budgeted ($)	Spent ($)	Encumbered ($)	Balance ($)
Salaries	129,175	32,294	---	96,881
Rent	9,000	2,241	---	6,759
Utilities	2,000	468	---	1,532
Telephone	700	183	---	517
Maintenance	1,000	52	197	751
Office Supplies	800	557	83	160
Postage	200	43	---	157
Travel	500	---	---	500

The program budget is one such example. It is intended as a planning and control tool in that it relates input to expected benefits. This encourages a more thorough review of the input-output relationship or effectiveness of the agency's activities.[8] The critical review of financial matters can, however, also lead to conflict and low morale among employees and volunteers, as the worth of their contributions to the general mission of the agency is scrutinized. It is therefore recommended, before introducing the innovation, to discuss any budget changes with all effected participants to ensure widespread support for the new approach. A well-written budget need not be presented as a top-down control device. Instead it can improve morale when it is treated as the proposed plan of action whose implementation requires the enthusiastic support of all.

The availability of new financial planning tools should not distract us from the benefits of the basic line-item budget. Clarity is one of its advantages. This is achieved because expenditures are expressed in standardized categories, such as salaries or office supplies. Ease of understanding is also maintained because the classic line-item document is prepared annually and presented in current dollars. Adjustments for inflation, program changes or a different service volume can be readily factored in. Finally, the incremental approach gives the budget process a certain degree of stability, continuity, and predictability, which reduces the anxiety that financial matters can readily generate in organizations that tend to be cash poor.[9]

Whether for a year or long term, the basic budget document and its variations provide guidelines for the future. As an additional administrative tool, performance evaluation techniques can be built into a program right from the start.[10] Such techniques allow for the constant monitoring of program implementation and avoid unpleasant surprises at the end of the fiscal year when new financial requests have to be justified to United Way and other funding sources. Other quantitative methods have been developed to measure the productivity of nonprofit operations. Baker and Murawski, for instance, propose a technique to calculate efficient management in terms of paid staff/volunteer ratios.[11] The final control device is the financial statement at the end of the fiscal year in that it summarizes the monetary transactions of the past funding period.

165

Conclusion

Many nonprofits are too small and underfunded to have a budget analyst or accountant on the staff, who can concentrate on finances. Employees and volunteers tend to come from the helping professions with little understanding about fiscal matters. This deficiency can be counterbalanced by the judicious appointment of specialists to the board of directors. Sometimes corporations can be persuaded to participate in a loaned executive program, by which budget officers of the business offer their services as an in-kind donation to the nonprofit entity.

For many years, nonprofits in Texas, like the rest of the nation, concentrated on meeting human needs. Financial management was haphazard, and spending occurred in spurts depending on the availability of funds. But administrators have recognized that good management and a dedication to professional standards improves the service delivery and enables them not only to do good, but to do even better.

Notes

1. Thomas Wolf, *The Nonprofit Organization*. Englewood Cliffs, NJ: Prentice-Hall, 1984: 90-112; and C.P. McLaughlin, *The Management of Nonprofit Organizations*. New York: John Wiley, 1986.
2. See, for example, E.C. Lashbrooke, *Tax Exempt Organizations*. Westport, CT: Quorum Books, 1985; P.B. Firstenberg, *Managing for Profit in the Nonprofit World*. New York: Foundation Center, 1986; H.J. Brice, *Financial and Strategic Management for Nonprofit Organizations*. Englewood Cliffs, NJ: Prentice-Hall, 1987; and J.M. Bryson, *Strategic Planning for Public and Nonprofit Organizations: A Guide to Strengthening and Sustaining Organizational Achievement*. San Francisco: Jossey-Bass, 1988.
3. United Way of America, *A Guide for the Self-Assessment of United Ways' Fund Distribution Processes*. Alexandria, VA: United Way of America, 1985.
4. United Way of Metropolitan Dallas, *Budget Manual*. Dallas: United Way, 1987; and United Way of Tom Green County, *Policies and Procedures Manual*. San Angelo: United Way, 1988. Typescript.
5. United Way of America, *Accounting and Financial Reporting*. Alexandria, VA: United Way of America, 1989.
6. United Way of Lubbock, Lubbock, TX: United Way , 1990. Typescript.
7. J.A. Byrne, "Profiting from the Nonprofits," *Business Week*. March 26, 1990: 66-74.

8. R.K. McLeod, "Program Budgeting Works in Nonprofit Institutions," in *Harvard Business Review. Management for Nonprofit Organizations: Part I.* Boston: Harvard Business Review, 1971: 59-69; and Irene Rubin, "Budget Theory and Budget Practice: How Good the Fit?" *Public Administration Review. Vol.* 50, March/April 1990: 179-189.

9. Aaron Wildavsky, "A Budget for All Seasons? Why the Traditional Budget Lasts," in K.V. Ramanathan and L.P. Hegstad (eds.), *Readings in Management Control in Nonprofit Organization.* New York: John-Wiley & Sons, 1982: 292-305.

10. J.S. Wholey, et al., *Performance and Credibility. Developing Excellence in Public and Nonprofit Organizations.* Lexington, Mass.: Lexington Books, 1986.

11. B.J. Baker and Kris Murawski, "A Method for Measuring Paid Staff Support for Volunteer Improvement," *Journal of Voluntary Action Research. Vol.* 15, July/Sept., 1986: 60-64.

13

PUBLIC-PRIVATE PARTNERSHIPS IN MEETING FUTURE NEEDS

Siegrun F. Fox

Joint government and business efforts to meet societal needs have a long tradition in Texas and the rest of the United States. For centuries, governments have ordered military supplies from private firms, had roads built by private contractors, and in general interacted with the private sector for the delivery of various goods and services. In return, the private sector has relied on government to educate the future work force, maintain a stable legal environment, and protect the private activities against internal or external threats.

Fiscal stress in the last decade heightened interest in public-private partnerships at all jurisdictional levels. Cities formed committees of leaders from the governmental, proprietary, and nonprofit sectors to survey their communities' resources and potentials.[1] States expanded their use of private firms in response to the tax rebellion that began in California in 1978 and spread elsewhere in subsequent years.[2] Also, changes in federal-state relations increased competition among states and encouraged them to mobilize their resources through public-private efforts.[3] At the federal level itself, the Carter administration introduced the partnership concept as a policy tool with the Urban Development Action Grant (UDAG) program.[4] President Reagan abolished UDAG in connection with his cutbacks in domestic programs, but he strongly endorsed other types of partnerships and private sector initiatives.[5]

The flurry of activities in practice has been accompanied by a steady stream of research studies. Since privatization, contracting out, and other forms of private involvement in governmental affairs have been controversial, they have been carefully scrutinized by researchers at universities, in think tanks, and government agencies.[6]

This chapter draws on the many insights from theory and practice to explore the possibilities and limits of public-private cooperation in major policy areas in the State of Texas. It describes partnerships in economic development, education and training, health and social services, and criminal justice.

Economic Development And Public-Private Partnerships

In the past, the political culture of Texas worked against government involvement in economic activities. Ranching, agriculture, the oil industry, real estate, and banking prospered without overt public support. The construction of highways and farm-to-market roads was one area where government was encouraged to be active, and as a result Texas has one of the largest road networks in the nation.[7] Otherwise, the regulation and promotion of the various extracting, manufacturing, and service industries were divided among many different boards and commissions to avoid the concentration of political power in a few department heads.

The rapid decline of all the traditional industries in the 1980s changed assumptions about the proper role of government. The consolidation of eight state boards and agencies into the Texas Department of Commerce in 1987 was a visible sign of the changed attitudes. The purpose of the new Department is to cooperate with the private sector in building a diverse and dynamic state economy and to create jobs. A description of the Department's six divisions further illustrates the new, active economic development mandate:

• The Finance Division: It offers financial and technical assistance to businesses and communities in Texas. It administers the Rural Industrial Loan Fund, the Enterprise Zone Program, the Public Facilities Capital Access Program, and the Community Development Block Grant Program.

• The Business Development Division: This division concentrates on retaining and expanding the state's existing business and industrial base and marketing Texas nationally and internationally as an ideal state for business location and expansion. It is a large division, and its functions are divided among eight offices.

• The Work Force Development Division: It administers job training programs statewide to ensure that a highly trained labor force is available to businesses. A network of 34 service providers develops, coordinates, and delivers the training programs.

• The Small Business Division: This division serves as the state's chief advocacy office for small, minority, and women-owned businesses in Texas. In addition to an Office of Small Business Development, it has an Office of Business Permit Assistance.

• The Tourism Division: As the name implies, it promotes travel to Texas with a national television and print advertising campaign. It works with communities and professionals in the tourism trade to market the state.

• The Support Divisions: They include the Research and Planning Division, the Program Compliance Division, the General Counsel, and the Marketing and Media Division.[8]

In addition to the institutional and financial support at the state level, the Texas Legislature passed three laws that enable communities to provide financial assistance to private entities. The statutes are the Public Improvement District Assessment Act of 1977, the Texas Tax Increment Financing Act of 1981, and the Texas Enterprise Zone Act of 1983. Public Improvement Districts (PIDs), which in other states are called special assessment districts, can be created to fund projects that only benefit a particular area in the community. The planned activity is financed by revenue bonds, which are retired from special tax assessments on the properties in the improved district.[9]

Tax increment financing (TIF) also involves special districts and the use of revenue bonds to improve a particular local area. Only the repayment mechanism differs from PIDs. In the case of TIFs, the difference between tax revenues from the unimproved and improved pieces of property is dedicated to the retirement of the bonds. A judicial ruling has all but invalidated the use of TIFs in Texas. The court ruled in *El Paso Community College District v. City of El Paso* that cities cannot capture tax revenues that belong to school districts.[10]

A 1983 amendment to the Texas Tax Increment Financing Act permits the designation of certain blighted areas as local or state enterprise zones. Austin was one of the first communities to make use of the new law. The city combined state and local tax incentives to direct manufacturing and commercial activities to areas of high and persistent unemployment.[11],†

Some economic development legislation required constitutional amendments, and several were passed in recent years. In the November 1987 election, voters approved House Joint Resolution (HJR) 5, which authorized the Legislature to provide economic development assistance in the state. Another carefully watched amendment was HJR 88, which permits the state to issue general obligation bonds for the superconducting supercollider research facility. A year later, another amendment was passed, which established a Texas growth fund and provides for the investment of certain state funds in businesses in the state.

In the 1989 election, voters approved three additional constitutional amendments dealing with economic growth. One amendment allows for the issuance of $75 million in state bonds for agricultural and business efforts that lead to the development of Texas products. Another measure authorizes the state government to issue additional $500 million of Texas water development bonds for water supply, water quality, and flood control purposes.[12] The voters also favored the "Freeport" Amendment. It removed from the tax rolls property that was in the state only temporarily for production purposes, unless local taxing units voted to override the exemption by the year's end.[13] This amendment has created a crazy quilt of taxing and tax-exempt jurisdictions across the state, since cities, counties, school districts, and community college districts all had the power to make their own decisions irrespective of the preferences of other taxing units in the area.

---

† In distinction to the state and local efforts, federal enterprise zone legislation has not been passed by Congress because the federal proposals not only provide for tax incentives but also involved relaxation of health and safety standards set by the Environmental Protection Agency and the Occupational Safety and Health Administration. Opposing legislators and labor leaders argue that relaxed rules would create second class citizens, whose lives would be exposed to greater hazards.

Taken together, the various financial incentive programs of the state and localities can be lucrative to corporations. A Taiwanese firm, for instance, is receiving $225 million in tax breaks and direct subsidies to locate a $1.3 billion chemical plant at Point Comfort, which is 100 miles southwest of Houston. Texas lawmakers phased out some sales taxes, dedicated state money, and supported tax abatements to attract the plant. The project, however, has received mixed reviews because the parent company has a very poor environmental record both in Taiwan and in Louisiana, where it has other chemical operations.[14]

In addition, the use of tax abatements for economic development purposes has been questioned. It is apparently unfair to established firms that do not enjoy the tax advantage, causes public services to trail behind private investments, and shifts the tax burden to homeowners and existing businesses.[15] Additional limits to public-private partnerships will be addressed below in the final section, after the review of government and business cooperation in other policy areas has been completed.

Public-Private Cooperation In Education And Training

Private support for schooling has a varied history in Texas. The settlers in the 19th century valued it so much that they listed the lack of education among their grievances in the Texas Declaration of Independence from Mexico in 1836. In the following decades, the questions of funding and popular control over education policy remained controversial.

The issue of quality education came to a head in the 1980s, when national and state studies documented a serious erosion of students' knowledge.[16] When the Texas government failed to obtain voter support for its legislative proposal involving pay raises for teachers and additional public school funding, it invited the cooperation of influential private-sector representatives. H. Ross Perot, the high-tech industrialist from Dallas, became the chair of the blue-ribbon Select Committee on Public Education. The committee proposed a series of changes, most of which were adopted in the comprehensive eduction reform legislation in 1984. It appears that the public-private cooperation was critical in getting the measure passed, considering that it cost $2.8 billion and challenged the traditional Texas emphasis of sports.[17],†

At the community college level, public-private cooperation also made things happen. In 1965, for instance, business leaders in Dallas encouraged the state to establish a community-college district in Dallas county, which in subsequent years

---

† While the renewed emphasis on academic subject matters is a necessary correction in Texas education policy, the economic value of sports should not be underestimated. Especially the export potential of the spectator sports football, baseball, and basketball may be undervalued. These three sports do not only have entertainment value for domestic consumption, but with proper marketing could conceivably also attract planeloads of Japanese and German tourists.

built seven campuses.[18] Other areas also formed junior college districts at the urging of the private sector. The mission of these educational institutions is to provide vocational-technical training beyond the high-school level, and to achieve this objective, community colleges cooperate closely with local industries to ensure that their students receive skills that the private sector needs. In this way, the colleges can make substantial contributions to economic development in the state.

The first four-year colleges in Texas were founded by private benefactors, but over the years public institutions eclipsed the private ones in size and prestige. It is, however, important to note that the growth of the Texas public higher education system occurred to a great extent due to private sector initiatives and that substantial amounts of private money have been donated to public institutions. To mention three examples, the Meadows Foundation has made large contributions to higher education and research in Texas since 1948; the Carr Scholarship Foundation has made millions of dollars available to students at Angelo State University; and the University of Texas Southwestern Medical Center at Dallas was founded and expanded through the active involvement of private leaders and private funds.[19]

In the wake of the criticism of public education, Texas higher education has also been subjected to scrutiny. The body in charge of conducting the review and making recommendations again consisted of representatives from the government and business community. The Select Committee on Higher Education hired a private accounting firm and used private funds to study the management of higher education in Texas. Its report, published in 1986, ignored traditional sentiments and recommended a massive restructuring of existing institutions. The Texas Legislature, however, could not overlook popular preferences. The alumni of the universities that were threatened with extinction or merger exerted so much pressure on the lawmakers that only a few changes have been implemented so far.[20]

A weakness was also discovered in proprietary schools in Texas. Some had apparently been set up with little concern for the quality of their training programs. The state was called upon to revise the Education Code and strengthen its oversight function. Furthermore, a committee was formed to study the long-term regulation of private, for-profit institutions in Texas. School dropouts and the chronic unemployed are especially vulnerable to fraudulent promises of education and training.[21]

Like other states, Texas is experimenting with various programs to improve the schooling and training of "at-risk" youths and adults. One effort in San Angelo has received state and national attention. It is called Preparing Area Youth for Success, PAYS for short, and combines money and in-kind donations from the local school district, the state, the federal government, and the private sector to offer an alternative education to that segment of the student population that tends to drop out before finishing school. Business can make meaningful contributions to the education of discouraged students by such simple steps as explaining the job interview process and job application forms in the non-threatening environment of the classroom.[22]

Some educational and training programs for the long-term unemployed are administered by so-called Private Industry Councils. They were initiated at the federal level with the Job Training Partnership Act of 1982, which mandated the establishment of public-private partnerships for job training purposes. Local educators, union representatives, and business people are supposed to meet and jointly analyze what jobs are available in the community and what skills the unemployed need to fill them. Under the Act, the states are expected to exercise administrative authority over the program by designating local service areas, dispersing discretionary funds, and overseeing implementation. It appears that Texas, along with other states, has been slow in assuming its responsibilities and spending the federally-provided funds.[23]

Supporters of these education and training programs point out that neither Texas, nor other states, can continue to ignore the school drop-outs without incurring long-range problems. As the U.S. economy increasingly becomes international and high-tech, unskilled jobs disappear or move to less developed countries, leaving uneducated Americans with fewer honest job opportunities. The ever expanding welfare and prison populations testify to the link between inadequate education, welfare dependency, and crime.[24] While schooling is the long-term solution, temporary measures are taken to deliver social programs and lock up criminals. Since voters are opposed to substantially higher taxes to pay for the many new welfare programs and prisons needed, public-private partnerships have been formed as alternative delivery approaches.

Public-Private Cooperation In The Delivery Of Social Programs

Partnerships between government and the private sector exist in a variety of social services. The relationships range from a regulatory role of an otherwise private economic activity, such as child care, to contracting out of an otherwise public function, such as food services in public institutions.

There are more than 21,000 child care centers in Texas, most of which are operated by private, nonprofit or proprietary firms. To ensure certain health and safety standards in these facilities, the state has issued rules and requires the licensing of child care centers and their administrators.[25] A few places in every city are funded jointly by the state and federal governments for the children of poor families. With the number of working mothers increasing, there is a great demand for inexpensive, but high quality child care, and it is an ongoing challenge for the public and private sectors to expand the supply. The situation is so acute in many states that a broad bipartisan coalition is lobbying for increased federal involvement in child care.

More public-private partnerships are also needed at the other end of the age spectrum. Longer life expectancy has increased the number of people in need of minor or major daily care, while the number of family members available for such work has declined. The alternatives are in-home care by paid housekeepers, to institutional services for persons in need of continuous medical attention. The providers of these services usually are proprietary or nonprofit firms. The state enters the picture as licensing agent and through the Medicaid program shares the costs of health care for the elderly poor with the federal government.[26]

To ensure the availability of health care for the general population, the state supplements private for-profit, private nonprofit, community-based, and federal efforts. The state makes a significant contribution to the training of physicians, nurses, and allied-health professionals. In addition, it makes health care available for the poor by subsidizing county health departments and community hospitals. Eligible families with dependent children can also sign up for the Medicaid program.

In the area of mental health and mental retardation, lawsuits and changed professional standards in the last fifteen years increased the demand for sheltered community homes in Texas. The profession has advocated housing in the least restrictive environment, and the courts have upheld this right. As a consequence, wherever possible, people are being moved out of large institutions into small residential settings. Many of these alternative facilities are operated by private nonprofit or proprietary corporations holding contracts with the state.[27]

In general, services that the state is expected to provide, but does not wish to handle in-house, can be contracted out to the private sector. In this arrangement the government still maintains control over the cost and quality of the service. Only its implementation is left in the hands of private for-profit or nonprofit entities.[28] Food services or maintenance work in hospitals can be arranged in this way. In-home care for the elderly or foster care for children is also usually provided by private individuals on contract with the state.

Contracting has its advocates and detractors. Supporters argue that the private sector can be more flexible and efficient in delivering services,[29] while opponents maintain that flexibility and efficiency are achieved at the expense of the service recipients and rank and file workers.[30] Real dilemmas have emerged. When the contract is loosely defined to allow for flexibility and reduce costs, the contractor is likely to exploit the loopholes and provide minimal service. When, on the other hand, the contract is detailed, flexibility and cost savings can be lost for the private provider and also for the state, which needs to retain a qualified staff that can write airtight contracts and supervise their compliance.[31]

If contracting at all, options offered by nonprofit versus proprietary entities have to be weighed. In the social service field, where the client may be young and innocent, old and frail, poor and intimidated or mentally retarded, the nonprofit sector may have an edge over the for-profit sector because of the different principles that guide their operations. A service attitude is necessary and a profit motive inappropriate when the primary customer cannot assume a critical "buyer-beware" attitude.[32]

With this difference in mind, governments at the local, state, and federal levels have encouraged the formation of private, nonprofit organizations by granting tax-exempt status to institutions that offer social services to people irrespective of the clients' ability to pay. In Texas, the legal framework for nonprofit entities is provided by the Nonprofit Corporation Act, which spells out in detail the selection of officers, handling of finances, and other important organizational features (Vernon's Ann. Rev. Civ. Stat. Tex. Art. 1396).

Whether for-profit or nonprofit, the private service sector is growing and meeting a variety of social needs. A relatively recent development is the business involvement in the criminal justice field, which is the subject matter of the next section.

Criminal Justice And Public-Private Cooperation

With the steady increase in crime, overcrowding of Texas prisons has become a serious and costly problem. A federal court ruled in *Ruiz v. Estelle* (1980) that the Texas Department of Corrections facilities were overcrowded, understaffed, and generally substandard. Further legal wrangling and poor economic conditions in the state delayed compliance with the ruling, but the state finally agreed to double the number of prison beds to 65,000 by 1993.[33]

What is interesting about the new Texas prison policy is the fact that the Legislature authorized the Department of Criminal Justice to contract with private, for-profit entities for the financing and operation of new facilities. Since SB 251 was passed in 1987, two firms, Becon-Wackenhut and Corrections Corporation of America, each constructed two 500-bed pre-release centers, which were fully operational under private management by the beginning of 1990.[34] N-Group Securities, a for-profit firm from Houston, is building several correctional facilities for other governmental entities in the state. The construction is being paid for by the sale of tax-exempt bonds to private investors. The cities where the prisons are located only contribute the necessary infrastructure, such as water and sewers.[35]

The private involvement has its share of supporters and opponents. Advocates point out that money can be raised more readily from private investors than from taxpayers and that private managers will operate more efficiently than public employees. Speed in construction and cost savings in maintenance are important considerations in Texas due to the discrepancy between court-imposed standards and funds available to comply with them.[36]

Critics have raised a number of objections. They maintain that the danger of inmate exploitation is too great in a for-profit facility and that savings will be achieved at the expense of prisoners and ordinary employees.[37] "Creaming" has also been observed. It means for-profit correction facilities only accept the easiest-to-handle prisoners, say nonviolent white-collar inmates, leaving difficult felons for the state institutions.[38] Moreover, the issues of liability and cooperation with law enforcement officers in case of a disturbance have created unanswered questions.[39]

Other public-private partnerships have existed in the criminal justice system of Texas for a longer time and have been more accepted. The state has, for instance, contracted out much of the medical and psychiatric care in prisons.

175

Private, for-profit or nonprofit entities are also used in counseling or training of juveniles and adults.[40]

The description of public-private partnerships in the four policy areas, economic development, education and training, health and welfare, and criminal justice indicates a variety of cooperative possibilities. Where appropriate, specific limits were also mentioned in the individual sections to clarify policy options. The following section summarizes additional obstacles that have emerged in Texas and other states.

Some Limits To Public-Private Partnerships

Financing of the public contribution to a joint development effort generally requires the approval of the population affected, and the ballot box tends to be the most effective weapon available to project opponents. Among possible detractors are those who dislike a particular feature of a project, say its location, size, or architecture. They can be called substantive opponents. And there are those critics who are against public-private partnerships as a matter of principle. The latter can be called ideological opponents and are identified in greater detail below because they have been influential in this and other states.

Among the ideological opponents are two political groups that have shaped Texas politics in the past, a conservative elite and populists. The traditional elite, whose wealth was tied to the land, wanted low taxes and limited government, and in return accepted a low level of public services. The decline of ranching, agriculture, oil, real estate, and financial institutions weakened the economic and political power of this elite. The rise of interest groups, representing Hispanics, African-Americans, and women, further reduced the influence of the "good old boys".[41]

In addition, an alternative elite whose wealth was in the new high-tech industries emerged. The new leaders recognized that Texas was losing ground compared to the thriving economies of other states and countries and that the key to prosperity was better schools and universities. The shift in wealth, power, and ideology explains the fact that Texas was willing to introduce educational reforms and raise taxes to pay for them during the severe recession of the 80s.[42] The most prominent representative of the changed guard is the previously mentioned H. Ross Perot, founder of Electronic Data Services and Chair of the Select Committee on Public Education. The power of the new elite, however, did not remain unchallenged either.

Populist sentiments can strengthen or curtail elite power. One of their trademarks is the belief in the abilities of the common people. They oppose big business and/or big government because they feel that the large institutions exploit them and stifle their own aspirations. To understand populist opposition to public-private partnerships, it is important to distinguish between a left-wing and right-

176

wing faction. As demonstrated in other states, left-wing populists oppose the partnerships concept because they fear that state officials are selling out to private interests, while right-wing populists fear that government gets too much involved in economic planning. Especially when the two factions of populism form coalitions with the conservative elite and other opponents, can public-private partnerships be defeated.[43]

Research on successful and unsuccessful economic development efforts in the north-eastern states provides the following lessons: Those who will apparently reap most of the benefits should also carry the main financial burden. In addition, to attract widespread voter appeal, projects should contain something for all geographical areas and socioeconomic groups. Retired people, for instance, may resent higher taxes for job creation programs, but may support them when the programs also promise better services for senior citizens. Finally, costs of projects should be kept in limits, since grandiose plans tend to be opposed by voters.[44]

The last finding can be confirmed by an experience in Texas. Voters in 1987 rejected a constitutional amendment that would have made $125 million available for new business development, but approved a scaled-down version of $75 million two years later.

An additional flaw in public-private partnerships is the divergent set of principles that guide government and business operations. To enable democratic accountability, governments have sunshine laws, which require public agencies to open their meetings and files to interested parties and the media. In Texas, they are the Open Meetings Act and Open Records Act. Furthermore, the public sector is supposed to be service oriented and treat citizens in an equitable, even compassionate, manner. Business, on the other hand, desires to operate in secret to stay ahead of the competition. And the private sector is supposed to be profit motivated and adjust the quality of goods and services to people's differential ability to pay.[45]

Conclusion

In recent years, courts have been called upon to interpret the reach of both public and private sectors. Under the U.S. Constitution, state governments cannot violate individuals' civil liberties and due process rights. Private businesses have no such legal restraints, as the U.S. Supreme Court made clear in two cases in 1982. In *Rendell-Baker v. Kohn*, the Court ruled that the First Amendment right of freedom of speech does not apply to a privately-owned institution, although it received most of its funding and operation guidelines from a state agency. In *Blum v. Yaretsky*, the Court argued that the Fourteenth Amendment due process requirement was not applicable to a decision made by a private entity, although the decision resulted in a reduction of public benefits, in this case Medicaid payments.[46] One can expect additional lawsuits in the future, as more public-private partnerships are formed.

The analysis of barriers that can stand in the way of joint government-business ventures in Texas uncovers possible obstacles, but no insurmountable ones. And that may be good. There are so many needs in the state, the nation, and the rest of the world that it is important to rally all public and private capabilities, and at times these potentialities can be optimized through public-private cooperation.

Notes

1. Perry Davis, "Why Partnerships? Why Now?" in *Public-Private Partnerships Improving Urban Life*. Proceedings of the Academy of Political Science 36, ed. Perry Davis. New York: The Academy of Political Science, 1986: 1.

2. Joan Allen et al., *Opportunities for the Greater Use of the Private Sector in Delivering State Services*. Washington, DC: Urban Institute and Council of State Government, 1987: I-1

3. John Shannon, "Competitive Federalism -- Three Driving Forces," *Intergovernmental Perspective*. Vol. 15, Fall 1989: 17-18.

4. Katherine Lyall, "Public-Private Partnerships in the Carter Years," in *Public-Private Partnerships Improving Urban Life*. Proceedings of the Academy of Political Science 36, ed. Perry Davis. New York: The Academy of Political Science, 1986: 4-13.

5. R.A. Berger, "Private Sector Initiatives in the Reagan Administration," in *Public-Private Partnerships Improving Urban Life*. Proceedings of the Academy of Political Science 36, ed. Perry Davis. New York: The Academy of Political Science, 1986: 14-30.

6. See, for example, CED, *Public-Private Partnership. An Opportunity for Urban Communities*. New York: Committee for Economic Development, 1982; C.W. Lewis, *Community Collaboration. A Handbook on Public-Private Partnerships in Connecticut*. Storrs, CT: Institute of Public Service, 1985; J.R. Henig, *Public Policy and Federalism. Issues in State and Local Politics*. New York: St. Martin's Press, 1985; and ICMA, *Service Delivery in the 90s: Alternative Approaches for Local Governments*. Washington, DC: International City Managers Association, 1989.

7. Mike Kingston (ed.), *1990-91 Texas Almanac*. Dallas: Dallas Morning News, 1989: 506

8. Texas Department of Commerce (n.d.), *Programs and Services*. Austin: Texas Department of Commerce. Brochure.

9. Susan Mead and C.J. Miller, "Texas Statutory Tools for Joint Development: Public Improvement District Assessment and Tax Increment Financing," in *Texas Economic Development in Transition: Opportunities in Public-Private Collaboration,* eds. S.M. Wyman and R.R. Weaver. Arlington, TX: Institute of Urban Studies, University of Texas at Arlington, 1989: 46.

10. Ibid., 57-59.

11. Joseph James, "The City of Austin Enterprise Zone Program," in *Texas Economic Development in Transition: Opportunities in Public-Private*

Collaboration, eds. S.M. Wyman and R.R. Weaver. Arlington, TX: Institute of Urban Studies, University of Texas at Arlington, 1989: 67-70.

12. T.L. Whatley (ed.), "Amendment Three," *Texas Government Newsletter.* Vol. 17, Oct. 9, 1989: 2.

13. T.L. Whatley (ed.), "The 'Freeport' Bill Comes Due," *Texas Government Newsletter.* Vol. 17, Dec. 11, 1989: 1.

14. Associated Press, "Tax Breaks Bestowed on Taiwanese Polluter to Build Texas Plant," *San Angelo Standard-Times.* Sept. 11, 1989: 5A.

15. H.T. Gross and B.L. Weinstein, "Are We Giving Away the State," *University of North Texas Perspectives.* Vol. 4, Nov. 1989: 2-3; and Michael Morrison, "Some Lawmakers Say Tax Abatements Hurt Texas," *San Angelo Standard-Times.* Dec. 27, 1989: 8A.

16. LBJ School of Public Affairs, *Education, Technology, and the Texas Economy. Vol. 1: Economics of Education.* Policy Research Project Report 85. Austin: University of Texas at Austin, 1988.

17. Eugene Jones et al., *Practicing Texas Politics.* 7th ed. Boston: Houghton Mifflin Co., 1989: 311-12.

18. W.E. Claggett, "Dallas: The Dynamics of Public-Private Cooperation," in *Public-Private Partnerships in American Cities,* eds. R.S. Fosler and R.A. Berger. Lexington, Mass: Lexington Books, 1982: 270-71.

19. Ibid., 267.

20. Jones et al., *Practising Texas Politics:* 315

21. Jennifer Dixon, "Loan default rate above 60% at 16 Texas schools," *Dallas Morning News.* June 2, 1989: 17A and 21A.

22. Keely Coghlan, "Dole Cites Local School Programs," *San Angelo Standard-Times.* Sept. 8, 1989: 1A.

23. Jose Martinez, "JTPA - An Inside Perspective," Angelo State University, 1989. Typescript.

24. T.L. Whatley (ed.), "Amendment Eight," *Texas Government Newsletter.* Vol. 17, Oct. 16, 1989: 2.

25. Kingston, *Texas Almanac:* 413

26. C.J. Fox and S.M. Kennedy, "Texas Health Policy: Progressive Impulses Searching for Means," in *Texas Public Policy,* ed. Gerry Riposa. Dubuque, Iowa: Kendall/Hunt, 1987: 171.

27. LBJ School of Public Affairs, *Contracting Selected State Government Functions: Issues and Next Steps.* Policy Research Project Report 75. Austin: University of Texas at Austin, 1986: 21-92.

28. Ted Kolderie, "The Two Different Concepts of Privatization," *Public Administration Review.* Vol. 46, July/Aug., 1986: 285-91.

29. E.S. Savas, *Privatization. The Key to Better Government.* Chatham, NJ: Chatham House, 1987.

30. AFSCME, *When Public Services Go Private.* Washington, DC: American Federation of State, County, and Municipal Employees, 1987.

31. H.P. Hatry, *A Review of Private Approaches for Delivery of Public Services.* Washington, DC: Urban Institute, 1983: 13-28.

32. H.B. Hansmann, "The Role of Nonprofit Enterprise," *The Yale Law Journal.* Vol. 89, April 1980: 835-901; and Dennis Young, *If Not For Profit, For What?* Lexington, Mass: Lexington Books, 1983.

33. Jones et al., *Practising Texas Politics:* 370.

34. T.J. Gillman, "Private prison opens in Texas," *Dallas Morning News.* Sept. 8, 1989: 21A and 26A; and A.D. Sapp, Letter explaining the status of

179

privately-operated prisons housing state prisoners in Texas. Huntsville, Texas: Texas Department of Criminal Justice, Institutional Division, Jan. 22, 1990.

35. Ross McSwain, "San Saba Detention Center Slowed by Construction Woes," *San Angelo Standard-Times*. Dec. 29, 1989: 1C.

36. T.J. Gillman, "Private Prison Opens in Texas." 21A and 26A.

37. Mick Ryan and Tony Ward, *Privatization and the Penal System. The American Experience and the Debate in Britain*. New York: St. Martin's Press, 1989.

38. Associated Press, "300 Prisoners Rebel in Eden," *San Angelo Standard-Times*. May 24, 1989: 1A.

39. Ross McSwain, "Eden Stand-in Raises Authority Questions," *San Angelo Standard-Times*. May 26, 1989: 1A and 4A.

40. Sapp, Letter, 1990.

41. Gregory Curtis, "Behind the Lines. All the Fine Young Men," *Texas Monthly*. Vol. 17, Oct. 1989: 5-6.

42. K.R. Mladenka and K.Q. Hill, *Texas Government. Politics and Economics*. Pacific Grove, CA: Brooks/Cole, 1989: 22.

43. S.F. Fox, "Who Opposes Public/Private Financial Partnerships for Urban Renewal?" *Journal of Urban Affairs*. Vol. 7, Winter 1985: 27-40.

44. Hilary Silver, "Is Industrial Policy Possible in the United States? The Defeat of Rhode Island's Greenhouse Compact," *Politics and Society*. Vol. 15, 1986-87: 359-64.

45. Christopher Hamilton and D.T. Wells, *Federalism, Power , and Political Economy*. Englewood Cliffs, NJ: Prentice Hall, 1990: 162.

46. H.J. Sullivan, "Privatization of Public Services: A Growing Threat to Constitutional Rights," *Public Administration Review*. Vol. 47, Nov/Dec 1987: 461-67.

14

BUDGET MANAGEMENT PRACTICES: A COMPARATIVE STUDY OF FOUR CITIES

Aman Khan and Douglas Davenport

Like many communities throughout the nation, Texas cities have been squeezed by tremendous fiscal stress and complex management problems during the past two decades. Significant changes have occurred in local budgetary practices, as municipalities have attempted to better allocate scarce resources. A crucial response to this pressure has been the implementation of more sophisticated budget management models, including performance and zero-base budgets.

This chapter examines the budgetary responses of four Texas cities to their local circumstances. It assesses their budget management practices in order to gain an understanding of current implementation. The following questions are addressed here: how are budget management models being utilized? What changes have been made in the budget process to make these models more suitable for current needs? What are the outcomes of these changes? These assessments are made from a descriptive-narrative perspective in which it describes the models these cities use and the constraints they face. The chapter also attempts to provide a normative assessment, describing the implementation in terms of a number of commonly used policy criteria.

Theory Vs. Reality

For many years, the budget process was characterized by the absence of any compelling theory describing how governments allocated their resources.[1] Budget requests were primarily 'laundry lists' which decision makers granted as long as money was available. However, with the tightening of funds came an increased concern for a systematic rationale to appropriate them. Citizens began voicing their desires that money be spent efficiently on programs that were effective. Hence, economic criteria entered the political arena.

In response to this need, various management approaches and models were developed which attempted to provide some means of justifying budgets through an explicit rationale. For years the federal government (and most state governments) experimented with such models, including Performance, PPBS, and Zero-Base budgeting. However, implementing these models proved more difficult than was first expected, often resulting in disillusionment with the methodology. Practitioners discovered that the real world is not identical to the theoretical universe in which models are created. It is this tension between theory and practice that this chapter wishes to examine as it evaluates local level implementation of budgetary tools.

This section begins by briefly describing the basic models currently in use, followed by an overview of their actual use. The following cities were selected for this purpose: San Antonio, Fort Worth, Austin, and Lubbock. Each of these communities represent a unique set of socioeconomic circumstances, with differing budgetary needs, which have influenced the selection of budget management tools as well as their implementation.

Performance Budgeting

The concept of performance budgeting represents one of the first budget reform efforts, suggested by the Hoover Commission of 1949.[2] By definition, a performance budget "would concentrate attention on the work to be done or service to be rendered, rather than the things to be acquired."[3]

The structure of a performance budget necessarily includes the following elements: (1) identification of work activities; (2) identification of work or output units for each activity; (3) identification of input units for each major resource to be used; (4) calculation of the cost per work or output unit; and (5) multiplying the cost per work or output unit by the projected activity workload for the year.

Of course, not every work activity is identified and measured, due to the magnitude of such a task. Instead, only key activities are used to determine budget projections. Furthermore, the matter of defining output units can be problematic. Many public goods are difficult to measure, because they are not quantifiable. Finally, performance budgeting requires maximal effort on the part of those preparing the budget. Unfortunately, many cities and towns do not have the time or expertise necessary to properly implement this system.

Program Budgeting

Program budgeting emphasizes ends rather than means, or activities to be performed rather than objects of expenditure. The budget is based upon a logical or physical grouping of activities performed, rather than a line-item list of expenditure classifications.[4] The key elements for a program budget are: (1) establish the various programs or objectives within each department; (2) create plans to achieve these objectives; and (3) determine fiscal resources needed to accomplish these plans. When this final step is completed, the department request is submitted for approval.

A key difficulty with program budgeting is the tendency of programs to overlap, both between departments and within the same department. This hinders

182

coordination of proposals, while creating additional work for budget preparation personnel.

Zero-Base Budgeting

The conceptual framework for ZBB is built around three basic elements: (1) the identification of "decision units"; (2) analysis of decision units and the formulation of "decision packages"; and (3) ranking of packages to arrive at a unified budget. Historically, other elements have been added during implementation, yet these three factors constitute a foundation for the ZBB model.[5] The hallmark of ZBB is a continuous, multilevel, managerial assessment of budget requests, focusing upon the total budget request.[6] This is a 'bottom up' approach, with evaluation beginning at the lowest levels of managerial control.

Decision units are the basis for this evaluation, representing the building blocks of the budget process. The initial identification of decision units is crucial, and should reflect the organization's structure. Such units may be programs, cost centers, functions, or even line items. After identifying the units, functional managers create decision packages: a series of prioritized budget requests for each set of services or activities. The highest priority package addresses the funding level necessary to maintain operations at a minimal level. This level, expressed as a percentage of the current budget, is often preset by upper level management, usually in the 70-90 percent range. Low priority packages will reflect allocations at current levels, as well as increased spending levels.

Finally, upper level management ranks all of the decision packages to create a total budget. The documentation accompanying decision packages provides input for evaluating the requests. Thus, more precise control of resource allocation is possible, tailoring the budget to reflect the most valuable options. Ultimately, all programs and services are evaluated and compared, in order to provide an assessment of the entire budget. Contrary to what the name "zero-base" implies, ZBB does not mean 'starting over' every year without reference to what went before. Such an approach was originally used by the Department of Agriculture in FY 1964, without success.[7] Yet ZBB does provide for a systematic review of current operations, in light of future fiscal constraints.

Target Budgeting

The final budget system used is Target or Goal Budgeting. Conceptually, this is the simplest of all the models used by the four governments. It contains only one essential element, an expenditure target, which is set by upper level management prior to departmental preparation.[8] In effect, the target is a ceiling for individual budget requests, and may be based upon a previously adopted budget or some expected revenue level. Though the idea of ceilings or targets is not new, implementation of the conceptual model is a recent phenomenon.

Levels of Implementation: A Descriptive Assessment

Implementation of a model is never perfect. In other words, no model is used in a vacuum, without regard to the political and fiscal realities of the local government. Thus, it is important to establish criteria for assessing relative levels of implementation, which will vary from city to city. Three primary levels of implementation are suggested: adoption, adaption, and addition. A fourth level, cosmetic, may be considered a dysfunctional model of implementation.

Adoptive implementation means that a model is being used without any alteration or modification. It also means that no other model is exerting influence over the budgetary practices. *Adaptive implementation* suggests that the model has been adapted, or altered in some minor way to accommodate local constraints. However, there are still no other models in operation. *Additional implementation* represents a new model being used to supplement a current model. The level of modification of either model may vary, depending upon the circumstances. The more harmonious or complementary the two systems, the more successful the implementation. *Cosmetic implementation* refers to significant changes, such that the system actually used is only a likeness of the model. The result is an operational version which retains the name of the system, but not the requisite elements. Keeping these descriptions in perspective, let us briefly discuss the constraints which determine these levels of use.

Constraints in Model Implementation

No model can be implemented without regard to the political and fiscal realities of a governmental entity. Conversely, the models themselves require adherence to their basic elements, noted previously, if implementation is to be functional. In reality, however, there must be some trade off between model constraints and the basic elements or structure of these models to determine the degree of successful implementation.   The following describes two such constraints, resource and legislative, that are important in determining the level of model implementation.

Resource Constraints. More than any other thing, the availability of local resources affects the degree of successful implementation of any model. It is important to remember that resources not only include money but also personnel, a constraint that is often overlooked when considering budget management tools.

To properly utilize a system, the government must evaluate the fiscal requirements. Most systems will demand additional hours of preparation and training, while some may require upgraded information technology. This can mean costly capital expenditures for computer hardware, or increased personnel costs. Furthermore, personnel requirements must be considered. Do current employees have the expertise to successfully operate the new model? Or, can we hire qualified individuals without reclassifying positions, at higher salaries? To select a budget model without answering these questions will certainly result in a dysfunctional implementation, or greater fiscal stress.

Legislative Constraints. Unlike the private sector, the public sector faces various legal constraints upon its budgeting process. Each government must meet local ordinances as well as state statutes and codes. Most of these laws hinder the full implementation of any particular model, since uniformity is the goal of such constraints. Furthermore, local "policy space" must be evaluated.[9] Certain budgetary alternatives may not be acceptable to policy makers, who may resist substantive change. This is aptly illustrated by Daniel K. Wanamaker, who describes such difficulties in his article, "ZBB is Light-Years Away from Rural America."[10] With this foundation in hand, it is now possible to examine the budgetary systems currently used by these four Texas cities.

Model Implementation

San Antonio. It is the third largest city in the state with a population nearing a million. The past two fiscal years have been economically difficult for San Antonio. Due to a combination of factors, the City faced a projected year end deficit of $5.2 million for FY 1989-90. Furthermore, FY 90-91 indicated even more significant deficits as a result of slow revenue growth and mandated expenditures (contractual obligations and legal constraints). To face this challenge, San Antonio immediately reduced current expenditures. For a more permanent solution, the City took the following actions regarding the FY 90-91 budget: 1) elimination of 284 positions; 2) reductions in appropriations totaling $13.9 million; 3) institution of a hiring freeze; and 4) proposal of a property tax increase of 7.9 percent. These steps, along with the implementation of a secondary budget model, produced a balanced budget.

Until FY 1989-90, San Antonio primarily utilized a performance methodology for establishing departmental budgets. However, because of the legislative constraints (contractual obligations) and resource constraints (a significant deficit), San Antonio employed a target budget system to supplement the previous performance measures. Those departments in the Enterprise Funds and Special Revenue Funds submitted a budget based upon their own revenue and expenditure projections, while all General Fund departments were given goals (targets) for budget preparation. These targets were based on Management Services estimates of projected revenues and the reduced expenditure levels mandated during FY 1989-90.

Despite the creation of goals, departments are still required to justify any changes in current service levels through performance measures. These measures are to reflect workload statistics, effectiveness and efficiency measures. Changes which are to be justified include: program improvements due to increased service levels, program reductions required due to lack of funding, and mandated program changes due to legal constraints.

San Antonio distributes budget materials to the departments at the beginning of April. On June 1st, Management Services Department provides Target Budget amounts to the General Fund departments. June 15th is the deadline for Group II departments (mostly smaller departments) to submit their budgets to Management Services. June 22nd is the submission deadline for Group III departments, such as Police, Fire, and Human Resources. This reduced preparation time is indicative of the reduced discretion available to individual managers in creating their departmental

185

budgets. Any problems in target compliance are to be discussed with the appropriate budget analyst. Issues not resolved at the analyst level are to be submitted by the departments to the Management Services Director. This process ensures that any variations from the departmental goals are approved by upper level management prior to submission to the legislative body.

Clearly, San Antonio uses an additive implementation of the target model due to the resource and legislative constraints. The foundational model is performance budgeting, since all changes must be justified in this manner, with the target element being added. It will be interesting to note whether future budgets will retain the target element, or if revenues will permit it to be eliminated. Conversely, continued fiscal stress may enhance the utilization of the target model, signalling its continued dominance over the performance elements.

Fort Worth. One of the fastest growing cities in the state, Fort Worth has also faced a recent period of significant fiscal stress. Like San Antonio, Fort Worth has addressed this problem by instituting overall departmental goals, or targets. For General Fund activities, the target is the adopted 1989-90 budget. The underlying budgetary system is a Zero-Base Budget (ZBB), along with various performance measures. This structure is retained for presenting program alternatives, labeled "decision packages," which go beyond the target. A *program continuation package* is used to describe continuation of current programs which could not be accommodated in the FY 1990-91 base budget request. *Program improvement packages* are used to describe the combination of program expansions or additions that would increase the base budget request.

The departmental preparation phase of the budget process begins in early March. Each department prepares a base (continuation) budget predicated upon a target figure supplied by the Office of Management Services. Departments must then prepare a prioritized list of program continuations for current programs which cannot be financed within the base budget figure. Additionally, a department may prepare a set of program improvements and additions. These packages include expansion of programs currently funded and any new programs that the department wants considered for funding. Again, such alternatives are to be ranked in order of priority. A departmental budget request is comprised of a line-item expenditure request that is supplemented with detailed justification. All requests for funding must be related to specific program needs and must be measurable in terms of effectiveness and/or efficiency.

Budget materials are distributed on March 1st, and the departmental submission dates vary, depending upon the group assignment. Smaller departments, such as Internal Audit and City Secretary, are to have requests submitted to the Office of Management Services by March 19th. A second group, including Finance and Municipal Court, have a March 28th deadline. A third group, which includes all public safety functions, must submit requests by April 11th.

Much like San Antonio, Fort Worth uses the target system to maintain hierarchical control over proposed allocations. The analyst assigned to the department evaluates the base budget request and all decision packages. This analysis culminates in a set of preliminary recommendations to the City Manager.

The departments, the Office of Management Services, and the City Manager's Office continue refining, coordinating, and negotiating the various programs submitted through the budget process until early June.

Despite this level of centralized control, the retention of a ZBB format allows for more department-level input into the budget decisions through the alternative decision packages. Again, Fort Worth exemplifies additive implementation of the target model. The continued use of ZBB indicates that targets may be a temporary element, depending upon the presence of increased revenues.

Austin. The City of Austin, the state capital, is currently recovering from an economic downturn that began in the mid-1980's. Unemployment has decreased slightly, sales tax payments are projected to increase $3.3 million over FY 89-90, and business expansion continues. However, property values continue to fall, decreasing 2.3 percent from FY 1989-90. Even though the overall economic situation is improving, the City budget for FY 1990-91 will not benefit significantly from this recovery.

The basic budgetary system used by the City of Austin is a variation of the ZBB model. With the continuing resource constraints, Austin recently incorporated a target model as a secondary, or supplemental tool. The target is provided by the Budget Office, and is based upon the FY 1989-90 adopted budget. However, it allows for program enhancements or new services included in FY 1989-90. In Austin's system, ZBB decision packages are labeled "budget types," which document incremental increases or decreases to the base budget. Budget types are to be made up of related program components, and can be grouped for all services and associated costs to the base budget. Furthermore, types may cross "budget organizations," a newer designation for cost centers. Increases or decreases must be presented in the smallest rational incremental changes possible. A series of budget increase or decrease types related to the provision of a specific service is to be used wherever possible to present options which do not force "all or nothing" decisions. Like decision packages, budget types are to be ranked in order of priority.

Austin's budget preparation process involves four phases, described as follows:

Guidelines Phase. During this phase, the actual expenditures and revenues reported for the last fiscal year and the current fiscal year budget are entered on the budget preparation computer system from the accounting system.

Agency Phase. During the agency phase, the departments prepare an expenditure budget submittal having three components: a base budget meeting together with a specified expenditure target; a prioritized set of budget increase types; and a prioritized set of budget decrease types. The increase types are increases associated with current services not accommodated in the base budget and proposed program changes. The decrease types reduce the base budget to a specified percentage of the current approved budget.

Analysis Phase. Once received by the Budget Office, the proposed expenditure and revenue submittals are analyzed. Recommendations are made to

187

the departments and to the City management, and is used for development of the Manager's Proposed Financial Plan.

Reconciled Phase. This phase corresponds to the adoption stage of the budget cycle, in which the budget is finalized and approved by the City Council.

As noted previously, the use of a target methodology enhances centralized control of the budget process. Providing each department with a target to be met forces program decisions which may not be in line with departmental goals and objectives previously established. However, the use of 'budget types' does allow for future accommodation of needed expansion during the analysis and reconciliation phases. As with San Antonio and Fort Worth, Austin has added the target model to a foundational system.

Lubbock. In many respects, the Lubbock economic situation resembles that of the other three cities. A severe downturn connected to the Texas energy bust affected every area of West Texas, including Lubbock, resulting in increased unemployment (peaking at 6.3 percent in 1983), and decreased revenues. The City responded to the downturn by restricting expenditures, increasing collection of delinquent taxes, and deferring some capital outlays. After bottoming out, the past three years have seen some economic expansion, and current projections show continued stable growth.

Though the economic situation is similar to that of the other cities, Lubbock has not drastically altered its budgeting system during this time, making only minor technological changes. Lubbock utilizes a modified form of ZBB which also incorporates program and performance elements. The City has used ZBB for the past decade, and has recently focused upon the program and performance budget aspects for evaluation and review.

The ZBB aspect of the budgeting process can be seen in the use of three decision packages: One, a "Reduced Level Package," which is to be equal to or greater than a 15 percent reduction of the current approved budget. Two, a "Current Level Budget," which outlines the proposed plan of operations of a center and details the expenditures necessary to operate at that level. Three, an "Expanded Level Package," which can be used to propose new programs or services, expand or improve programs, request additional personnel or equipment, or other actions that will result in additional costs. Performance elements are incorporated into the Current Level Budget request as part of the justification requirements. Where program goals and objectives are quantified, department heads are asked to provide activity and performance measures. These figures are used to establish funding levels for each cost center within the department. Reduced level packages are evaluated in terms of impacts upon service delivery, and expanded packages describe additional performance measures to be used if implemented.

In terms of decision making, the use of a ZBB format allows more department level flexibility than the target approach utilized by the other three municipalities. Though final approval lies in the hands of the City Manager (and ultimately the Council), the decision packages prepare an agenda for reconciliation between administrative revenue constraints and departmental expenditure needs.

Comparative Assessment

This section examines the assessment of model implementation. Table 1 is a matrix for comparing the systems used by the four cities. Obviously, the use of ZBB as the primary model dominates the budgetary structures of the cities examined here. It demonstrates the flexibility of the model and its applicability for local use. Only the largest of the cities, San Antonio, utilizes another model (performance) as a basis for budgeting. However, the presence of tremendous deficits has resulted in new pressures on the budgetary systems, with a similar reaction by the governments - three of the affected cities have added a target model to address this constraint.

TABLE 1
Implementation of the Models

City	Primary Model	Additional Model(s)
San Antonio	Performance	Target
Fort Worth	Zero Base	Target
Austin	Zero Base	Target
Lubbock	Zero Base	Program/Performance

As stated previously, the resource constraint represents the primary situational variable. Though a model may be capable of addressing limited revenues, the manner of implementation may preclude its effectiveness. The experience of the three largest cities examined supports this supposition. Rather than expanding or modifying the (then) current system, they added a secondary or supplementary model - in each case a target system.

Figure 1 is a diagrammatic representation of the models as implemented by the four cities. It is designed to express the influence of each system as well as the interrelationships between the models.

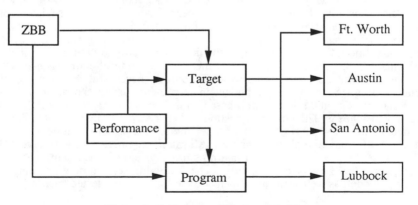

Figure 1. Influence of Budget Models

For three of these cities, the basic mode for requesting revenues is 'filtered' through an allocation target or ceiling. Despite the presence of adequate justification through effectiveness measures, performance measures, or high prioritization, the final decision is largely determined by the previous ceiling. For the fourth city, Lubbock, certain program and performance measures are used in conjunction with decision packages to justify requests, which also provides a secondary filter.

These observations support two distinct, yet interdependent conclusions: one, no single model has been created that suits every local situation; and two, none of the models have been implemented so as to adequately address all of the constraints of any of these cities. These conclusions are not an indictment of either the governments or the models, only observations regarding the difficulties of implementation. These matters are addressed more fully in the conclusion, but let us first assess these budget practices from a normative perspective.

Levels of Implementation: A Normative Assessment

Simply comparing the implementation of budget management tools by these cities will not provide a correct assessment of the value of the models. To compare the unique circumstances of City A to those of City B will not answer the question, "Who has done a better job with a budgeting tool?" Instead, it is wiser to examine the models, evaluating their strengths and weaknesses in terms of certain fixed criteria. The question one can ask is, "Has City A chosen the best model to meet its local constraints, in terms of these criteria?" If the chosen model's strengths are well-suited to that city's needs, then the implementation will be relatively successful.

The following criteria have been used as standards for evaluating the models: economy, efficiency, and effectiveness. Though many other criteria could have been included, these criteria were chosen because they represent the most important 'success gauges' in the public sector, where (for the most part) profit is not the 'bottom line.'[11] However, to the degree that program outcomes and costs are quantifiable, these criteria provide the most meaningful comparisons. Thus, budget systems must be selected which encourage 'successful' program selection and funding. Since no single budget management system can meet all of the criteria, cities should select models based on their relative strengths, in light of the community needs. The ultimate question is, "Has each city implemented the best model(s) for its situation?" If the proper model has not been implemented, no amount of 'massaging' will enable the system to operate effectively. This reinforces the previous assertion that no single system can be a panacea for the budgeting ills of every municipality. The following section now examines the various models as well as the implementation in light of the selected criteria.

190

Performance Budgeting

A performance budget is clearly *efficiency-oriented*, which is the most common criterion for economic evaluation of programs. In operational terms, efficiency means maximizing the use of resources. Thus, a more efficient program will produce a greater level of benefits from the same dollars than a less efficient one. From a more formal policy perspective, Nagel defines efficiency as "the ratio of benefits achieved to costs incurred."[12] This criterion is particularly important when comparing competing options with quantifiable measures. In terms of a budget management system, an efficiency-oriented model should provide justification requirements that measure program efficiency. In other words, the model ought to force unit managers to calculate costs and measurable benefits for every program, so that upper level management can compare the options.

The use of performance measures and per unit costs provide decision makers the necessary information to evaluate programs in terms of efficiency. When various departmental budgets are compared, performance measures will indicate where the smallest amount of resources are producing maximum outcomes. Of course, a performance budget is not well-suited for those programs where outcomes cannot be quantified. Unlike ZBB, there is no consideration of the qualitative factors or the political necessity of continuing certain programs regardless of cost.

By selecting a performance model, coupled with a target element, San Antonio appears committed to programs that are efficient yet least expensive. This combination of models signifies a desire to reduce costs, even at the expense of valuable social services. Indeed, upon examining the current financial condition of the city, one finds it is attempting to emerge from a significant deficit situation. At stake is the survival of essential government services, though other good programs may suffer.

Perhaps the question should be asked, "Could the performance model have been adapted to serve the immediate needs of San Antonio?" Only those within the city itself can respond appropriately to that question. However, it seems that San Antonio's situation speaks more about the model than about those implementing it. As we stated before, the performance model is "labor intensive," that is, it requires massive amounts of time and many personnel to effectively implement it. Restricting budget requests (a form of cutback management) through a target model effectively revamps the goals of departments in preparing budgets. Establishing a ceiling prevents wasting time justifying programs that cannot be expanded or in some cases implemented. Clearly, San Antonio has retained the strengths of the basic performance system, while dealing with the urgent situation at hand through the addition of targets.

Zero-Base Budgeting

ZBB is perhaps the most difficult model to categorize, because its strength is flexibility. Yet, in terms of the criteria used here, ZBB has a strong *effectiveness-orientation*. This criterion contrasts with economy, for it asks how well a policy meets its objectives.[13] This is usually expressed in relation to program costs as cost effectiveness, even though the outcomes may not be monetary.[14] For that reason, cost effectiveness is often used to compare competing programs with similar goals and outcomes that cannot be reduced to monetary terms. A budgeting model that is effectiveness-oriented will enhance selection of the most effective programs, even though some others may be less costly.

As originally conceived and subsequently operationalized in the public sector, ZBB is well-suited for comparing the effectiveness of programs. The use of decision packages and ranking techniques provides managers with the mechanisms to meaningfully compare programs.

Lubbock's use of ZBB principles for determining proper program expansion has helped it emerge from the doldrums of the mid-eighties in a healthy posture. Through the use of effectiveness measures, budget increases have encouraged the emergence of better programs. Furthermore, the justification requirements inherent in the creation of decision packages has forced departments to evaluate their objectives. Though the purpose of ZBB is not to 'start from scratch,' this annual justification of programs reinforces the vision of management. The result is a clearer picture of governmental goals on the part of lower level decision makers, which can be communicated to all employees.

Target Budgeting

The entire focus of a target budget is to provide an appropriation ceiling, which is at the core of the *economy perspective*. A target budget does not address how well the program reaches its goals, or whether another program might reach a higher priority goal. It is a 'bottom line' approach to government spending, which often characterizes the concerns of constituencies.

In today's world, everyone is 'economy minded,' which refers to the most inexpensive route to reach a goal. As Rehfuss notes, economy is a powerful political term, which speaks of the lowest possible cost.[16] This can refer to lower monetary costs or savings of time and resources. This criterion ignores the relative value of a policy (results), considering only its costs. While efficiency is generally expressed as a ratio, economy simply compares the absolute costs of various programs.

As discussed earlier, three of the cities are currently using a target approach as a secondary model. San Antonio's use of targets is clearly motivated by a serious fiscal crisis, which demanded quick action. The use of targets ensures compliance with the overall governmental goal of restricted spending. Fort Worth, like San Antonio, has also faced a serious revenue shortfall. Furthermore, Fort Worth has responded to this problem in a similar manner, by implementing a target model. It is apparent that targets have been set to prevent unrealistic requests which waste valuable budget preparation time. Departments are fully aware when justifying their budgets that only the highest priority decision packages face any chance of approval; thus, managers will carefully weigh their choices. The final city using targets, Austin, seems to be using the model for a slightly different reason. Rather than a ceiling, the targets appear to represent a reasonable range of alternatives for which to strive. Additional justification through the ZBB format may permit increased allocations beyond the original target.

192

Program Budgeting

In terms of the model, a program budget does not address any of these criteria. In implementing the model, elements can be included to reflect efficiency, effectiveness, or economy. However, such justification measures would be an indication of dysfunction, not simply an adaptation. To add efficiency measures to a program budget results in a performance budget, while adding effectiveness measures would overlap the boundaries of ZBB. Of course, no model is completely distinct from the others; they must all reflect the various budget stages and be flexible enough to be implemented in the real world. However, a program budget is more a reorganized/expanded line-item budget rather than a new budget philosophy.

The additional use of a program structure by Lubbock provides a logical network for budget coordination. Where overlap exists among services offered, this structure can assist management in addressing the issue. Furthermore, the elements of a program budget are complementary to the ZBB format. The program budget does not hinder the creation of decision packages, and can be helpful in formulating decision units.

Each of the four cities have modified their basic budgeting structure through the addition of a secondary model. For the three largest municipalities, this was borne out of an urgent financial crisis, and they responded with the most economy-oriented model, a target system. However, the limitations of the target model are apparent. None of the governments replaced their original system, for a budget ceiling does not enhance either effectiveness or efficiency.[17] Since targets do not provide justification for programs, these cities retained a basic system which does. The presence of extreme fiscal constraint resulted in a spending lid; relaxation of that constraint may remove it. Municipal governments recognize that targets do not provide the most effective or efficient services; whether they continue such ceilings is highly speculative.

Conclusion

In conclusion, many lessons can be learned from the practices of these cities, if we look carefully. Though each community faces a unique set of circumstances, numerous valuable principles are applicable wherever budgeting takes place. The following observations, based upon the experiences of the four governments, provide some food for thought.

The budget management system selected is modified to fit local needs. No 'canned' approach is truly feasible; no model can be transferred from theory to reality without adaptation. Each of these cities has varied the models to some degree, yet all have retained the crucial elements. Thus, one observes that the models utilized are sufficiently flexible to permit effective implementation in 'real world' settings.

Old models are not replaced, but are incrementally adapted to new models, and vice versa. The experiences of these four cities support the notion that incrementalism still thrives at the local level. Fine-tuning is far more prevalent than systemic overhauls. Even in the face of extreme deficits, the new model has been molded to the existing system, rather than replacing it completely. Change is more fluid and less dramatic, reflecting the human dislike for extreme reorganization. Systems that are familiar will be adapted to meet most needs, with the use of additional models when necessary.

No model appears capable of responding to all the demands of every local government. As stated previously, no 'supermodel' has emerged which can handle every constraint. Though ZBB is extremely flexible, the volatile economic climate of some metropolitan areas may force additional model implementation. This is the testimony of two Texas cities, which added budget targets to their ZBB structure.

Along with these observations, certain future trends appear to be fairly certain. One, there will be continued expansion of model adaptation and addition. The 'stand pat' philosophy will go by the wayside, as cities seek to prepare for uncertainty and fiscal constraints. Old systems may be stretched beyond repair, if not continuously adapted to reflect current circumstances. If that happens, newer models may be added to deal with fiscal stress. Yet, some vestiges of the old system will probably remain, due to the natural resistance to change.

Two, there will be continued focus upon both effectiveness and efficiency. Budgetary systems which allow both criteria to be satisfied will be used, as cities seek to offer better and more efficient services. Currently, ZBB offers the most promise in this regard, though other models may be adapted to answer this challenge.

The cumulative impact of this assessment is fairly straightforward: even the best models cannot solve all of the financial woes of a community. To select a system because it is 'all the rage' will not guarantee proper budgeting; only the correct evaluation of the constraints, followed by a thoughtful review of the available models will prepare management for success. In the final analysis, however, even the right model will not work if it is not implemented properly. This means molding the system to the circumstances, not vice versa. To put it another way, measure the feet before you buy the shoes, because they may not fit. Wise is the city manager who remembers this lesson when facing pressure to "do something" about the budget.

Notes

1. This is the thesis of V.O. Key in his article, "The Lack of a Budgetary Theory," *American Political Science Review*, 34 (December, 1940): 1137-40.
2. Fremont J. Lyden and Marc Lindenberg, *Public Budgeting in Theory and Practice*. New York: Longman, 1983.
3. Ibid., 69.

4. Texas Municipal League, Budget Manual For Texas Cities. Austin: Texas Municipal League, 1983: 46.

5. Graeme M. Taylor, "Introduction to Zero-Base Budgeting," in Thomas D. Lynch (ed.), *Contemporary Public Budgeting*. New Brunswick: Transaction Books, 1981.

6. Ibid., 7.

7. Ibid., 5.

8. Gloria A. Grizzle, "Five Great Issues in Budgeting and Financial Management," in J. Rabin (ed.), *Handbook of Public Administration*, New York: Marcel Dekker, 1989: 200-201.

9. This term, which is widely used in program evaluation literature, refers to the range of programs which are politically acceptable to the constituency. For a fuller discussion, see P. H. Rossi and H. E. Freeman, *Evaluation: A Systematic Approach*, 4th ed. Newbury Park: Sage Publications, 1989: 418ff.

10. Daniel K. Wanamaker, "ZBB is Light-Years Away from Rural America," in Thomas D. Lynch (ed.), *Contemporary Public Budgeting*. New Brunswick: Transaction Books, 1981.

11. For a fuller discussion of additional criteria, see William N. Dunn, *Public Policy Analysis: An Introduction*. Englewood Cliffs, NJ: Prentice-Hall, 1981: chs. 7 and 9.

12. Stuart S. Nagel, *Public Policy: Goals, Means, and Methods*. New York: St. Martin's Press, 1984: 33.

13. Nagel, op. cit., 33.

14. Rossi and Freeman, p. 377.

15. John Rehfuss, *The Job of Public Manager*. Chicago: Dorsey Press, 1989: 12.

16. Grizzle, op. cit., 217.

BUDGET PRESENTATION: NORMATIVE CRITERIA VS. ACTUAL PRACTICE

Robert C. Rickards

The term "budget presentation" means different things to different people. Nowadays, it can connote a multimedia display mounted by a government finance director to introduce the executive's draft to councilmembers and the public. Traditionally, though, the "budget presentation" refers to the budget document itself.

Typically, a budget document has a cover, table of contents, governmental organization charts, a transmittal letter, financial summaries, statements of goals and objectives, divider pages, revenue estimates, departmental and activity budgets, program budget summaries, performance measurements, enterprise and internal service fund reports, capital outlay plans, special analyses, accompanying documents, reader's guide, and explanations of budgetary preparation and adoption procedures. These components of a budget presentation are important because of their usefulness in explaining an administration's policies to legislative officials and the public.

This chapter introduces a set of normative criteria the Government Finance Officers Association (GFOA) thinks budgetmakers ought to meet. It uses the criteria to evaluate a large number of budget presentations made by Texas cities during the 1980s. It analyzes the presentations' specific strengths and weaknesses, and examines them for evidence of systematic variation in their quality. The chapter concludes with several suggestions for sharply narrowing the gap between normative criteria and current budgetary presentation practices.

Budget Presentation And Budgetmakers' Common Concerns

All municipal finance directors have at least four major concerns about formulating and explaining their budgets: 1) they must produce, on a timely basis, a draft budget meeting state statutory requirements to balance current expenditures with current revenues; 2) they strive to improve the general level of city government management, while 3) insuring that top officials maintain control of city policies; and 4) they also try to raise the level of budgetary debate both within government and among members of the general public.[1]

In addressing these concerns, budgetmakers (often unwittingly) assume a moral responsibility because they effectively define reality for most people. They do so by describing the status of city government in terms of its revenues and expenditures, classifying them by source and activity. Better budgets furthermore describe such activities and what they accomplish.[2]

The extent of a city's reliance on various income sources, together with the amount of its expenditures on different activities, constitutes a statement of policy preferences. Those preferences may reflect the particular tastes of a few individual decisionmakers. Or they may represent a set of collective choices arrived at through complex bargaining among numerous officials.

Regardless of whose preferences they may reflect, the budget commits city government financially to pursuing certain policies. It, therefore, is indeed a work plan with a dollar sign attached.[3] However, some budgets are more than that. They include and carefully use workload statistics, performance accounting, and evaluation standards and thus serve as instruments of good management too.

Budgetmakers' responsibility to define reality in this fashion is especially important in democratic governments, where the main purpose of the budget system is accountability. Voters hold city council accountable through the electoral system. At the same time, city council holds executive agencies accountable by reviewing their budgets, setting the appropriation levels people want, and letting agency heads know, through statements of legislative intent, how people want their money spent. Hence, it is crucial for budgetmakers not only to define reality accurately, but to communicate their definition to city councilmembers and voters effectively.

Unfortunately, though, public budgets are mysterious documents to most people, including government officials. People are aware that chief executives propose budgets to legislative bodies. They also know that these bodies then make decisions on taxes and how much money to allocate various programs. If they work in government, people may even know about materials prepared to "justify" the budget, and detailed controls which frequently prohibit simple management decisions. Yet anyone meeting regularly with councilmembers or the general public soon gains the impression that few of them really understand their respective city budgets.

Why People Don't Understand Public Budgets

If scholarly descriptions of the budgetary process are correct, this lack of understanding is not surprising. The literature emphasizes the dominant role of executive branch experts in the budget formulation process. That has crucial

197

implications for the nature of their work. Because they do not run for popular election, they are better insulated from the external pressures than councilmembers are. The pressures felt by executive branch experts at budget preparation time instead come mostly from the need to make thousands of individual expenditures decisions before the next fiscal year begins. Moreover, they must make these myriad decisions in such a way that the sum of planned expenditures does not exceed anticipated revenue. In other words, they must propose a balanced budget.

So the executive's experts tend to focus their thinking on things to be bought and to ignore potentially controversial considerations like policy issues and service levels. That means they concentrate their attention on numbers representing various amounts of money, but spend relatively little time interpreting the numbers' policy significance for the budget's readers.

To aid themselves in reaching resource allocation decisions, the executive's experts supposedly rely heavily on a few simple rules, rather than observed changes in external conditions.[4] Lacking a better alternative, they begin by accepting "historical precedents" as a guide for recommending how to allocate anticipated revenue. Thus, their initial estimate of an administrative unit's expenditures next year usually is the same amount authorized for it in the current year.

Next the executive's expert adjusts most estimates on a "fixed-percentage, across-the-board" basis. This procedure "satisfices" the administrative units' spending demands, while assuring that a balanced budget is attainable. It does so by providing each unit with a "fair share" of the projected net addition to municipal revenue. Guaranteed an incremental allocation above its expenditure "base," every unit can carry on and expand its activities. Maintaining most administrative units' "fair share" avoids creating many "winners" or "losers," and thus minimizes dissatisfaction among participants in the budgetary process.

Finally, the comptroller forwards the marginally adjusted, balanced budget draft to the chief executive, who formally proposes it to city council. Due to the periodic necessity of standing for election, councilmembers are more directly exposed to environmental influences than the executive branch's experts. Yet environmental influences scarcely affect resource allocation decisions because council seldom alters the chief executive's proposed budget much.

The reason for council's minimal budget impact arise from the line-item format of most city budgets and a legislature's inherent disadvantages in handling fiscal matters. First, line-item budgets direct the reader's attention to relatively unemotional subjects such as salaries, travel, and supplies. When the chief executive recommends funding changes, they occur at the margins. Hence, the line-item formats tends to limit budgetary debate rather than raising its level. That allows the chief executive to avoid wholesale policy revisions and the battles with council likely to accompany them.

In addition, councilmembers typically are part-time officials, who receive modest salaries at best. Consequently, they have little time for revising the thousands of spending recommendations made by the executive. Councilmembers also lack in-depth financial expertise and adequate staff support to interpret budget numbers for themselves. These inadequacies severely handicap council's various finance subcommittees. They therefore confine their efforts mainly to checking for blatant errors and omissions in the chief executive's draft.

Statutory balanced budget requirements encourage such behavior. Accordingly, no proposal to increase expenditures for a line-item above the chief executive's recommendation can stand alone. Instead, a second proposal either decreasing another item's allocation or increasing taxes must accompany it. But neither option can be chosen without causing a fight over which items (whose taxes) to decrease (increase). As a part-time official, with little financial expertise, a councilman has slim prospects for winning such a struggle. So, sooner or later, council approves the chief executive's spending plan largely as submitted.

Of course, the general public is even less well-equipped to consider the executive's budget proposals than councilmembers are. Voters simply have less time and expertise, and no staff with which to analyze public budgets. Thus, budgets really are unfathomable enigmas to most people -- a situation which seriously weakens the democratic principles of government accountability.

GFOA Criteria And Texan Cities Studied

Besides viewing budgets as communication devices, the GFOA also sees them as policy documents, financial guides, and operations guides. In evaluating annual budget presentations, members of the GFOA's Special Review Committee therefore uses a checklist divided into four sections, each corresponding to one of the functions just mentioned. The individual sections contain from 15 to 12 normative criteria that budgetmakers ought to meet, as well as a general rating for the entire section. Table 1 displays the criteria on this checklist.

GFOA reviewers use a five-point scale to grade budget presentations on each criterion. The scores range from 1 (very weak), through 2 (marginal), 3 (acceptable), and 4 (distinctive), to 5 (exemplary). In addition, they are grouped into three categories: 1 and 2 (does not satisfy criteria); 3 and 4 (proficient); and 5 (especially notable). The standard for proficient documentation is the thoughtful presentation of information by financial professionals for the benefit of the budget's readers. While the checklist can be helpful to budgetmakers in preparing their own presentations, its use does not guarantee that an applicant will earn one of the GFOA's prestigious certificates of proficiency. A sufficient number of low scores in one sections, or throughout the whole checklist, very well may disqualify an applicant.

The study reported in this chapter employed a slightly modified version of the GFOA checklist. The modification made was the introduction of a 0 score (missing) for budgets altogether failing to address a given criterion. Otherwise the rating scale used here was identical to the GFOA's.

TABLE 1
Criteria for the GFOA's Distinguished Budget Presentation Awards Program
----

Section 1: Budget as a Policy Document

1. The budget should include a coherent statement of budgetary policies. These may take the form of goals and objectives, strategies and other mechanisms.

2. The document should explain the budgeting process. If not, the attached application material *must*.

3. The document should describe and articulate basic policy changes. Explain the substantive impact of policy changes on operations, service levels and/or finances.

3. The rationale for the policies should be explained.

4. The budget document should explain how policies (particularly new policies and revised policies) will be implemented and monitored.

Section 2: Budget as a Financial Plan

1. The budget should explain the financial structure and operations of the government. It should explain major revenue sources, how funds are organized, etc.

2. All operating funds and all resources should be included in the financial plans provided in the budget. This need not mean that all activity be subject to an appropriation budget, but rather should provide for deliberate financial planning of governmental activity.

3. The budget document should include projections of the government's financial condition at the end of the proposed fiscal year.

4. The budget document should explain any conditions, or projected events, that require changes in operations in order to ensure financial stability or solvency.

5. The budget should include projections of current year financial activity, and provide a basis for historical comparisons (e.g., last year, this year, next year).

6. The budget should include both an operating and capital financing element. If a separate capital program exists, the operating budget should explain the relationship between the two documents.

7. The budget should include a consolidated picture of all operations and financing activity, in condensed or aggregated form.

8. The budget should be prepared in such a way that budgetary performance can be measured and accounted for.

9. The budget should address debt management issues, particularly those that affect current and future operations.

10. The budget should explain its basis, whether GAAP, cash, modified accrual, or some other statutory basis.

Section 3: Budget as an Operations Guide

1. The budget should explain the relationship between organizational units and programs, where appropriate.

2. The budget should include an organizational chart, descriptions of work force organization (e.g., personnel count comparisons) and sufficient data regarding past operations to provide a basis for comparison.

3. The budget should explain how capital spending decisions will affect operations and operating expenditures.

4. The budget should provide specific objectives and performance measures/targets. If appropriate, timetables and deadlines should be included.

200

5. The budget should describe the general directions given to departmental heads or line managers. This could be accomplished through:
- goals and objectives
- reorganizations
- statements of functions
- appropriation or staffing limits
- delegation of authority or
- other methods that clarify the responsibility of managers or supervisors.

Section 4: Budget as a Communication Device

1. The budget document should be available to the public in some draft form prior to governing body action.
2. The document should provide summary information suitable for use by the media and the public.
3. The document should avoid complex technical language that cannot be understood by the reasonably informed reader.
4. The document should include a transmittal letter or a budget message that outlines key policies, strategies, etc.
5. The document should provide a table of contents and/or an index.
6. A glossary of key terms is recommended.
7. Basic units of the budget, whether they be funds, programs, departments, or whatever, should be concisely explained.
8. Simple charts and graphs should be used to highlight key relationships. Interpretation is needed to explain the graphs.
9. The document should disclose sources of revenue. Explain assumptions underlying the revenue estimates and highlight key revenue trends.
10. The budget document (or the application material) should explain the procedure to be used for amending the budget during the coming fiscal year.
11. Related financial and operational activity should be cross-classified or cross-indexed to assist the lay reader.
12. Statistical and supplemental data should be included in an appendix or throughout the text.

After a training period to familiarize themselves with the modified checklist, two reviewers evaluated recent budget presentations from 68 Texas cities. These cities included virtually all the state's major population centers. Their total 1980 population of 7.7 million included 54.2% of all Texans.[5] The study thus is highly representative of the budgeting systems in place where most Texans live.

Table 2 displays summary statistics describing the cities and budgets covered by the study. As shown in that table, the average city studied had a 1980 population of 111,865. In addition, the average budget presentation evaluated was for the 1987-1988 fiscal year, called for total spending of $103,926,723, or $995.79 per capita, and 241 pages long. Also noteworthy is the large amount of variation around each mean value.

201

TABLE 2
Summary Statistics Describing Texas Cities and their Recent Budget Presentations

Variable	N	Mean	Standard Deviation	Minimum	Maximum
1980 Population	68	111,865	238,846	1,511	1,595,138
Presentation Year	68	1987.28	1.96	1981	1989
Budgeted Spending	68	$103,926,723	$225,739,016	$452,514	$1,116,988,613
Spending Per Capita	68	$995.79	$1,292.31	$88.59	$9,088.76
Presentation Length	68	240.66	223.09	17	999

Budget Presentation Ratings And Analysis

At first, the two reviewers worked independently in evaluating budget presentations. After completing their evaluations, they compared scores and reconciled any differences. They then entered the reconciled scores into a computer data bank for analysis. Table 3 and Figures 1 and 2 report the distribution of reconciled, section and overall scores, together with their mean and standard deviation across all 68 city budgets.

As Table 3 reveals, the mean overall score is 3.26, which indicates that the average city's budget presentation scores somewhat higher than "acceptable" on the 5-point rating scale. The same is true for mean scores on three of the four sections: policy document (3.33); financial plan (3.51); and operations guide (3.37). Only the mean score for the budget as a communication device (2.97) falls, just barely, below the acceptability point. So, on average, municipal budget presentations in Texas appear to be "acceptably proficient."

A close look at individual criterion scores reveals the things the average budget presentation does best. Its highest scores are for: projecting current year spending (4.67); having table of contents and indices (4.13); showing all operating funds (4.10), and giving revenue projections and the assumptions behind them (4.03). It also does very well in providing consolidated financial statements (3.97); summary information (3.96); budget performance measures (3.96); letters of transmittal (3.93); general operations guidelines (3.77); projected year-end financial condition (3.74); organization charts and performance data (3.71); and statements of budget policies (3.71).

Unfortunately, though, Table 3 points to several serious shortcomings as well. To begin with, budget presentations score best as financial plans (3.51), then as operating guides (3.37) and policy documents (3.31), while scoring worst as communicating devices (2.97). That means they are most beneficial to budgetmaking "insiders," whose technical expertise can compensate for the presentations' less than "exemplary" communication of information. Likewise,

202

TABLE 3
Summary Statistics Describing Section and Overall Scores for Texas Cities' Budget Presentation

Variable	N	Mean	Standard Deviation	Minimum	Maximum
Presentation as a Policy Document	68	3.33	1.38	0.00	5.00
Presentation as a Financial Plan	68	3.51	0.91	1.30	5.00
Presentation as an Operations Guide	68	3.37	1.48	0.40	5.00
Presentation as a Communication Device	68	2.97	1.14	0.67	4.83
Overall Presentation (Weighted)	68	3.29	1.16	0.68	4.89
Overall Presentation (Unweighted)	68	3.26	1.09	0.83	4.89

they are least beneficial to "outsiders" (e.g., city councilmembers and voters), who lack such expertise.

In Table 3, one can see there is great variation around the overall and section means. That variation is apparent at first glance in Figures 1 and 2. Figure 2a shows the distribution of overall scores resulting from summing the individual criteria scores and dividing by 32. This overall score weights the communication and financial plan functions most heavily, because there are more criteria in these two checklist sections. In the distribution, 23 presentations are in the range between "distinctive" and "exemplary," but 20 others are below the "acceptable" level.

Figure 2b depicts another distribution of overall scores. In calculating them, the four section scores were added and divided by four. Hence, these overall scores reflect equal weighting of each section. The shape of the distribution, though, is not much different from the one in Figure 2a. Although 25 of the 68 presentations here are in the range between "distinctive" and "exemplary," 20 others still fall below the "acceptable" level.

Similar variations in quality are apparent in Figures 1a - d. As policy documents, 31 budgets are "distinctive" or better and 19 less than "acceptable." For budgets as financial plans, the numbers are 27 and 19, respectively. As operations guides, they are 33 and 18. But as communications devices, just 16 are in the "distinctive" range and none are "exemplary," while 35 are less than "acceptable."

Another close look at the individual criteria scores pinpoints the things done least well in the average budget presentation. The lowest scores are for: the

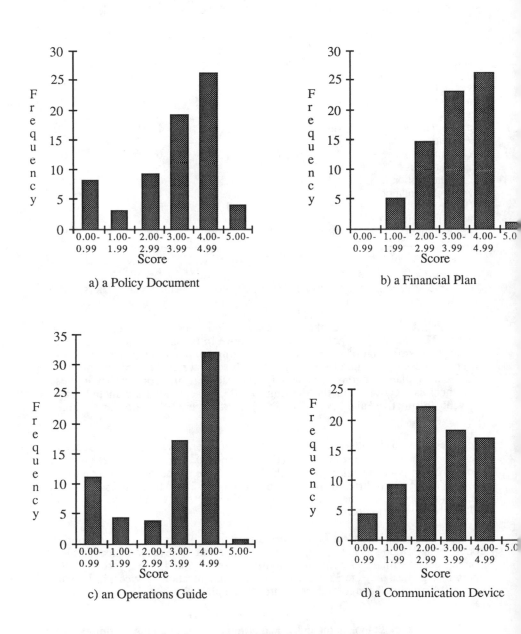

FIGURE 1
Distribution of City Scores for Budget Presentation

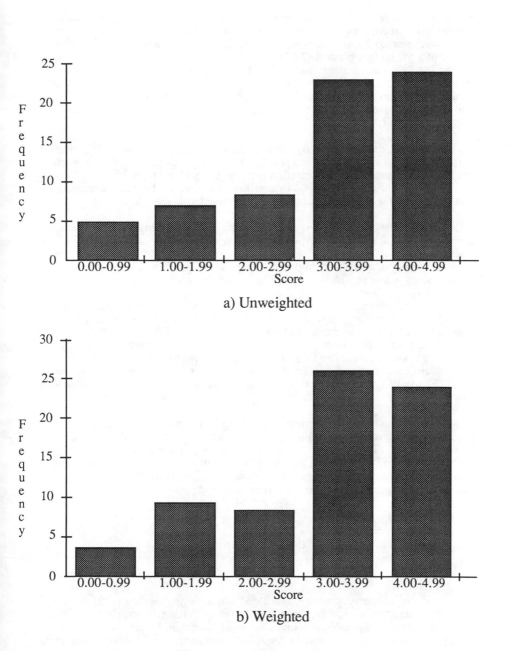

a) Unweighted

b) Weighted

FIGURE 2
Distribution of City Scores for Overall Budget Presentation

205

glossary of terms (1.17); specifying the accounting basis (1.68); and explaining budget amendment procedures (1.77). Less than "acceptable" scores also go to: crosslisting related financial activities (2.15); easily read graphs and charts (2.44); explaining the budget process (2.62); discussing capital spending impacts (2.68); addressing debt management issues (2.68); making budget drafts available to the public (2.77); and statistical and supplementary data (2.83). Every one of these shortcomings leaves budgets harder for councilmembers and voters to understand and thereby weakens the ability of such "outsiders" to hold executive agencies accountable.

Thus far, the analysis shows that municipal budget presentation in Texas do some things well and other things poorly. However, it does not indicate whether the observed variation in presentation quality is systematic. A bit of additional analysis, though, reveals several interesting associations between presentation quality and certain characteristics of the cities studied.

First, 1980 population size and budgeted spendings are moderately associated ($r = .38$ and $.43$, respectively) with one criterion, disclosing revenue sources and the assumptions made in projecting revenue trends. That implies cities with larger populations and higher total spending tend to make better budget presentations in this regard.

Second, presentation year correlates with scores for: explaining the rationale for policies, policy implementation and monitoring, and the financial structure and operations of government; including all operating funds in financial plans; projecting year-end financial conditions; providing a glossary of key terms; disclosing revenue sources and assumptions made in projecting revenue trends; and using statistical and supplementary data. All the above correlations are in the range from .30 to .38. Apparently, there is a weak trend for budget presentations to improve in these respects over time.

Third, the budget document's page length is significantly related to every one of the normative criteria, with most of the correlation values falling in the range from .35 to .45. This variable's general importance is not at all surprising. By including more of the requisite information to be clearer policy statements, better financial plans, more accurate operations guides, and more effective communication devices, budget presentations necessarily become longer.

Suggestions For Improvement

Be that as it may, greater length alone will not improve the overall quality of budget presentations. Surely, there is no point in further festooning them with unusable statistics, inadequate bridges between capital and operating budgets, or overly-long sentences written in polysyllabic "bureaucratese." City governments should devote their scarce resources only to those budgetmaking efforts likely to yield meaningful additions to current presentation documents.

206

Fortunately, remedying 7 of the 10 shortcomings cited above ought not to be an input-intensive task. One merely need to include a glossary of terms, specify the presentation's accounting basis, explain the budget process and amendment procedure, discuss capital spending impacts and debt management issues, and furnish draft budgets to the public. With just a little effort in these areas, budgetmakers could improve the overall quality of their presentations dramatically.

Improvement in the three remaining areas, crosslisting financial activities, creating easily read graphs and charts, and publishing useful statistical and supplementary data, admittedly will require greater efforts. In making them, budget officers should keep in mind their responsibility to produce readable interpretations of the information presented. Many presentations still read like accounting reports, with much of the text and numbers unintelligible to anyone except the persons preparing them. In this regard, councilmembers and voters no doubt would welcome the use of shorter sentences, clearer language, and more active verbs.

Beyond such recommendations, there are no universal prescriptions guaranteed to transform "very weak" presentations into "exemplary" ones, The problems emerging in any city's environment create unique presentations tailored to those unique requirements that separates budgetary mastercraftsmen from their less-skilled colleagues. As in any craft, one can learn helpful lessons by studying the work of better budgetmakers. The best budgets covered by this study contain a number of useful alternatives for meeting various requirements. Those budgets are at the top of the list of (weighted) presentation scores displayed in Table 4. Although published in 1982 and therefore slightly dated, *Effective Budget Presentations: The Cutting Edge* remains another source of good examples, which many Texas cities still might want to emulate.

Conclusion

On average, budget presentations by cities in Texas are better than "acceptable." Indeed they serve some budgetary purposes quite well, particularly financial planning. However, there is great variation in the presentations' overall quality, with almost 30% of the budgets reviewed falling short of the GFOA standards for acceptability. The most common shortcomings have to do with the budget's function as a communication device. These shortcomings are particularly serious because they limit "outsiders'" understanding of executive agencies' operations and thus the agencies' accountability for their actions.

Budgetmakers can remedy the bulk of the shortcomings cited here rather easily, though, simply by expanding their presentations to include more relevant materials. Numerous good examples showing alternative ways to present such materials are widely available. Councilmembers and voters should insist that chief executives use those good examples to improve their own budget presentations.

TABLE 4
Individual Overall Scores for City Budget Presentation in Texas

Rank	Score	City	Year	Rank	Score	City	Year
1	4.89	Ft. Worth	1988-89	35	3.46	Groves	1988-89
2	4.83	Plano	1986-87	36	3.37	Tyler	1988-89
3	4.54	Bellaire	1988-89	37	3.34	Amarillo	1987-88
4	4.54	San Marcos	1988-89	38	3.34	Longview	1984-85
5	4.51	Abilene	1987-88	39	3.29	Bryan	1988-89
6	4.49	Mesquite	1988-89	40	3.26	Midland	1987-88
7	4.46	Grand Prairie	1988-89	41	3.26	Brownweed	1987-88
8	4.34	Irving	1988-89	42	3.23	Beaumont	1982-83
9	4.29	Garland	1988-89	43	3.20	Texarkana	1987-88
10	4.26	Plainview	1986-87	44	3.20	Port Arthur	1987-88
11	4.26	Corpus Christi	1987-88	45	3.20	Edinburg	1986-87
12	4.26	Greenville	1987-88	46	3.17	Wichita Falls	1987-88
13	4.20	Lubbock	1987-88	47	3.14	Bedford	1985-86
14	4.20	Galveston	1988-89	48	3.14	Pasadena	1987-88
15	4.17	El Paso	1987-88	49	3.06	NewBraunfels	1987-88
16	4.17	San Antonio	1987-88	50	2.91	Victoria	1983-84
17	4.14	Dallas	1987-88	51	2.69	Waco	1988-89
18	4.09	Big Spring	1987-88	52	2.60	Baytown	1987-88
19	4.09	Sea Brook	1982-83	53	2.54	Round Rock	1982-83
20	4.09	Ennis	1987-88	54	2.29	Lockhart	1987-88
21	4.06	Sundown	1988-89	55	2.26	Richardson	1987-88
22	4.03	Odessa	1987-88	56	2.26	Brownsville	1987-88
23	4.00	Carrelton	1986-87	57	2.17	Universal City	1987-88
24	3.94	Austin	1988-89	58	1.89	Temple	1987-88
25	3.89	Cleburne	1987-88	59	1.80	San Angelo	1986-87
26	3.89	Harlingen	1984-85	60	1.80	Georgetown	1984-85
27	3.86	Orange	1988-89	61	1.74	Weslaco	1987-88
28	3.86	Denison	1987-88	62	1.40	Raymondville	1987-88
29	3.86	Addison	1987-88	63	1.34	Andrews	1985-86
30	3.83	Arlington	1988-89	64	1.26	Laredo	Sept. 87
31	3.71	Alice	1980-81	65	1.03	Llano	1983-84
32	3.69	Gainesville	1988-89	66	1.03	Texas City	1986-87
33	3.66	Duncanville	1987-88	67	0.94	Jasper	1981
34	3.63	Houston	1984-85	68	0.94	Nacogdoches	1987-88

Notes

1. For a discussion of the latter three concerns, see T.D. Lynch, *Public Budgeting in America* (3rd edition). Englewood Cliffs, NJ: Prentice-Hall, Inc., 1985: 103.

2. R.D. Lee, Jr., and R.W. Johnson, *Public Budgeting Systems* (3rd edition). Baltimore, MD: University Park Press, 1983: 3.

3. Sydney Duncombe cited in Lynch, op. cit., 3.

4. See J.P. Crecine, *Governmental Problem-Solving: A Computer Simulation of Municipal Budgeting*. Chicago, Il: Rand McNally, 1969: 69-98; and Aaron Wildavsky, *Budgeting: A Comparative Theory of Budgetary Processes*. Boston, MA: Little, Brown Co., 1975: 220-9.

5. Bureau of Census, U.S. Department of Commerce, *1980 Census of Population and Housing: Summary Characteristics for Governmental Units and Standard Metropolitan Statistical Areas TEXAS*. Washington, DC. U.S. Government Printing Office, 1982: 1-18.

6. Girard Miller (compiler), *Effective Budgetary Presentation: The Cutting Edge*. Chicago, Il: Municipal Finance Officers Association, 1982.

16

CHANGING BUDGETARY PRACTICES AT THE LOCAL LEVEL

Douglas Davenport

Budgeting has been a vital part of local government for much of this century. In fact, one of the earliest signs of municipal reform resulting from the Progressive era was the adoption of a budgetary process for fiscal control.[1] Since the days of the New York Bureau of Municipal Research, budgets have emerged as the most important annual document produced by city governments, portraying in written form the guiding philosophy and goals of the community. Yet, a careful examination of local budgets reveals many changes over the years. Most obvious are the physical changes in presentation: budget documents are certainly larger, and more professionally produced than in the past. However, other changes are far more significant, relating to shifts in the fiscal position of municipalities. The majority of these budget modifications have been a response to a range of pressures, which will be discussed shortly.

Texas cities provide the context for this chapter. Like many other regions, Texas has not been immune to fiscal difficulties. In fact, it can be argued that in the previous decade Texas has faced some of the greatest monetary constraints experienced in the country. The budget practices which have emerged in response to those constraints are not unique to this state, though each municipality has its own methodology and context. Certain common currents may be observed with regard to Texas cities, which are applicable to the rest of the nation.

This chapter has a three-fold objective: (1) to describe the economic and social forces at work in Texas cities; (2) to examine the changing character of local budgeting in Texas; and (3) to suggest future needs and directions for budgetary practices. We begin by discussing the various factors which brought about the changes we have observed.

Economic And Social Forces

Though each community has a unique socioeconomic context, none are isolated from the larger forces at work. Some of these pressures are national in scope, while others directly impinge upon Texas. The following sections summarize the most crucial factors which have affected the local budget process.

Federal Fiscal Policy

Beginning with the "War on Poverty" inaugurated by the Johnson administration, the federal government began massive income redistribution programs. Such programs provided central cities with increased funds through grants-in-aid, though they failed to significantly alter the plight of the inner city poor.[2] Federal support peaked in 1978, then shifted significantly under the Reagan administration.

When President Reagan began his fiscal policy of "New Federalism," the total amounts given to local governments decreased. He also reorganized the intergovernmental revenue structure, by combining 77 categorical grant-in-aid programs into nine block grants. Much statutory control was also handed over to the states, in an attempt to reduce "big government."[3]

The ultimate result of this policy was a marked decline in total local revenue. The decreases in federal monies were not compensated by increased state funds. This is demonstrated in the Texas data, where funding from Austin remained relatively flat while federal funds dropped. Table 1 depicts the historical changes in intergovernmental changes for Texas cities.

TABLE 1
Federal and State Revenues to Cities
(Percent of General Revenues)

	1971-72	1976-77	1981-82	1986-87
Federal	8.6%	17.7%	11.1%	5.0%
State	1.5%	2.2%	1.0%	1.6%

Sources: U.S. Census Bureau, Census of Governments, 1972, 1977, 1982, 1987.

Declining Revenues

The decrease in intergovernmental funding was exacerbated by the "tax revolt" of the late 1970's. Measures such as proposition 13 in California and Proposition 2 1/2 in Massachusetts resulted from public outcry regarding the local tax structure, primarily high property taxes. Nationwide, the property tax decreased in importance during the period of 1977 to 1982. In 1977, property taxes represented 31% of total revenue; in 1982 that proportion had dropped to 25%.[4]

Texas municipalities have increased their property tax levies, growing from $1.051 billion in 1980 to $2.147 billion in 1988. However, this has been accompanied by shrinking property values, which declined by $22.6 billion in 1988 from 1987 levels.[5] Thus, increased collections have resulted from increased rates, rather than local economic growth. Table 2 graphically illustrates the historical shifts in local government revenues. The declining role of property taxes has created a fiscal vacuum, which has been largely filled by increased user fees.

TABLE 2
Shifting Revenue Sources
Texas Municipalities

	1971-72	1976-77	1981-82	1986-87
Property Tax	39.8%	31.5%	17.2%	17.1%
Sales Tax	14.1%	13.7%	10.3%	8.3%
Charges/Fees	29.8%	28.2%	46.1%	45.0%

Sources: U.S. Census Bureau, Census of Governments, 1972, 1977, 1982, 1987.

Increasing Expenditure Demands

Though federal and state transfers have declined, demands for expenditures at the local level have increased. Several factors have contributed to this increasing demand, which we will discuss briefly. Obviously, not all of these factors have the same effect on all municipalities. Some are more directly affected, particularly the larger metropolitan areas. However, all communities face the need to increase budget allocations. The following considerations highlight those reasons:

Aging Capital Infrastructure. As revenues decline, funding for new facilities are usually the first area to be cut. However, if older buildings are not replaced, maintenance costs on those existing structures continue to increase. These costs are relatively inflexible, since repairs and renovations cannot be safely avoided. Texas (and the Southwest in general) is more fortunate in this regard, due to the relatively young metropolitan areas. However, with the rapid growth of major Texas cities, the issue will become increasingly crucial.

Personnel Pressures. In spite of 'cutback management' techniques, personnel requirements remain fairly constant. Some positions may be deleted, yet a minimum staffing remains which is necessary to carry on vital governmental functions. Furthermore, pensions must be funded, incremental step increases in pay will continue, and training costs for new personnel must be absorbed. Various cities, including San Antonio and Austin are currently wrestling with this matter in a significant way. Both cities have eliminated numerous positions, while attempting to retain an acceptable service level.[6]

Demand for Improved Services. No one wants their local government to provide second-rate services. Garbage collection should be timely, water must be clean, parks and recreation facilities should offer a variety of programs. Much of this is taken for granted, yet each improvement means a significant cost increase. Voters are often vocal in demanding government service, yet most are equally opposed to any tax increase.

Technological Growth. The past twenty years have witnessed an accelerating application of new technology in the private sector. This has resulted in new "growth industries," many of them related to information technology.[7] However, these advances have affected government much more slowly and in unique ways.

Although one might expect large government units to arise to exploit new technologies and manage large public service plants more effectively, this has not been the case. Instead, the boundaries of general governments have remained fixed and limited, special-purpose governments have emerged. Nationwide, the number of special districts has increased from 12,339 in 1952 to more than 28,500 in 1982.[8] Texas has also seen a similar increase, with an average growth of 350 per decade. Table 3 illustrates this change. It should be noted that school districts, the most common special district, have declined during the past 40 years.

TABLE 3
Growth of Special Districts in Texas

Year	Total Government Units	School Districts	Other Special	
1950	3,963	2,479	491	---
1960	3,485	1,792	645	(+31%)
1970	3,446	1,318	1,001	(+55%)
1980	3,624	1,138	1,425	(+42%)
1989	4,180	1,113	1,892	(+33%)

Sources: U.S. Census Bureau, Statistical Abstract of the United States, 1961, 1971, 1981, 1990.

This proliferation has resulted in an increasingly complex set of exchange relations among governments, and has effectively resliced the revenue pie into smaller pieces. With each new special district, the existing governmental units have faced new taxes for their constituencies, without the benefit of added revenues.

Demographic Shifts. America had witnessed a tremendous shift in population distribution during the past twenty years. This growth has been a regional shift, as many families migrated from the "Rust Belt" of the Northeast, to the "Sun Belt" of the Southwest in search of new employment in energy related fields. For Texas, this tremendous influx of population has produced fiscal stress, as cities seek to keep pace with the demands for increased services. Table 4 represents the population trends that have occurred in Texas.

Volatile Oil Prices. As discussed elsewhere in the book, the entire Texas economy has been deeply affected by the sharp decline of world oil prices in 1986-87. The effects were observed immediately in state revenue collections, yet it ultimately reached local communities as well. As energy-related industries collapsed, local economies suffered. Concomitantly, municipal governments scrambled to tighten their belts and to seek alternative revenue sources.

During the summer of 1990, energy prices skyrocketed with the Iraqi invasion of Kuwait. More than likely, Texas cities will benefit from renewed investments in energy exploration and refinery improvements, assuming oil prices continue at increased levels. However, the ultimate monetary impact is difficult to predict, and will be slow in coming. Prudent forecasting and planning are crucial to keep municipalities in step with shifting revenues.

TABLE 4
Texas Population Trends
(Figures Rounded)

Year	State Population	U.S. Rank	Percent Metropolitan Population
1940	6,415,000	6	--
1950	7,711,000	6	--
1960	9,580,000	4	69.5%
1970	11,197,000	4	79.6%
1980	14,228,000	3	79.4%
1989	16,991,000	3	80.5%*

*U.S. Total Percentage of Metro Population: 77.1%

Sources: U.S. Census Bureau, Statistical Abstract of the United States, 1961, 1971, 1981, 1990.

Clearly, Texas' deteriorating economic conditions have influenced local government finances. The continuing pressure of increased expenditures, coupled with uncertain revenues, has forced communities throughout the state to modify their budgetary practices to withstand these forces. The next section describes specific ways cities have adjusted those practices.

Budgeting Changes In Texas

The budget process provides the conceptual framework for local resource allocation and outlay. This process, commonly called the budget cycle, has changed very little over the past few years.[9] However, recent advances in the areas of computer technology and methodological tools have greatly impacted the various stages of this cycle. This section examines some of these changes and traces the developments that have affected the budget cycle in general.

Technological Changes And Budgeting

Operationally, technological changes can be seen in all four stages of the budget cycle: preparation, appropriation, implementation, and evaluation. Until recently, most Texas communities have not utilized state of the art technology in the budget process. However, even smaller cities are now seeking to implement advanced budgeting tools. Budgeting practices have been greatly impacted by the growth of technology in several ways. Two of the most significant changes have been (1) the use of more sophisticated forecasting tools, and (2) the increased use of information technology throughout the budget process. We will briefly describe those changes below.

Use of Forecasting Tools. Forecasting local revenues and expenditures has been transformed by the application of advanced mathematical techniques. By way of contrast, local forecasting among Texas cities used to be limited to judgmental, or qualitative techniques: estimates made by 'experts,' based upon their knowledge and experience with the local economy. These estimates were short-term, dealing only with the upcoming fiscal year.[10] Toulmin and Wright, in their 1983 text on expenditure forecasting, observed that methods are relatively sophisticated at the federal level, while decreasing in sophistication at the state and local levels.[11]

This generalization, which was a fairly accurate description in the late 70's, is no longer applicable. Many state and local governments now utilize multi-year forecasting techniques, based upon sophisticated econometric models.[12] In the state of Texas, long-range, multi-year projections are becoming more widespread. Dallas County, the City of Fort Worth, and San Antonio are representative of local governments using more complex methods to determine future economic trends.

Texas municipalities are using more complex methods for projecting future revenues and expenditures, a trend associated with two divergent events: the increasing importance of future projections at the local level, and the advent of more powerful computer applications. The need for future projections is based upon the increasing strain upon budgets, which we have discussed earlier.

Use of Information Technology. Many of the procedural advances in local government budgeting are related to the proliferation of large scale computer applications. The growth of information technology has allowed municipalities to perform many analytical functions 'in house,' rather than hiring outside consultants. Thus, the preparation stage of the budget process can be more closely monitored by departmental staff, without relying upon non-agency analysts. The advances in technology can be described as either hardware or software improvements.

Information systems are at the cutting edge of rapidly converting theoretical advancement to application. The computer technology available just a decade ago scarcely resembles what is in use today. At the local level, the most crucial changes in computer hardware have been: (1) smaller, more powerful units; (2) decreased overall cost; and (3) better network systems.

Due to these factors, many cities have computerized their budget preparation. Rather than distributing printed forms to be duplicated and filled in, budget departments often provide forms and instructions on diskettes, or distribute materials through electronic mail systems (E-Mail). This allows each division to complete their requests and transmit them electronically, reducing computational errors and time requirements. For example, the City of Lubbock recently implemented 'electronic' distribution of budget preparation forms on diskette. With a network of personal computers, each department is able to prepare lower-level budgets in a fraction of the time and labor formerly necessary.

A wide variety of significant events have occurred in the area of software development. Primary among these are integrated financial software, ready-made statistical and spreadsheet programs, and the advent of 'desktop publishing,' all designed for personal computers.

Integrated financial software packages have been utilized in the private sector for some time, particularly on mainframe systems. However, they are now becoming more popular in the public sector. These packages are characterized by the interrelationship of the various modules, enabling accounting entries to be reflected in the budgeting data, as well as providing for cash management. This has played a vital role in the implementation of the budget, an area often overlooked. With the increased size of local budgets, control over execution has become critical in order to avert cash flow crises. This development has become crucial in the day-to-day operations of larger municipalities, and is illustrated by the City of Austin, which recently implemented an integrated package throughout their offices. This has given Austin much better control over the daily budget activities and a more accurate annual portrait of budget execution.

Commercial statistics packages and spreadsheet programs are a concomitant development. Many cities are using spreadsheets and statistical packages to assist in budget preparation, which can eliminate many repetitive entries and speed accurate computations. Austin, for example has utilized a popular electronic spreadsheet package in city-wide budget preparation for several years.

Finally, the graphing and presentation capabilities of available programs permit finance and budget data to be presented visually without the need for specialized external graphics resources. This has dramatically affected the adoption phase of the budget cycle, for the rise of desktop publishing has encouraged end users to prepare their own documents. Thus, budget directors of smaller cities can effectively communicate their objectives to council members and the public through easily understood graphs and illustrations.

Clearly, the impact of information technology upon governmental operations has been significant. This is most obvious in finance and budget departments, particularly for small cities. The ability to upgrade systems at reasonable costs, while decentralizing information availability, has allowed more accurate data to be used by everyone. The added impact of presentation graphics and easy to use software has aided the proliferation of information technology in the public sector.

Methodological Changes And Budgeting

From a methodological viewpoint, perhaps the most significant change taking place has been in the area of budget management tools. The budgeting systems used by Texas cities have undergone significant changes during recent years, moving away from the philosophy that the budget is simply a means of allocating resources and managing expenditures. To be sure, that concept still remains a vital part of the budget system. However, municipalities have begun recognizing the tremendous economic and political pressures facing the budgeting process, seeking new ways to justify fiscal policy.

In a simpler time, the straightforward line-item budget sufficed. In fact, the Texas Budget Manual states that "almost without exception, smaller Texas cities use line item budgets."[13] In many respects, line-item budgeting is the heart and soul of every system, no matter how sophisticated. Every expenditure is a journal entry, which is booked in line-item fashion. Thus, it is necessary to retain some basic understanding of unit costs for financial management. However, the current fiscal demands, coupled with increased policy constraints, have forced several changes in local budgeting systems. A conceptual examination reveals several trends, which we will now discuss.

Decentralization of preparation activities. The sheer size and scope of local budgets require careful preparation that is beyond the capabilities of most budget offices. Therefore, virtually every city involves each department in the preparation process.

Departmental involvement occurs on two levels. At the lower level, clerical staff are utilized to complete budget forms. Though this may appear insignificant, the volume of paperwork necessary to prepare an annual budget requires highly coordinated staff participation. At the upper level, managers assist in formulating departmental goals and objectives through allocation requests. Therefore, the involvement of managers at the early stages of budget planning is important for coordinating city-wide objectives.

Increased justification requirements. Continued fiscal distress has forced a drastic reevaluation of budget systems by all cities. The philosophy of "creeping incrementalism," which has been used to describe local budget justification, simply states that no budget undergoes comprehensive evaluation on a regular basis.[14] Rather, the previous budget becomes a "base," to which is added a small (3-5%) increase. Thus, budget decisions are made 'around the margins,' not from the center.

At the local level, particularly in Texas, this is simply no longer true. Severe revenue shortfalls have forced municipalities to reconsider the entire proposed budget, asking departments to suggest specific ways to make reductions without curtailing significant city services. Thus, departments are now asked to 'explain,' or justify their requests for funds, regardless of its place in previous budgets. This justification is often incorporated into the basic budget forms compiled at department levels.

To accomplish this goal, many cities incorporated performance budgeting into their system. This approach requires that budget requests be made according to activities to be performed, and focuses upon workload or output to justify expenditures. The basic premise is an analysis of cost-benefits, attempting to cost out each activity performed. Thus, upper-level administration has an accurate picture of the expenditures and benefits connected to those activities, and can fund them accordingly.

While the notion of efficiency in government is laudable, attaching costs and benefits to public sector goods is difficult. Many of the activities performed by municipalities cannot be properly evaluated on a cost basis, nor can tangible benefits be assigned to them. Furthermore, the complexity of determining per unit costs, total number of outputs to be produced, and the number of inputs required for those outputs is enormous. Very few local governments have the expertise or the personnel to accurately assess efficiency, or to perform the analyses on a regular basis.

In response to the problems associated with performance budgeting, many governments have opted for a variation of zero based budgeting (ZBB). In simplest form, a zero base budget requires each unit to compile 'decision packages,' based upon percentages of the previous budget. Terms such as 'reduced level,' 'expanded level' or 'base level' are indicators of a ZBB approach.

The strength of ZBB is flexibility. Though budget directors may hesitate to call their city's system 'zero based,' and may use different terminology, yet the underlying philosophy is a derivative of ZBB. This hesitation is due to a mistaken notion of what zero based budgeting implies. For many managers, ZBB conjures ideas of 'starting from scratch' in every department each year. This is a caricature of ZBB philosophy which is unworkable at any level of government. Rather, ZBB is a means of offering fiscal alternatives to upper-level city management. As functional managers provide input regarding desires for their units, broader municipal goals can be addressed that still allow for departmental discretion.

A combination of methodologies appears to be the most common solution. For instance, the City of Lubbock currently uses a variant of ZBB, while incorporating performance elements. This allows the flexibility of a ZBB format, while retaining a cost-benefit analysis in the framework of the budget document. Furthermore, performance oriented departments can present more convincing decision packages based upon known workload costs.

Regardless of the approach taken, it is clear that cities no longer incrementally increase budgets without regard to justification. Though the political aspects of policy still affect budget preparation, the proliferation of performance and zero based budgets indicate a more rational basis for budgeting. Due to the legal requirements of a balanced budget, local governments have been forced to reassess every expenditure, which has resulted in new budget management techniques.

Comprehensive budgetary controls. The fiscal distress which brought about the adoption of new budget systems has also forced more 'top down' approaches. While this may appear to be contrary to the decentralization of preparation activities mentioned above, it is not. Lower level managers are being used to plan the budget, however, this still occurs under the parameters established by top administration.

Primarily the use of a top down approach results in coordinated requests focused upon long range city-wide goals, rather than a hodgepodge of individual department 'wish lists'. This clearly demonstrates that the budget document is becoming just as important as a management tool as it is a financial plan. For example, various cities have instituted target budgeting, which means that upper level administration sets a 'target' (or ceiling) for each department. The department heads are then asked to complete their budget requests so as to fall within this guideline. This can be combined with either performance or zero based formats, permitting further evaluation. Such an approach was recently used by San Antonio in preparing their Fiscal 1990-91 budget.[15]

Looking At The Future

The budgeting trends currently observable in local Texas governments are likely to continue, since the causal factors cited previously remain in effect. The increased expenditure demands, coupled with rising competition for revenues and the demographic shifts that occurred, will not dissipate soon. They are significant, entrenched forces that will continue to affect the budget process.

Future trends can be characterized as follows: 1) continued growth in sophistication; 2) increased emphasis upon conservation; and 3) expanded search for alternative revenue sources. Let us briefly examine each trend.

Continued Growth in Sophistication. This refers to the sophistication of various budgeting aids, such as forecasting techniques and information technology applications. As more budget analysts become familiar with econometric modeling and regression analysis, they will find such tools very useful. Furthermore, information technology expansion continues unabated. Managers have already grown accustomed to more powerful hardware and software; they will continue to expect more advanced technology as it becomes available.

Increased Emphasis Upon Conservation. The decade of the 1960's witnessed a rapid expansion of federal programs, many of them aimed at the local level. The 1970's saw a 'tax payer revolt' against perceived waste and inefficiency in city and county governments, putting new stress on local finances. As federal funding diminished in the 1980's, cities faced even greater pressure to balance their budgets. Obviously, this pressure will not wane in the near future, but will require continued conservation of resources.

The goal of conservation will require the expanded use of cost-benefit analysis in all phases of the budget cycle. Performance budgeting may have little utility in the future (due to the extensive measurements it requires) but the need for understanding costs remains. Furthermore, evaluation activities will continue, with emphasis upon more comprehensive evaluations performed in-house. As internal personnel with knowledge of evaluative techniques are added, local governments will better utilize them to assess local programs.

Expanded Search for Alternative Revenue Sources. The most crucial long-range trend on the horizon is a renewed emphasis upon alternative revenues. The volatility of energy prices have made severance taxes a difficult revenue to forecast. At the state level, this has proved disastrous during the past five years. Local governments have also suffered, though more indirectly through the accompanying economic downturns.

Likewise, shifting federal policies have shrunk the intergovernmental revenue pie. Since state funds have not been shifted to compensate for this decrease, cities have been forced to cut back or find new revenues. It would appear that 'cutback management' has reached its maximal feasibility, for municipalities can only reduce service levels to a certain degree.

219

Therefore, the future will most likely see increased taxation, combined with larger user fees and charges. However, raising taxes always brings with it the danger of taxpayer revolt, as witnessed in the late '70's. Thus, most governments will concentrate on increasing user fees and charges. Since most citizens do not see such fees as a tax, they are less likely to complain. Also, it is much easier to explain the need to increase charges, since a tangible service is being purchased. This is comparable to private sector marketing strategy in which the consumer is educated regarding the increased costs of providing such service.

Conclusion

The budget practices of local Texas governments have been significantly modified during the past decade. These changes were not the result of long range strategic planning, but were pragmatic reactions to various socioeconomic pressures.

The responses of municipalities fall into certain broad patterns, even though each community is unique. Conceptually, budgeting is no longer a piecemeal activity done by a small number of administrators. Rather, it is a comprehensive and strategic activity involving all levels of management, as evidenced by the use of zero based and performance budgets.

From an applied perspective, forecasting techniques and information technology have increased in sophistication. These tools, once the exclusive domain of state and federal governments, are routinely utilized in even the smallest local entities. Such tools enable cities to perform their own analyses, and monitor budget implementation in a timely manner.

The future will continue to witness the growth of local government technology. It will also witness a search for viable alternative revenue sources and increased fiscal conservatism. For Texas cities, budgeting has grown from infancy to adolescence. Much naivete has been lost, along with some idealistic perceptions of "doing things the way we always did them." Expansion of the budgeting process continues, along with the attendant 'growing pains'. However, a realistic perspective of economic life in the 1990's makes such changes essential if Lone Star communities are to thrive.

Acknowledgement

The author would like to thank Dr. Aman Khan for the topic as well as his ideas and suggestions on the chapter.

220

Notes

1. R.K. Fleishman and R.P. Marquette, "Origins of Public Budgeting." *Public Budgeting and Finance*. Volume 6, Spring 1986: 71-77.

2. Julius Margolis, "The Fiscal Problems of the Fragmented Metropolis" in J. Richard Aronson and Eli Schwartz (eds.) *Management Policies in Local Government Finance*. 3rd ed. Washington, DC: ICMA, 1987.

3. Leonard Ruchelman, "The Finance Function in Local Government" in J. Richard Aronson and Eli Schwartz (eds.) *Management Policies in Local Government Finance*. 3rd ed. Washington, DC: ICMA, 1987.

4. U.S. Bureau of the Census, 1982 Census of Governments. Vol. 4. Washington D.C.: U.S. Government Printing Office, 1982: 31.

5. Legislative Budget Board, *Fiscal Size-Up*: 1990-91 Biennium. Austin, TX, 1990: 2-18, 2-19.

6. An expanded discussion of both cities' budgetary concerns and processes can be found in the chapter on comparative budgeting at the local level.

7. Niv Ahituv and Seev Neumann, *Principles of Information Systems for Management*. 3rd ed. Dubuque, IA: Wm. C. Brown Publishers, 1990.

8. P.B. Downing and T.J. DiLorenzo, "User Charges and Special Districts" in J. Richard Aronson and Eli Schwartz (eds.) *Management Policies in Local Government Finance*. 3rd ed. Washington, DC: ICMA, 1987.

9. John Rehfuss, *The Job of the Public Manager*. Chicago: Dorsey Press, 1989.

10. C.K. Zorn, "Issues and Problems in Econometric Forecasting: Guidance for Local Revenue Forecasting." *Public Budgeting and Finance*. Volume 2, Autumn 1982: pp. 100-110.

11. Lewellyn Toulmin and Glendal Wright, "Expenditure Forecasting" in Jack Rabin and T. Lynch (eds.) *Handbook on Public Budgeting and Financial Management*. New York, NY: Marcel Dekker, 1983.

12. Zorn, op. cit., 100.

13. Texas Municipal League, *Budget Manual for Texas Cities*. Austin, 1983.

14. Aaron Wildavsky, *The New Politics of the Budgetary Process*. Glenview, IL: Scott, Foreman and Company, 1988.

15. Management Services Department, *City of San Antonio Budget Process Procedures Manual for Fiscal Year 1990-91*. San Antonio, TX, 1990: 10.

Bob Bullock is Lt. Governor of the State of Texas and is recognized as the man with all the facts in state government. As former State Comptroller, Mr. Bullock earned a reputation as an expert on taxes, finances, and Texas Government. Both the business community and other public offices have acclaimed his achievements in the accuracy of the official state revenue estimates, in regional economic studies, in state tax analysis, and in assisting local governments, to improve their accounting systems. Since 1975, his tax collection programs have been noted for simplicity as well as for establishing quick, convenient access for taxpayers who need answers and assistance. Mr. Bullock, who has served as Secretary of State, assistant Attorney General, aid to the governor and member of the House of Representatives, was born and raised in Hillsboro. He attended Hill Junior College, Texas Tech University, and Baylor University Law School.

Douglas B. Davenport is currently serving as an officer in the major crimes unit of the Lubbock Police Department in Texas, after years of management in the non-profit sector. He completed a B.A. in 1979 from Central Bible College (MO) and has just completed an M.P.A. in finance at Texas Tech University.

Thomas Finke is a graduate of Texas Tech's Masters of Public Administration program. While at the university, he worked on numerous grant projects with the Center for Public Service. He is now employed with the Communicable Disease Center in Atlanta.

Siegrun F. Fox holds a Ph.D. from the Claremont Graduate School. She is an assistant professor of Political Science and Public Administration at Texas Tech University. Her research interests include public/private partnerships and the third sector. Her previous works were published in *Public Administration Review*, *Review of Public Personnel Administration*, and *Journal of Urban Affairs*.

Keith E. Hamm is an associate professor of Political Science at Rice University. He has published numerous professional articles and book chapters on state politics and administration. His major research has dealt with such topics as committee decision making in state legislatures, interest groups and lobbying, formation of subgovernments, and gubernatorial transitions. Currently, he is working on a study of state legislative committee assignments and their impact on public policy. He is past vice-president of the Southwestern Political Science Associates.

Kay Hofer obtained her Ph. D. from the University of Nebraska-Lincoln in 1978 and her Masters Degree in Political Science from the University of North Texas in

1973. She has taught public finance at the University of South Dakota, Oklahoma State University, Pan American University and currently the Director of the MPA Program at Southwest Texas State University in San Marcos. She also served as Director of Comprehensive Health planning for the State of South Dakota and has been a senior policy analyst with the State. Her activities have included professional consulting in the areas of public finance administration, grant writing, development of program and performance indicators, long-term care of the elderly, health care facility evaluation and evaluation of management systems. In addition, she has testified before committees of the United States Senate as an expert in the area of long-term health care.

Aman Khan is a member of the graduate faculty in Political Science and Public Administration at Texas Tech University where he teaches applied quantitative methods, public budgeting and financial management. He is one of the founding editors of the *Journal of Management Science and Policy Analysis*, and has served as a guest editor of *Public Budgeting and Financial Management*. He has also served on the review board of several national and international journals, including *European Journal of Operations Research Society*. His current research interests are in the area of budget forecasting, capital budgeting, and finanical planning at the state and local level. Trained as an economist and planner, he has a Ph.D. in Public Administration.

John P. Moore is Deputy Comptroller of Public Accounts with responsibilities for Legislative Affairs and Revenue Estimating. He joined the Comptroller's Tax Publications, Tax Information and Research divisions. He was the first director of the Comptroller's new Economic Analysis Center and became Associate Deputy Comptroller for Fiscal Management in 1987, responsible for revenue estimating, fiscal policy research, fund accounting and claims against the state. Mr. Moore was named Deputy Comptroller in November 1987. He is one of four members of the Comptroller's Tax Policy Committee and since 1979 has been involved in the preparation of each edition of *Fiscal Notes*, winner of the National Association of Governmental Communicator's Blue Pencil award on 1987 and 1988. He represented former Comptroller Bob Bullock on the Select Committee for Tax Equity. A graduate of Midwestern State University in Wichita Falls, John Moore was a newspaper reporter and editor before joining the Comptroller's Office.

Jim Oliver is Director of the Legislative Budget Board and one of the foremost budget practitioners in the country. Since 1960, he has served the state government in various capacities, as an assistant director of LBB, administrative assistant for program development for Governor Preston Smith, Director of the Governor's Office of Budget and Planning, and as an assistant director of LBB. In addition, he also served as a number of the Executive Committee of the National Association of Legislative Fiscal Officers, and as President of the Western States Legislative Fiscal Officers Association. Active in various social, cultural, and religious organizations, Mr. Oliver has a Bachelor of Business Administration in Engineering/Business from the University of Texas at Austin.

Jerry Perkins is Director of the Center for Public Service and Professor of Political Science at Texas Tech University. He has previously served at Georgia State University and the University of Miami (FL). He has published in the leading political science journals, including the American Political Science Review and the

223

Journal of Politics. Currently, his focus is on grant activity for the university in energy/environment and nonprofit management.

M. Ray Perryman is the Herman Brown Professor of Economics at Baylor University. He is the architect of a variety of complex modeling systems for all parts of the country. A prominent scholar, he holds a Ph.D. from Rice University in Economics and a B.A. in Mathematics from Baylor. His hundreds of articles and presentations span a wide variety of topics, gaining him international respect and acclaim. Among his most recent awards are (1) the Nation's Outstanding Young Economist and Social Scientist (National Science Foundation), (2) Outstanding Young Person in the World in the Field of Business and Economic Innovation, (3) Member of the World Hall of Fame, (4) Member of the Hall of Fame of Distinguished Americans, (5) One of Ten Outstanding Young Persons in the World. He has also received citations from both the Congress of the United States and the Texas Legislature. Dr. Perryman authors the *Texas Economic Forecast*, a subscription service providing details of the state's economic development, and *The Perryman Report*, a series of executive-level forecasts on state and national economies. He has served on dozens of federal and state task forces, as editor of both academic and trade journals, and in leading conference roles within the fields of economic, statistics, forecasting, modeling, and simulation. Through economic development and legislative studies, he tirelessly demonstrates his commitment to using economic information for business expansion and job creation.

James B. Reed obtained a B.A. in Political Science from Colorado College and a Master of Public Affairs from the Lyndon B. Johnson School of Public Affairs at the University of Texas at Austin. He has worked for U.S. Senator Lloyd Bentsen, former Texas State Representative Gerald Hill and the Texas Advisory Commission on Intergovernmental Relations, an agency of state government. At ACIR, Mr. Reed authored or directed studies in financial trends in state and local government, the socioeconomic impacts of high-level nuclear waste disposal in Texas, the environmental and regulatory impacts of the superconducting supercollider, the feasibility of revenue bonding to finance a low-level radioactive waste disposal facility, and an analysis of the state organizational structure for environmental regulation and natural resource protection. He also served for three years as an elected director of the South Austin Growth Corridor Municipal Utility District #1. Mr. Reed currently works for the National Conference of State Legislatures in Denver, Colorado as a policy specialist in energy, science and natural resources. He has authored reports in the policy areas of radioactive and hazardous materials transportation, science education and state-tribal relations during his tenure at NSCL.

Robert C. Rickards is an assistant professor in the Lyndon B. Johnson School of Public Affairs, the University of Texas at Austin. He conducts research on public financial management in a wide variety of institutional and national settings.

Charles W. Wiggins is a professor of Political Science at Texas A&M University, where he served as the director of the Master of Public Administration Program from 1981 to 1989. He has published several books, chapters, monographs, and articles on state government and administration in the area of public administration, interest groups and lobbying, the legislative process, and

224

gubernatorial activities. He is quite active in several professional associations, and has served as the President of the Southwestern Political Science Association, as well as the Texas Association of Schools of Public Affairs and Administration.